© Stephanie Stuart

Maryalice Huggins has worked in New York for twenty-five years as a restorer of high-end antiques and mirrors. She lives in Middletown, Rhode Island.

Aesop's Mirror

Maryalice Huggins

PICADOR

SARAH CRICHTON BOOKS
FARRAR, STRAUS AND GIROUX
NEW YORK

To my sister and brothers,
Susan, Bob, and Bill

www.picadorusa.com

Picador® is a U.S. registered trademark and is used by Farrar, Straus and Giroux under
license from Pan Books Limited.

For information on Picador Reading Group Guides, please contact Picador.
E-mail: readinggroupguides@picadorusa.com

Grateful acknowledgment is made for permission to reprint the following
material: Excerpts from "The Magnificent Nicholas Brown Desk and Bookcase"
reprinted with permission of Christie's Images Ltd. 2009. Excerpts from Alva Woods
Family Papers and Washburn Family Papers reprinted by permission of the Rhode
Island Historical Society, Providence, R.I. Correspondence from Marshall Woods
to Richard Upjohn, from the Gowdy Collection, reprinted by permission of the
Providence Preservation Society, Providence, R.I.

Designed by Jonathan D. Lippincott

The Library of Congess has cataloged the Farrar, Straus and Giroux edition as follows:

Huggins, Maryalice, 1952–
    Aesop's mirror : a love story / by Maryalice Huggins.—1st ed.
      p. cm.
    "Sarah Crichton books."
    Includes bibliographical references and index.
    ISBN 978-0-312-65532-7
    1. Mirrors—United States.   2. Antiques business—United States.   3. Art—
Provenance.   I. Title.

NK8440.H84   2009
749'.3—dc22

                                                                         2009015218

Picador ISBN 978-0-312-65532-7

First published in the United States by Sarah Crichton Books,
an imprint of Farrar, Straus and Giroux

First Picador Edition: October 2010

Beauty, like Wisdom, loves the lonely worshiper.

—Oscar Wilde

All things that pass
Are woman's looking-glass;
They show her how her bloom must fade,
And she herself be laid
With withered roses in the shade;
With withered roses and the fallen peach,
Unlovely, out of reach
Of summer joy that was.

—Christina Rossetti, "Passing and Glassing"

Contents

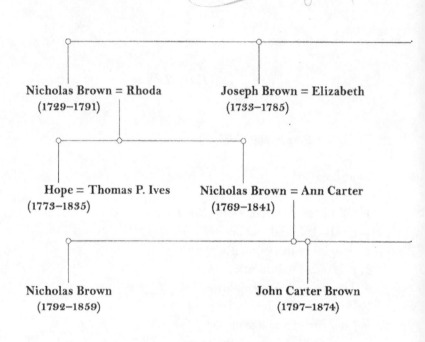

Nicholas Brown = Rhoda
(1729–1791)

Joseph Brown = Elizabeth
(1733–1785)

Hope = Thomas P. Ives
(1773–1835)

Nicholas Brown = Ann Carter
(1769–1841)

Nicholas Brown
(1792–1859)

John Carter Brown
(1797–1874)

THE BROWN FAMILY TREE

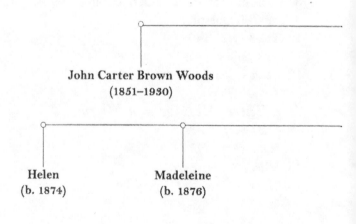

John Carter Brown Woods
(1851–1930)

Helen
(b. 1874)

Madeleine
(b. 1876)

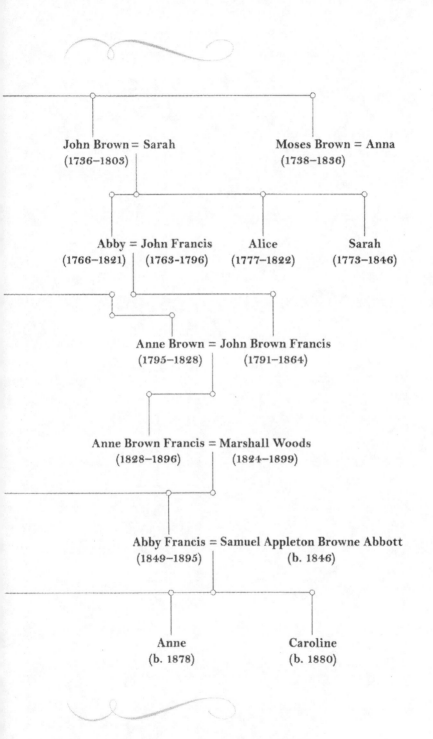

John Brown = Sarah
(1736–1803)

Moses Brown = Anna
(1738–1836)

Abby = John Francis
(1766–1821) (1763–1796)

Alice
(1777–1822)

Sarah
(1773–1846)

Anne Brown = John Brown Francis
(1795–1828) (1791–1864)

Anne Brown Francis = Marshall Woods
(1828–1896) (1824–1899)

Abby Francis = Samuel Appleton Browne Abbott
(1849–1895) (b. 1846)

Anne
(b. 1878)

Caroline
(b. 1880)

Aesop's Mirror

Prologue

I am living in the wrong century. Friends joke I was born in a hoopskirt. Every day, I think of what it must have been like to have lived in the past. Even at night I sometimes have vivid dreams in which I am a character in another time, in a different country, where people are dressed in period costumes and wander about rooms furnished in the decor of a featured era. If there is such a thing as reincarnation, I, like most adherents, picture myself not as one of the common folk but as belonging to the higher caste of society. In that tableau, I am among those who patronize the artisans of my time, thus setting the standards of fashion; my peers and I are so on the mark about taste that centuries later people are still enthralled with the pieces we commissioned.

Since a time machine has not been invented, the closest I have come to participating in another age is to surround myself with antiques. My whole career has been spent in the decorative arts. I am a restorer. Touching the surfaces of objects created long ago, I connect to history in a visceral way. When I work on antiques, I get to glimpse several personalities at once: the designer, the artisan, the owners, past and present. The living and the dead are my clients. I consider all of them before I pick up a tool or a brush.

People love antiques for a variety of reasons. At the high end of the field, experts create the market. Investment-minded collectors follow their lead. New discoveries are made more frequently now, when more people than ever collect (everything) and dealers have to make a living. For others, like me, who don't have a million dollars to spend, appreciation is enough reward.

My niche is American and French decorative arts from the eighteenth and nineteenth centuries. I am drawn to Americana for its charming simplicity. I love French pieces for their rich ornamentation, sophisticated construction, and use of a wide range of materials. My favorite categories are seating and mirrors. Chairs, both sculptural and practical, are to me the most intimate of all furniture since they are designed to encase the body.

Mirrors are fanciful. As the saying goes, a mirror never lies. They reflect how we feel about ourselves in every possible way. When people, and even animals, put their faces to a mirror, they tend to remain absolutely still for a few seconds. Whenever I'm working on an old mirror, I am amused to think about the variety of characters who once posed before the glass.

Mirrors, once considered precious in every civilization, are now common. As far back as 400 B.C.E., artists were inspired to embellish mirrors with mythological narratives—themes having to do with poetry and love, both exalted and sexual. In ancient Greek divination ceremonies, a small polished steel disk would be lowered on a string into a well. When raised, the mirror was believed to have the power to show the face of the person on whose behalf the ritual was performed. What follows is a story about a mirror I discovered at an auction in Rhode Island. Even in poor condition, the carved figures captivated me. The frame of my mirror depicts a fable—Aesop's "The Fox and the Grapes." In much the same manner as the ancient disk on a string, this particular mirror had a story to tell about the people who owned it.

PART ONE

Treasures of the Past

CHAPTER ONE

A Rhode Island Auction

When people discover I am in the antiques business in New York City, they never hesitate to ask my advice. Often, I am invited to their houses to see what they have. In most cases, such hospitality is extended when a change in residence is imminent. After people tell me the stories of how they came upon their cherished antiques, two questions inevitably arise: How much are they worth? And how can we best unload them? Right away, I set the record straight. I am not an appraiser. I am an antiques restorer. I have more exposure than most to the world of dealers, collectors, and specialists, and thus I know a thing or two about old furniture, but I know far from everything. The truth is no one really does.

The question of an antique's value is tough to answer. It is not like the Blue Book value of a car, although the sale price is based on similar criteria: model, year, and condition. With the market for art and antiques in constant flux, not even the pros can predict with absolute certainty how much pieces will bring. Recent sales of similar things in the same category serve as a barometer for rough estimates only. But what one person chooses to pay for one object, at one particular time, does not always set value. I can attest to this from firsthand experience. Often I have found myself the happy owner of some unusual piece that I possibly have paid too much for. The fact that so few wanted what I now own has not diminished the pleasure of living with my beautiful "mistakes."

How should you sell your antique, the one you have been hoping will allow you to quit your job and ease you into retirement? If by slim chance you own an outstanding piece with extraordinary, documented provenance, you won't have to go looking for buyers. Chances are the dealers and specialists already know your name. Eventually they will be in touch. If, on the other hand, what you own is of purely sentimental value, you may as well let it serve its purpose. The rule of thumb for midrange antiques is "Easy to come by, hard to sell." Such is the world I work in.

In the summer of 1995, a new friend named Tracy Hall told me her family was planning to sell their farm in central Rhode Island, as well as the contents of the outbuildings. Mrs. Miller, Tracy's mother, had spent sixty years collecting antiques in Rhode Island. At that point, I had spent twenty-five years working in decorative arts, so I offered to go through the family's household furnishings as a favor. Having never been to their home, I could not wait to see what was there.

Tracy, a top horse handler, is recognized for her ability to work with horses no one else can train, turning wild creatures into Palm Beach polo ponies. The farm where the family lived was used mainly for this purpose. Although I like horses, for me the best vantage for viewing them is at a distance, preferably when they are grazing in a faraway field. Horse people are notorious for clean barns and messy houses, so I happily anticipated finding a trove of neglected antique furniture at the farm.

Navigating the country roads through central Rhode Island, I arrived at Brigadoon Farm in the town of Clayville. The family compound resembled a scene from a Currier & Ives lithograph. Rows of beech trees shaded a split-rail fence that ran along both sides of a long dirt road. Set beyond two granite pillars was an eighteenth-century colonial house bordered by a vast reservoir. As I passed through the opened gate, I could see Tracy, surrounded by a milling assembly of mixed-breed dogs. Tall and lean, she had the erect posture of an equestrian. Her dark hair was tucked behind her ears, her large Prussian blue eyes smiling. Together we walked around the grounds, accompanied by the dog pack crisscrossing our route. On a lawn overtaken by weeds, we passed a disused swimming pool where a broken diving board dangled by the threads of its torn canvas cover at a forty-five-degree angle.

By footpath, we arrived at the edge of a lake. Tucked beneath an umbrella of tall pines were two log cabins built in the 1890s. Unoccupied for years, they were furnished in organic Adirondack decor: chairs and tables were constructed of twisted twigs; chests of drawers covered with peeling white birch bark sat across from metal bedsteads, whose mattresses sagged in the middle like hammocks. On a dressing table, a girl's vanity set was laid out in a fan-shaped pattern; a hairbrush, comb, and handheld mirror with handles made of walnut burl were placed atop a rust-stained linen table runner embroidered with violets and edged in scalloped crocheted lace.

In contrast to the forlorn cabins, the leather-and-hay-scented barn was immaculate. Only one stall out of the ten was occupied; it belonged to a young, edgy thoroughbred, recently arrived from Virginia. The horse, deemed unworthy of a career on the racetrack, had been destined for the slaughterhouse before Tracy interceded. In the shadowy interior light, we passed a line of tack hanging on beam posts. When we approached his stall, the horse's eyes flickered with fear. He moved skittishly, scraping the floor with his hoofs. He turned from us and stuck his head out a window that faced the meadow where he longed to run and join his new friend, the goat. Tracy tried to tempt him with an apple, all the while praising him by name in a gentle singsong voice. But the horse could not be swayed by flattery or sweet reward.

Finally, Tracy led me to the carriage house attic. The place was packed tight with layers of stacked furniture, making it impossible to walk around without toppling things. It was hard to see with only shafted light filtering through boarded windows. Tracy turned on the single bare bulb dangling on a cord from a rafter. From my vantage on the top rung of a ladder, most of the furniture appeared to be American. Although authentic, the style was simple country. The painted cottage chests, sets of stenciled Hitchcock chairs, spinning wheels, and primitive tables, although charming, did not strike me as particularly valuable.

The main house had a colonial American character, with most of the original interior architectural features intact. Mrs. Miller's eclectic collection created a relaxed New England atmosphere. Given that it belonged to a woman with a rack-roofed station wagon and a reputation for mining the fertile antiquing ground Rhode Island once was, it was not as cluttered as I had hoped. I chose a few pieces for my friend to consider keeping, based on decorative charm rather than market value.

Tracy was not interested in any of the inventory. Nothing I could say tempted her. "I am moving across the road to a house my mother gave me," she said. "I've already taken all I want from here."

That said, there was no point in pressing or continuing to poke around further. I was anxious to see her house across the road, as I was still unconvinced she could not somehow squeeze in a few more antiques.

Once inside her modest two-bedroom house built in the 1940s, I saw Tracy had selected the best of what I had seen that day. A small collection of good early American pieces such as highboys, clocks, and primitive paintings made her home personal and cozy. One piece, however, struck me as incongruous. A Roman garden statue—a lion cub—reclined on the floor between a pair of potted ferns. Its limestone features had softened from years outside. It would be a while before I figured out where it came from.

Several months later, in October 1995, I vacillated about attending the Millers' auction. Not until the morning of the sale did I decide to go. The clincher for me was the weather and time of year. The sky was cerulean blue, and the sun looked as though it was going to stick around. Instead of being holed up in my New York City apartment, which offered unappealing views of the façade of the Holiday Inn across the street and a symphony of honking taxis and idling tourist buses, I decided the day warranted a trip to New England. The leaves were turning, the autumn air was crisp and earthy. Because during my previous trip I had not seen anything I was dying to have, I headed for "Little Rhody" with empty pockets. Cruising through the center of Clayville, with its white steepled church, Grange building, and tiny post office, I was reminded of photographs in a propane gas company calendar one might receive at Christmastime. I arrived for the preview about forty-five minutes before the auction was to commence and parked my car in line with others on the bank of a freshly cut hayfield.

Mike Corcoran had been chosen to handle the auction. Mike is the best-known society auctioneer in Rhode Island. His clientele is from the old money set; the mansion-encrusted coastline of Newport and Watch Hill has been his primary district. A born showman, he is funny, outrageous, irreverent, and handsome. According to local legend, Mike once was Aquidneck Island's most desirable bachelor, and so far nothing has changed. He started in the business in the 1950s, working for Gustave White, auctioning off the contents of thirty-room mansions as robber baron descendants either died or grew weary of maintenance and property taxes on their titanic summer residences. If a wealthy buyer or arsonist could not be found, a popular alternative was to gift estates to tax-exempt institutions like the Catholic Church or the Preservation Society of Newport County. Original household furnishings and fine art were offered to the public. These auctions drew dealers from Boston, New York, London, and Paris. Medieval tapestries, Persian rugs, Old Master paintings, and period European furniture were routinely sold under value and carted away by the truckload, ultimately landing in the hands of the next batch of nouveaux riches.

When Mike is not holding on-site sales, he conducts auctions from his own white-shingled warehouse in Portsmouth, Rhode Island. The quality of his merchandise varies from the horrible (which he will admit publicly) to meriting the occasional prize. Mike touches everything he sells. He's tried on an Australian fire brigade helmet and dozens of top hats and derbies. He cracks himself up as he swings a Scottish sword made in 1745 or aims the empty barrel of a broken antique shotgun at people in the audience he pretends to not like. If there is a baby grand on the block, Mike steps off the stage, saunters to the back of the room, and plays a few bouncy jazz riffs from the 1940s. His talent at the keys reels in the old ladies. He will go to any length to keep his audience entertained, integrating those present into the theater of the auction. He never forgets a name, so one doesn't need a paddle with a number, only to register at the front desk with Elsie, his secretary of forty years. If he spots new faces in the crowd, he walks right up to their seats and in front of everyone asks their names, where they are from, and if they have cash.

A top-notch Newport estate auction will attract hotshot antique dealers to a Corcoran event. But a sale in Clayville, advertised in *Antiques and the Arts Weekly* and featuring stoneware crocks and spinning wheels, did not lure heavy hitters. Only small-time local dealers and curious neighbors attended the Millers' auction. Past auctions had prompted me to observe that locals did not go to a Corcoran event with the intention of buying. They came to see Mike's act under a tent, mingle with friends in privileged surroundings, and enjoy a catered lunch. On this day, I planned to dovetail into that category myself. But one never knows. A testament to Corcoran's wizardry is his ability to cajole the tightest Yankee into an impulse buy in a matter of seconds. After a sale, a common sight was the remorseful expressions on the victims' faces as they lined up at the receipt counter. However, because, I've been told, Mike neither spends his time studying antiques and art nor pays attention to current market prices, people have been known to score at his estate sales. I was about to do the same.

During the preview, I was surprised to spot two large crated Rococo mirrors leaning against a wall inside the carriage house. One was the most unusual mirror I had ever seen. Rapture and intrigue hit me at once. It was as if my brain was shot with a sudden blast of dopamine, the hormone that neuroscientists believe triggers cognition, motivation, reward, and . . . compulsive gambling.

The frame's figurative design was based on Aesop's fable "The Fox and the Grapes." The carvings displayed a whimsical Rococo repertoire. Frolicking babies carrying baskets of grapes on their heads climbed a ladder across a divided section of glass at the top. Two other babies perched on opposite ledges. One stood beside a rustic, grape-filled bucket while his twin pulled a resisting goat on a leash. From among rocks gushing golden water at the crown, bold clusters of fruit, vines, and flowers cascaded down the sides. Tucked into two central cyma curves at the base, an alert fox sat in the grass with head raised, thirsting for the grapes he could not have. Designers working in London in the eighteenth century often used such allegory. As I gazed at the frame, one in particular came to mind: Thomas Johnson. A master carver and furniture designer, Johnson worked in London in the mid-1700s, at the height of the Rococo period. His first book of plates for carving pieces was published in 1758, and his work became so popular that the core design was reinterpreted in the nineteenth century. The question was, was this mirror made during the official Rococo period in the eighteenth century, or was it manufactured later?

The word *Rococo* is derived from the French word *rocaille* (rocky), and the Rococo style evolved from the weightier seventeenth-century Italian Baroque. The Rococo movement originated in France in the eighteenth century and was promoted by Madame de Pompadour, Louis XV's trendsetting mistress and patron of the arts. From Versailles the style quickly spread to every nation in Europe. Like the lifestyle emphasized at the French palace, the compositions are lighthearted and gay.

Hallmarks of Rococo design are its asymmetrical proportions, made up of scrolls, curves, and surprising forms. Carved and gilded ornaments convey the interaction between man and nature in a surreal world filled with action and fantasy. Wild beasts and putti often appear amid masses of intertwining foliage, shells, rocks, and dripping water. Chinoiserie characters holding umbrellas, seated on raised platforms beneath pagoda roofs, are often part of the design. These, plus baskets, fruit, flowers, trophies, and human masks are frequently cast together in a variety of schemes meant to jolt the imagination and evoke timeless stories and fables.

For collectors of Rococo, the period from 1730 to 1770 is the most desirable. Indisputably, the art of carving both in France and England was at its apex then. Two artisans collaborated: the carver and the gilder. But the success of the end product depended on the gilder's finesse at tooling into thin layers of white gesso built up with a brush over the raw wood. The gilder's smoothing of the gessoed surface, carving of tiny veins on leaves, and creation of intricate patterning on flat planes all lent refinement and dimension, enhancing the effect of shadow and light once the piece was sheathed in gold leaf and raised decoration burnished with an agate-tipped tool.

In the 1830s the Rococo style experienced a revival in Europe and America, which lasted well into the 1870s. Familiar designs were reintroduced and reinterpreted. And thanks to the advance in technology, for the first time in history enormous glass plates were within the means of the expanding bourgeoisie. But there was a difference.

Mass production of mirror frames became cheaper when the woodcarver and gesso worker could be eliminated. Cast plaster often replaced solid wood. Identical pieces were cranked out in volume to satisfy the droves of people who could not tell the difference between them and artful, custom-made pieces and who were not inclined to pay or wait for something better. In the Victorian age of clutter, there were vast rooms to fill and walls to cover. If mirrors were large, ostentatious, and covered in shiny gold, most customers were satisfied.

What puzzled me about this mirror was that its size appeared to be Rococo revival while the primitive carvings on the frame were reminiscent of the eighteenth-century American school. Then there was the matter of inconsistency. Some sections were artfully managed, while others were handled awkwardly. The carver excelled at fruit and flowers, whereas his human figures were disproportionate, static, squashed, and quirky, strikingly similar to those on American labels, etchings, and paintings from the mid-1700s through the 1830s. Perhaps what one famous observer said about furniture could apply to a mirror. Thomas Jefferson, who preferred to buy his own in Paris, noted, "Furniture of quiet elegance could be made in Philadelphia, as well as furniture with burdens of barbarous ornament." Indeed, the Fox and Grapes mirror, raucous and bold, had nothing "quiet" about it.

It was this primitive, self-taught American-like quality to its figures that attracted me to the Fox and Grapes frame. If it was made even as early as 1800—rather than in the 1830s—the mere thirty-year difference would substantially increase its value. If that were the case, it would rise above the category of simply decorative and might almost be museum-worthy. Regardless, in my long career as a restorer and gilder of mirrors, I had never come across one like it.

Colonial mirrors made between 1760 and 1800 have always presented experts with problems determining country of origin: England versus America. In the mid–eighteenth century, shops along America's Eastern Seaboard regularly carried imported English-looking glasses as well as frames. Despite the colonists' hatred of the English, almost everything made in England was precisely what everyone wanted to own. But imported mirror plates were often refitted to frames made by colonial craftsmen. Carvers and furniture makers working in places like New York, Baltimore, and Philadelphia used British design books as they strove to imitate the much sought after English models. Artisans took license in reinterpreting forms according to their own skills and their clients' budgets. Though England's Rococo period was winding down in the 1770s, the style remained popular in America, where it extended to as late as 1800.

Unfortunately, the original glass had been replaced in the Fox and Grapes mirror. This would detract from its value and create one more obstacle in determining the frame's age. It was hard to say when the change had been made. Judging from the thickness and clarity of the glass, my off-the-cuff guess was that it had been replaced after 1850. Earlier mercury-backed glass plates blemish over time, one reason why so few examples exist. As the art of mirror making improved, people often pitched out tarnished glass for more reflective surfaces. Even American mirrors displayed in museums seldom hold their original plates of glass.

Another tall gilded Rococo mirror stood beside the Fox and Grapes. A shell adorned the crown, and from there, flowers and graceful leaves descended, looping around ten divided glass sections. This ornate yet refined mirror was a perfect example of high standard 1860s Rococo revival. The frame was in pristine condition and had never been restored. The original glass was spotted with age. Harmonious proportions made it pleasing, and the vibrant carvings were of wood rather than composite. It was not common to find a revival frame made entirely of wood. As mentioned, cast plaster over wood was generally the method for producing frames during the later part of the nineteenth century. A Victorian with a discerning eye and a flush bank account had purchased it. This mirror's flawless state guaranteed a quick sale to one of my decorator clients in either New York or California.

Outside on the lawn was what appeared to be an American Greek Classical sofa. It was so shocking to see it there, my first thought was that it was a reproduction. Several dealers gathered around the sofa. I tried not to generate more interest by getting too close. A top-quality antique here in Clayville seemed too good to be true. The days of finding treasures in attics and barns were over.

Yet, even from a distance, the proportions of the sofa looked right and period. A pair of dolphins constituted the arms and extended to the feet. The sculptural form, bold and sleek, manifested exquisite balance and grace. In place of fins, long leaves suggestive of wings lent the piece lightness, as though at any moment it might lift and fly away to a mythological island in Greece.

In early America, maritime merchants were the main clients to order pieces featuring the benevolent dolphin, believed to rescue drowning sailors. Cetaceans had long been described as the embodiments of peace and uncontained joy, and as guides to another world.

After the dealers moved on, I planted myself in front of the sofa. Brown, gloomy paint applied after the date of production covered the dolphins' bodies. At closer range, a glint of gold flashed in the sunlight from beneath a tiny chip in the paint. My heart raced when I realized the original gold and the wash of blue-green verdigris on the scales might still be intact. My restoration skills began to click in. I visualized how the sofa had looked originally and the steps I would take to salvage what I hoped was still there. Low-relief carvings of oak leaves and raised acorns in tight-grained mahogany flanked the upper back rail. There, the crackled finish looked old and perfect. The bulky Victorian springs in the seat could easily be replaced with its intended webbing. A few rosewood veneer sections on the front rail were missing, as was a hardwood seat stretcher and both fishtails on the arms. Other than those minor shortcomings, the sofa had survived relatively unscathed. The distinct design fit squarely into the Classical period, around 1825. It was just what the antiques community could relate to and thus a safe purchase for quick resale. Having expected nothing so tempting, I kicked myself for how financially unprepared I was to participate in the sale. If I could buy the couch at the right price, it would defray the cost of the one piece I now wanted more than anything: the Fox and Grapes mirror. I went to register with Elsie at the picnic table that served as Corcoran's makeshift desk. I couldn't let the sofa vanish into an antiques dealer's van.

With time to kill before the auction, I returned to the carriage house to inspect the mirrors again. Whereas the dolphin sofa was easy to identify, pigeonholing the Fox and Grapes mirror was a conundrum. I managed to get Tracy's attention as she walked by.

"Where did these things come from?" I asked, pointing to the mirrors. "Were they here when I came by this summer?"

She confessed she had not seen the mirrors, which had been sealed in their crates for forty years until just a few days ago. She briefly explained that several of the mirrors, as well as some other items, had come from an estate in Providence called the Woods-Gerry Mansion. The hyphenated name stood for the two prominent families who had once lived there. The Woodses were the original owners of the house, built in the mid–nineteenth century. In the 1950s, Tracy's father had purchased the property and quickly sold it to the Rhode Island School of Design. The goods inside were shipped to Clayville and had remained in storage in the barn ever since. That was all Tracy was willing to offer me at that moment. With the auction about to start, she grew distracted and scurried off into the crowd.

I compared the two mirrors. Though the gilding was hard and bright on the revival mirror with the shelled crown—the workmanship so flawless it had survived 120 years of domestic use followed by 40 years in an unheated barn—it was, as they say disparagingly in the antiques world, just decorative.

To me it lacked the soul of the Fox and Grapes mirror. Although I knew many might prefer the more traditional revival mirror, I was enchanted by the awkwardly carved figures on the Fox and Grapes.

Thomas Johnson's designs were challenging and time-consuming to produce. As a result, most of his volumes of etched plates remained on paper, serving only as inspiration. The carver of the Fox and Grapes frame had clearly struggled to interpret a complex design scheme that stretched him beyond his range. Despite this struggle, he had, with determination, found his own way. I admired his courage to undertake one of Johnson's most replicated works, however incapable he was of giving the figures true proportion and movement. The carver's naïve hand and subject matter lent a gentle humor that resonated with me. The potbellied babies echoed American folk art simplicity. His unique interpretation was seductive. The carving stood outside the standards by which most objects are judged. Personal and individualistic, to me the frame was a work of art. It had a pulse. It had life.

The three pieces I wanted stood apart from everything else the Millers put up for sale that day. Their preference for colonial furnishings made it clear that flashy gold mirrors were not their style. The two mirrors and the Classical sofa had a sense of formality about them, signaling to me they were part of a group that had originally belonged to a sophisticated family of city dwellers. Despite the different periods, they were bound by a single thread: a generational insistence on quality.

My dilemma was that I wanted both mirrors: one for quick sale, the other for love. And I was determined that the gutsy Classical sofa, the unquestionable prize of the day, would be mine as well. Because of my financial circumstances, it seemed unrealistic that I would be able to have everything. To pacify the voice of reason, I played a familiar game: "If I had to choose just one thing, which would it be?"

My short-lived exercise in compromise was futile. Acting like a true dealer, I decided to buy everything and figure out how to pay for it later. I justified my behavior by relying on a platitude always handy when a situation felt scary but my instincts screamed I was right: "Everything that is meant to be will work out as it should." It was stupid not to have prepared for the auction, but I quickly forgave myself by recalling one of my aunt Googie's many aphorisms: "He who acts too late misses the opportunity."

Out on the lawn, Mike Corcoran was working the crowd, shaking hands, asking women about their families, and saying hello to as many people as he could in fifteen minutes. "How ya doin?" I'd hear him cheerily ask passersby. Should anyone get too chatty before an auction, Mike's cutoff line is "Huh. Is that so?" His expression is sympathetic, but with the show about to begin, the eyes read "gotta go." I overheard a woman with an earnest face ask if he could tell what period a chair was from. Mike, who detests any sort of pretension, took a moment before saying, "That, my dear, is from the lousy period." She stood flabbergasted while he waved his hand over her head to a dealer in the distance.

The auction was about to start. "Okay! Everybody ready?" Mike called out to a circling crowd, rubbing his palms together. "Let's get started!" People hurried to stake their positions under the white tent. Dealers stood on the periphery near the tent poles, arms folded, intently looking straight ahead. I took a seat in the middle.

At each auction, Mike chooses someone in the audience as straight man for his jokes. This day it was an elderly gentleman with a florid face, sitting front row center.

"Hi, Judge," Mike said. "How ya doin today? Good? Great! Now, let's begin with the rugs. Murf, bring that Chinese one up here."

With humor as his selling tool, once Mike gets people laughing, he digs in. "This rug is eight by twelve. It's in pretty good condition except for"—he poked a finger through—"one small hole in the middle. Who'll start the bidding at two hundred dollars? Two hundred dollars, anyone? How about a hundred? Jim, you in at a hundred? Yes! Good. I have a hundred. Anyone want to give me one fifty? Yes! And now I have one fifty. Do I hear one seventy-five? No? Okay. Take it away, Bruce, for one fifty! Good goin, Bruce! Ladies and gentlemen, Bruce comes to Rhode Island about twice a year all the way from Albany to buy things from us, and we appreciate that. He gets some good buys here. That's why he always comes back."

Four men carried an Edwardian pedestal table up and tilted it onto its side so everyone could see the figured top. "Lot fifteen is a dining room table with four leaves. Walnut, I believe. Look at that carving! Who'll open the bid at five thousand?" When no one raised a hand, Mike tried again. "How about twenty-five hundred for the table? Okay. I have two thousand. Do I have any takers for twenty-five? Yes, I do! Tom, you're in at twenty-five. Now I have three thousand from Jackie. Thirty-five anywhere? Ed, you're in at thirty-five." Mike noticed that Ed still had his hand in the air even though the audience had stopped bidding. "Ed," Mike said, shaking his head. "I already have your bid. Never bid against yourself. That's the cardinal rule. Any increases? Tom? Any interest? Nope. Tom doesn't want it. Sold to Ed Collins for thirty-five hundred dollars. Nice buy, Ed! Next we have a set of six dining chairs."

The last bidder, Ed, interrupted the proceedings. "Wait, Mike, I thought the chairs went with the table. I misunderstood. I can't take the table without the chairs."

"What are you talking about?" Mike snapped. "This is an auction. You own the table!"

"Mike, I'm sorry." Ed sounded embarrassed. "I can't buy it without the chairs."

"Okay," Mike said disgustedly. "Jackie, you were the last bidder at three. Do you still want the table for three?"

"No, Mike," Jackie replied, relieved she didn't get the table after all. "I thought the chairs went with the table, too."

"Ladies and Gentlemen," Mike announced. "I'm going to start over. This time it's *just* the table. Everyone clear about that? Here we go."

The judge bid the table up to $3,000, but a second after Mike declared the item sold, a voice chimed in from the sideline offering more.

"Too late," Mike said. "You're out. The judge got it. A judge always trumps the layperson."

China cups and plates went quickly and cheaply to the first bidder because Mike is bored by selling the little stuff. The audience was getting distracted. The din of private conversations was drowning out Mike's voice. Something had to be done to rein in attention. Desperate, Mike resorted to one of his old standbys. Holding up a giant porcelain punch bowl, he spun it on the tip of his fingers, then, using both hands, tossed it into the air and offstage, where it was caught below by Murphy, his assistant. This trick, which I've seen him use many times, never fails to elicit great gasps. The bowl, unsurprisingly, is never very valuable.

As the auction progressed, I focused on what I wanted while candlesticks, drop-leaf tables, and an assortment of housewares were sold and carried off by hand and dolly. (To this day I regret not bidding on an American eighteenth-century bonnet-top highboy that went for a price equal to that of a pair of shoes at Bergdorf Goodman.) An hour into the session, the sofa appeared. Two staff members, grabbing opposite arms, hoisted it above the heads of the spectators. The price was climbing at a clip in $500 increments. Suddenly, the bidding slowed down, hovering around $5,000. The auctioneer was pressing for $5,500. As the audience grew quiet, I shouted, "Fifty-three hundred."

Mike did his best to humiliate me for beating him down a measly $200. Rolling his eyes and swerving side to side, he shot me a flirty grin. The man was worth every penny of his 15 percent commission. With his left hand in his coat pocket, the right hand pointed two fingers to the crowd from an outstretched arm. He challenged his audience to top me. Mike allowed silence to last for ten seconds to give people the opportunity to think before the gavel hit the block. With nothing more he could do to escalate the price, he leaned forward from his pulpit and, in a pope-like gesture, bowed his head and swept his arm over the crowd. Looking up, he solemnly announced, "Sold. To the lady from New York City." There was an instant burst of applause, a display of support I had never experienced at a city auction.

At a city auction, every attendant's pinkie is raised to brow while the other hand jots down the hammer price in the margins of a catalog. The Clayville crowd was different. In unison, all turned in their seats to get a look at the sucker from the city will-ing to pay what they felt was a hefty price for a ratty old sofa in serious need of new upholstery.

The Fox and Grapes mirror was next. Mike knew I wanted it, and it was to his advantage to keep his winning streak going by focusing on me. Because the piece was so broken, and so cumber-some, it had remained stowed in the carriage house during the auction. Without the advantage of a refreshing second look, attendees had to rely on their short-term memories to decide how much they would pay for it. In broad daylight, the mirror's con-dition would become more obvious and discouraging.

I was optimistic about the lowball figure Mike had quoted me earlier in the day, when we were face-to-face in the driveway. His hands in the pockets of his Harris Tweed jacket, he had been non-chalant. "About a thousand," he'd said. Intuitively, he knew how to deliver the right answer: the one I wanted to hear. Like every victim of a salesman, I believed him. A tolerable price, I thought, for what I recognized as one hunk of a gorgeous piece in need of months of restoration.

It did not help that Mike had purposely announced my New York City residency to the crowd after my successful bid on the sofa, falsely signaling that I was either a dealer or a savvy collec-tor. After that, people assumed I knew something they didn't, which resulted in a contagious round of auction fever. Why was it, I asked myself, that whenever I really wanted something at auction, regardless of its limited value, one paddle-wielding maniac inevitably appeared who wanted the same thing based solely on the fact that I did? Predictably, my contender erupted out of the sidelines just as the bidding came to a crawl. When I turned around in my seat to see who I was up against, I spotted him right away. With his legs spread and his hands clasped tightly behind his back, he winked at me, his face plastered with a self-satisfied smirk. I was certain he was not any more informed about the history or value of this mirror than I. He was obviously a dealer out on a limb, and his audacious bid for something so atypical was as perplexing as it was infuriating.

Briefly I considered dropping out of the bidding war and letting the little guy in the back overpay through the nose. But I ended up paying more than eight times Corcoran's earlier estimate. My victory instantly morphed into a malaise of buyer's remorse. I did not need a huge restoration project for which I would not be paid. Every square inch of floor space in my studio in Manhattan was booked weeks in advance for antique furniture belonging to actual paying clients. The mirror was too tall and too grand to go on the wall of my nondescript New York apartment, and I was not keen on the idea of hauling it to my house on Block Island by ferry. If I ever decided to sell it, I might have a difficult time finding a buyer who was as drawn to its primitive beauty as I was. Nonetheless, the mirror was now mine.

In all, I purchased two ballroom-size mirrors—the revival shell-topped piece from the 1860s and the Fox and Grapes—a six-foot-tall mirror with a gilded bolection frame, the sofa, and some worthless bric-a-brac Corcoran bamboozled me into buying: the inevitable outcome of attending a Corcoran auction. I had no clue how I would pick up the five-digit tab for the day's spending spree. Even the shipping cost was more than I could come up with on the spot.

Calculating the damage, I had to think of something fast. In a dazed state I wandered into the main house to make a phone call. I regretted my standing disregard for money, a proud attitude that up until this moment I had never questioned. Moral and legal questions raced through my mind. Was it against the law to buy at auction when unable to settle the bill? Did the town of Clayville have a sheriff? Would the Millers sue?

Everything inside the house had been sold except a series of large, dingy paintings, the canvases glued to wooden panels. On the kitchen linoleum I spotted a black rotary phone. Sitting on the floor among packing materials, I placed the phone on my lap. With both hands frozen on the receiver, I summoned strategy. Since I seldom looked at my checkbook, I had no estimate of my available funds. My accounting method generally fell into the realm of vagary.

With not a little trepidation, I called the bank. Dialing zero, I spoke with a representative who told me my account held $900 and went on to explain how to apply for a loan. I would have to go back to New York, meet with an officer, sign a document in her presence, and wait over a week to be approved. By this time, my auction euphoria had been supplanted by embarrassment and fear. I considered making an arrangement with Mrs. Miller, whom I did not really know, to pay her in the near future. It seemed likely I might have to head back to New York and secure a business loan, thus establishing myself with a line of credit for what appeared to be my new sideline career as an antiques dealer.

With the auction over, Mrs. Miller, Tracy, and Mike Corcoran stood together talking beside some foldout display tables. I casually joined the circle. "Would it be okay with you if I paid you next week for the things I bought today?" I timidly asked. Like Pompeian statues, the cluster locked eyes on me. The star bidder, the New Yorker who had outwrangled all (for the most expensive pieces), was a potential deadbeat. Without awaiting further cue, I assured them of a check later in the day, to unison nods and faint smiles. Eyes glued to the ground, I marched back to the kitchen for fresh ideas.

Tapping family connections seemed my only option. Some went unconsidered, most being in similar straits as I. But there was one black sheep in the family who had the good sense to have a conventional job. My younger brother, Bill, was an upstanding mortgage banker and lived in Rhode Island. Miraculously, he was at home when I called.

I tried my best to explain my bind. To put it in his terms, I was asking for an instant loan of a sum that could be a down payment on a waterfront condominium.

"I'm quite desperate to be able to pay my bill at the

moment," I said, sounding like an Edith Wharton character on a losing streak at cards. "Just by selling one of the very valuable things I bought today, I am certain I will be able to pay you back in no time. I'll share some of the profits with you. How about that?"

"Well, Mary," Bill said, after a pause, "I suppose you know what you're doing. You've been at this antiques thing for a long time. Twenty-five thousand dollars is a lot of money, so give me a few hours to make arrangements."

I walked around the house's empty rooms until I felt calm enough to go back outside. Bursting with confidence thanks to my generous brother, I strode across the lawn to join Mrs. Miller, Mike, and Tracy, and reassure them of a check by late afternoon. They seemed so relieved that I was invited to join the Miller family for a celebratory lunch at their favorite diner, the Shady Acres.

As people organized to leave, I went back to look at the mirrors I now near-legally owned. I packed the loose elements lying at the bottoms of the crates into a paper bag for safekeeping. Standing in a corner where the mirrors were arranged, I saw my image at two angles. Something mysterious seemed to be taking place. "From antiquity onward, mirrors were believed empowered to capture the souls of those reflected in their lifetimes." I had to wonder, was there something to that? I felt charged with a sensation subtly electromagnetic. The spooky idea that the spirits of the dead could contact the living through mirrors oddly enough seemed rather possible.

The sum I paid for the fable mirror was nothing compared with what it was to cost me in the future. Owning it was like owning a beloved pet elephant that followed me around, forcing me to keep working in order to feed and house it. But that's love for you. You don't keep tabs.

CHAPTER TWO

Imagining the Past

My interest in the past is rooted in childhood. During summers and holidays, my family lived on Block Island, twelve miles off the coast of Rhode Island. In 1661, my Baptist ancestors were among the original purchasers of the island, who settled there to share religious ideas without Puritan restrictions. Some were part of Anne Hutchinson's group, who promoted the separation of church and state. The first democratic charter in America was written on Block Island. It stated that "no authority was able to control the opinions of men." Three hundred years later, many of their descendants still held on to their land and independent way of life.

When I was growing up, in the 1950s, the island's winter population was less than it had been two hundred years earlier. Being there, one felt transported into a bygone era. Islanders had a reputation for being clannish, not welcoming to strangers or open to change. For many year-round residents, life was not that different than it had been in the nineteenth century. Many still farmed and were self-sufficient. They seemed content to do without the conveniences offered on the mainland. Most did not have a phone or a TV. There were few cars on the road. Ostentation of any kind was quietly discouraged, even among the blue-blooded rich who came to rent places in the summer.

The Block Island landscape resembles the Irish countryside.

Miles of stone walls run along treeless hills, enclosing fields shot with wildflowers. The sky is wide and changing. On a clear day the sun reflecting off the ocean casts a bright, painterly light upon the earth, illuminating everything in its path. White-shingled buildings shimmer against a cloudless sky, and from their roofs shadows fall to the ground in crisp plumb-line angles. Migrating birds en route along the Atlantic flyway flock to the island in spring and fall, seeking refuge near lupine-bordered ponds, secluded marshes, and saltwater tidal pools. Harsh winds that blow from the northeast in winter die down to a light breeze by June, infusing the summer air with the scent of rugosa roses, honeysuckle, and bayberry.

My three siblings and I were raised in Manchester, New Hampshire. Our family moved there from New York City after my father was offered a better job. As in so many cities in New England, much of Manchester's architecture was a grim series of wooden clapboard multifamily structures built to house mill workers. Acres of monotonous brick factories lined the banks of the majestic but polluted Merrimack River. In winter we skied the White Mountains and skated on the ponds and lakes outside of town. Even though we spent more time in New Hampshire, we regarded Block Island as our real home, and all of us looked forward to going there whenever we could.

The ferry was the only way to and from the mainland then, making its passage once a day. Off-season, we made our Atlantic crossing on a low-slung vessel called the *Sprigg Carol*. Built in 1903 and named after a Confederate general, it had originally been a steamship. The 150-foot side-loader had the capacity to carry several cars secured by lashings on the deck and a small number of scruffy passengers, including chickens, goats, and cows. Approaching the island, I would climb to the top deck and stand at the bow in anticipation of seeing our house set beyond the beach.

We were the seventh generation to live in the house my mother inherited from her father when she was just sixteen. Built in 1750, our homestead was a wood-shingled Cape with a mas-sive center chimney, anchored on a fieldstone foundation. Additions extended from the central structure. Every room was sunny and cheerful, having been sited for the purpose of seeing both sunrise and sunset over water. Thin paneled doors covered in milk paint were set on forged hinges. Iron thumb latches clicked when lifted and lowered, a sound heard throughout the day when the house was fully occupied. The rooms were small, and every wall was covered in hand-blocked wallpaper, the patterns saturated with rich pigments. The stairs to the second floor were narrow and steep. At the top landing, a dormer window provided a view of what was once New England's largest Victorian hotel, four miles away in town.

Unlike my parents, I loved growing up in an old house. My mother, being an only child and the last of her line, was saddled with other houses besides the one we lived in. Her legacy, unfortunately, did not include cash for maintenance. My parents were burdened with the responsibility of keeping up the buildings by sheer ingenuity and their own hands. They tried to hire people to help out, but a sober man with any skills was hard to find. Day laborers came and went, a job half done their trademark.

Luckily, my father was a born handyman. He was a short, stocky man with a ruddy complexion, thick, shaggy dark eyebrows, and a wide, gap-toothed smile. Racing from one household calamity to the next, he relished every task as a unique problem to solve. His toolshed, which smelled like machine oil, contained every kind of used screw, fitting, and gadget that could be recycled when the occasion arose.

Just about everything had to be brought over from the mainland. Limited resources meant not much was thrown away. Even the most basic things in life were passed down to the next generation or to those who were struggling. Proof of the Yankee mentality was evident in my great-great-uncle Edward Mott's will, dated 1870, kept in a pine desk drawer in the living room. In a faded, winding script, he bequeaths a fellow islander his clothes.

My maternal great-aunt who raised my mother lived with us. Her name was Ethel Gertrude Mott, but we called her Googie. Born on the island in the nineteenth century, she was a member of the New England Baptist Church and the Daughters of the

American Revolution. When I was eight, she was in her eighties. Frail and thin, she had short, curly gray hair. She wore bifocals that made her eyes look enormous in comparison with her tiny head.

Aunt Googie could usually be found in the same spot in the living room. Dangling from a chintz wing chair, Googie's feet barely touched the floor. Beside her rested a bamboo cane she needed to get around. By holding the rubber end of her cane and bending forward, she used the handle hook to capture children by the neck.

Her birdlike body took up only a small portion of the seat cushion, leaving enough room for me to squeeze in beside her whenever I needed attention. For my entertainment, Googie would blow smoke rings from her Salem cigarettes, which she passed to me when my parents were not looking.

Smoking was sometimes followed by a reading. My favorite was a slim volume of poetry with a midnight blue leather cover, embossed with gilt lettering. Inside were cameo etchings and photographs of writers such as Tennyson, Longfellow, and Whitman. Men with long hair and wild beards were dressed in formal black coats with high-collared shirts. The ladies, Dickinson and Eliot, posed in dark crinoline dresses similar to the one I found preserved in mothballs in a trunk in our attic and wore one year for Halloween after taking the hem up with scissors.

The poetry, referring to ancient myths, battles, and death, struck me as arcane. Most of the time I focused on the daguerreotypes, the writers looking possessed, their eyes intense, shiny, and otherworldly. No one smiled for the camera. It seemed having one's picture taken was serious business back then. The etched images were more flattering and made the writers appear pensive and kind, posed dreamily beside their desks and inkwells, heads tilted with cheeks resting on their hands.

Despite her age and physical handicaps, Aunt Googie had a youthful spirit and a sharp mind. She supplied my sister, two brothers, and me with accounts of the "olden days." Reaching back into distant history, she answered our questions about her childhood on Block Island, and what New York City had been like before there were cars. These stories imprinted on my young mind an appreciation of history. As a household elder, my great-aunt provided advice about practical skills to prepare me for the future. "You should learn how to do a little needlework, dear. Someday it will come in handy," she would say, as her paralyzed fingers, wrapped in cotton string, loosely held a crochet hook. Her handicrafts were draped over every armchair, table, bed, and pillowcase edge. I admired the things Googie made for us but was too impatient to count stitches.

Sometimes my aunt took me with her to call on ancient cousins. Most lived off rutted dirt roads. All of these relatives were unmarried, childless women who lived by themselves in rooms filled with family heirlooms. They seemed awestruck that a child from the same gene pool existed and were just delighted to have me with them. Whenever I showed signs of curiosity about something that caught my eye, like an antique porcelain doll dressed in Victorian fashion, they would have a story to go with it. Brown-eyed dolls were brought back from England or France as gifts for daughters of clipper ship captains who sailed during the China trade. Maps would be brought out to show me the routes of sailors traveling from Rhode Island to different parts of the world before the Suez Canal was built. Inevitably, I would leave each cousin's house with a keepsake. Through my growing collection of historic objects, I began to fantasize about the past. I thought of antiques as having the power of a genie's lamp.

When I was a young girl, there were not many children around to play with. There were no clubs to belong to, or teams to join. You had to use your imagination to entertain yourself. Complaints of boredom or loneliness elicited little sympathy from my parents, who blamed "idleness" as the cause of my misery. Daydreaming or moping was considered "doing nothing" and an unconstructive way to live. "Can't think of anything to do?" my father would ask, as he hurried by with a tool in hand to fix a leaky plumbing fixture. "Then pick up your room. Do the dishes!"

Everyone was expected to help out around the house, and I

was not keen on that arrangement. My recourse was to slip out the door early in the morning, before my parents rose. Out of earshot, I found ways to spend my time other than doing housework, or planting and weeding the vegetable garden.

In the early sixties, people from the mainland began arriving and buying property. The old houses were sold furnished, a standard practice in those days. Once the new owners moved in, they pitched out everything inside. This suited me perfectly. The town dump became a treasure trove for me, a budding antiques collector with no money. The location was superb, set behind a rocky beach, with views of a granite lighthouse to the north.

I learned to be selective. The stock at the dump was constantly replenished with discarded inventory. There were others—even adults—up to the same thing, but the competition was far from fierce. Although a few arty types could present conflicts of interest, swapping usually settled matters amicably. At eight years old, I was by far the youngest aesthete on the littered turf. Most of the grownups—local tradesmen and weekend handyman dads—hunted for the practical, like a spare part for a rototiller or a hose that might do to mend a leaky wringer washing machine.

"Why would anyone throw that out?" I often wondered, dashing through a crowd of seagulls to retrieve a treasure glimpsed underneath a heap of twisted bicycles. I developed a keen eye for spotting and sorting, an ability to determine the merits of a broken wicker doll carriage, for example. Once the coffee grinds were hosed off, I could repair it myself with glue and string. The dump had substantial categories to choose from, including photographs, rugs, furniture, trunks of clothing and linens, and signed prints and paintings, most from the Victorian era. A Chinese hand-embroidered man's robe with solid gold buttons was discovered at this site, as was an oil portrait of President Grant painted at the time he was in office and was vacationing on Block Island.

I never told my parents where I spent my mornings, and they were too preoccupied restoring several old houses to notice I wasn't around for a good part of the day. Unfortunately, someone who had spotted me at the dump ratted me out. Afterward my father had a discussion with me about my compulsion to retrieve "old junk." As much as I tried to explain the beauty of each tattered object parked near the shed and outdoor shower, he still could not fathom my peculiar behavior. Likely he thought my urge to collect discarded things might be an early manifestation of a mental disorder. I think he feared I would become one of those people who cruise neighborhoods with shopping carts and I'd end up living in rooms piled to the ceiling with newspapers. Nothing I said could change his mind. My valuables were returned by jeep, and I was restricted to normal childhood activities, like spending the day at the beach. There, I entered a driftwood-collecting phase, but it did not last long, the sculptural pieces having but limited potency when it came to conjuring histories. For me, the tide had tumbled things too far from their original estates.

I began to wonder whether the dump was the only repository on the island or whether there might be an untapped trove of pristine antique inventory to be tracked down, a source no one had combed over. During my walks to ponds to fish, I started to notice abandoned buildings. These sites seemed worth exploring on days too foggy for the beach. I convinced other kids of varying ages to accompany me on outings that bordered on breaking and entering. I viewed excursions to these historical sites as anthropological in nature.

As the morning mist rose off the earth, a small band of children followed me through cow pastures. After tearing away vines that had sealed the entrances of eighteenth-century shingled Capes, we would begin our inspection.

Newspapers and magazines recorded dates of departure generally around the time of the First World War, when the U.S. government urged residents to evacuate the island. Some never returned. The interiors of these deserted houses conjured images of people who left with only the clothes on their backs. Furniture was in place. Beds were made up with sheets and quilts. On a bedside table a pair of folding reading glasses rested atop a book. Glass jars filled with homegrown food were stocked in pantry cupboards. Kitchen tables were set with flow blue china, a tea strainer resting on a saucer. Just curious, we were never acquisitive. The out-of-time experience was what we were after.

Keep Out signs posted in front of the condemned hotels in town did not deter us. I had been told never to read letters unless they were addressed to me, even if they were opened, but when so many years had passed and the envelopes were still sealed, that rule did not seem to apply. Seated in an overstuffed mohair chair in a hotel lobby, I spent hours ripping open mail that had spilled onto the carpet from a soiled canvas bag, hoping to find a lost love letter. But the post never divulged more than a request for a reservation.

My siblings and I had a pact that these more unusual activities were best kept undercover. Instinctively, we knew that our parents would not approve of the fun we had at the beach when we found a crate with the red stenciled lettering EXPLOSIVES that had washed ashore from a World War II submarine. We never ignited the dynamite packed in metal cylinders, but there were plenty of crayonlike red flares for each of us to use to set fire to rocks.

I did not like to think of myself as a tattletale, but I had a big mouth and could never keep a secret for long. One day I made the mistake of describing one of our recent finds to my mother while she was busy caulking a window sash. She was dressed in her painting clothes—a red bandanna, a checked shirt tied at the waist, turquoise capri pants, and white canvas sneakers. As she scraped and sanded, I took a seat below her on the lawn and began describing the tottery house we had discovered near a popular clamming spot on the salt pond. By her distracted expression, I sensed she was only half listening, as she often did when I would follow her around talking incessantly.

Suddenly she put down her putty knife. "Stay away from the hermit's house," she said sternly. "I don't want you playing in there. It's dangerous."

A real hermit? Before this moment I had assumed all hermits lived in Black Forest cabins or stone beehive huts on steep cliffs far from our civilization. Now it seemed these outsiders had migrated to windswept New England islands.

Alarmed by the consequences of my mother's edict, I rose to plant myself at her side. Grinding paint chips into the grass with the heels of my sandals and hopping from one foot to the other, I tried to think of something to say to make her change her mind. There was no reason to worry, I assured her. When inside the hermit's house we wore shoes to protect our feet from the glass shards carpeting the floor and were careful to avoid the opened hatch in the center of the room that dropped to the cellar and was filled with empty whiskey bottles.

Her attention now caught, she looked at me anxiously. "Promise me that you will not go there again," she said.

Looking at my toes, I nodded, half believing that, if I did not actually say the word, it would not count as a lie.

The next morning I headed directly to the hermit's. I felt sorry for him having lived alone in his ramshackle house. He did not have a mother like mine to paint and wallpaper his bedroom. If only he had ordered some new curtains and nicer furniture like we had from the Sears catalog, he might have felt more like having people over.

In time, I began combining house tours with bicycle trips to the cemetery. Orange-lichen-covered headstones with corroded epitaphs were set into steep graduated mounds that rose from a hill overlooking the harbor. I recognized some of the names from stories Aunt Googie had shared and mulled the possibility that the spirits of the dead might still be in circulation. I imagined myself endowed with paranormal abilities, able to receive and relay messages from beyond. If I could tap into the right technique, perhaps they would rise from their graves in an ectoplasmic haze, the only way the dead had of communicating. At the very least, I thought they would be pleased someone had come by to visit, as my old relatives seemed when I appeared before them with Googie.

Standing in front of a slate tombstone from 1730, I wondered if the spirit underground felt my presence. Using a method of my own invention, I stood straight, arms slightly raised and fingers extended, closed my eyes, and repeatedly called out the names in a low-pitched drone. After many attempts with no results, I gave up my graveyard experiments. The things these people had once used and had left behind gave me a greater sense of who they were.

My brother Bobby had a bent for history, too. While I was firmly a fan of the eighteenth- and nineteenth-century New Englander of European descent, he had a fascination with North American Indians. On a spring vacation, we had visited the American Museum of Natural History in New York, and my brother was highly influenced by the dioramas of Native Americans with bows and arrows and Indian moms dressed in fringed deerskin—with papooses—preparing food over campfires. In almost every scene, a body of water against a setting sun was the painted backdrop, prompting the notion that there may have been encampments buried at the edges of our pond.

Googie had also been reading Livermore's *History of Block Island* to Bobby, which resulted in an unshakable obsession with the Manisean, Mohegan, and Narragansett tribes native to Rhode Island. Seeking evidence of their lives on the island became Bobby's prime pursuit. At the age of eleven, he was perhaps the first person to investigate the ancient native settlements of Block Island with a shovel.

Bobby was the archaeologist, and I was his artifacts assistant. He enlisted my help, as he usually did when there were not any boys around. Together we built a rectangle-framed rack out of leftover timber using a porch screen as the bottom, nailed to the four sides. We lugged the sieve and garden tools through thickets of briars and poison ivy until we reached the small pond on our property. There, my brother was certain, Indians had lived, fished, and made clay pots.

Instinctively, he was onto something big. Twenty-five years later, in 1985, a group of scientists on a grant discovered within their first week of exploration "the earliest known year-round Native American site in Northern New England." It was located on the Great Salt Pond, near New Harbor, and was 2,500 years old.

But the afternoons my brother and I spent in the August sun, looking for arrowheads, primitive hand tools, and pottery shards in the pond lot near our house, were somewhat less productive.

As Bobby dug down about a foot in sections over a five-foot range marked with sticks and kitchen string, I would stand by, waiting for direction. He shoveled the dirt into the huge sieve, and once it was filled, I was told to get on the other end. Barely able to lift the loaded frame, we would shake the crib back and forth until nothing was left on the screen but pebbles. At first, I thought archaeology would be fun, but digging seemed an awful lot like work. I complained incessantly about the heat, the bugs, the heavy equipment. When not one arrowhead had surfaced over several days, I grew too discouraged to continue. What evidence, I demanded, did he have to place a lost tribe on the edge of our pond when there were hundreds of ponds on the island? What about Sachem Pond? Or Seneca Swamp? We might have more luck at a site with an Indian name. Our pond had no name other than the one we had given it—Mommy's Pond. Stomping my foot, I yelled, "I quit," and marched off to the beach with a towel. I looked back once from a wooden gate at the dirt road to see if Bobby would follow, but he did not. Defiant, he stood waist high in tall grass, with one hand wrapped around the long handle of a spade shovel.

Feeling guilty about leaving my brother in the lurch over the Indian expedition, I was eager to make up, and I did not want to be left out of any future escapades. Days later, when he claimed to have caught what he estimated was the biggest pickerel on record, yanked from the selfsame mystical pond on our property, I agreed to help. It was obvious, I said, that such a catch should be preserved for posterity. Using a book on taxidermy, we followed the pictorial instructions. After Bobby gutted the fish, I held its mouth open while he poured sand down the gullet. We ignored the sand that seeped out of the belly in sections missed with needle and thread.

Eventually, we needed the help of our older sister, Susan, who spent her time copying Flemish masters from art books my parents bought for her. From the age of seven, Susan had been given private drawing and painting lessons by a French nun in a studio at a convent in New Hampshire. At this juncture, she was painting posthumous portraits of our ancestors posing with various farm animals inspired by old photographs pasted on thick black paper in family albums. Dressed in a bathing suit and smock, she stood for hours by herself at a wooden easel placed on the lawn, wielding brushes and an oval wooden palette smeared with oils.

In her role as family artist, Susan was accustomed to interruption by our requests to draw realistically. As a supreme favor to us, she agreed to apply her skills to highlighting the scales of the trophy fish. Finally, the pickerel was mounted on a pine board, varnished, and inscribed with the weight and date of the catch. The three of us thought of this mounting as a collective contribution to the house decor, one that would hang on the wall for generations to come, eventually reaching the status of a cherished antique. And the pickerel did remain on view over the pine fireplace mantel for several years. Every season, to our amusement, the fish shriveled and buckled, contorting into surprising new shapes and colors, until one day it was tossed into the fireplace flames by my mother on one of her cleaning rampages. Mom was a tough art critic.

After high school, I worked with my boyfriend in Connecticut restoring early American furniture for antiques dealers. My parents thought I was floundering. Since I refused to go to college, they offered to send me to a one-year finishing school for women in London that trained students in the Montessori method of teaching children. The school and dormitory were contained in a beautiful white eighteenth-century building across the street from Hyde Park. My fellow students were daughters of barristers, Arab royalty, and titled English. It seemed strange to me that girls from such high-profile families received what in my opinion were shoddy educations, compared with those of their male peers, who attended prestigious colleges such as Cambridge and Oxford. I always hated school, so nothing changed once I got there. Skipping classes, I spent my days in the decorative arts galleries of museums. On weekends I hung around the antiques stalls on Portobello Road. By looking at finer things, I was honing an ability to differentiate levels of quality. This was the first step of my education.

My mother used to recall my grandfather's advice to her when she was a girl. "Alice," he said, "never sell the land. I like to know that everything as far as I can see belongs to me or my relatives." Referring to the tourists who stayed at his hotel in the summer, he was more specific: "Let them come, but never let them stay."

But when I returned in the early 1970s, Block Island was transforming into something much different. It had been widely publicized in metropolitan newspapers as an undiscovered place of idyllic beauty and an inexpensive second home destination. And the old order was changing. As members of the established families—like the Littlefields, the Dodges, the Motts, and the Champlins—either died or left the island for opportunities on the mainland, large tracts of land were sold by their descendants (or by the town for back taxes) to speculators for a song. Two centuries of architecture were practically wiped out when old buildings were condemned and torn down. Developments of prefab beach houses built on the highest hills and near the beach interfered with the extended views. The island was fast losing its wild charm.

What stayed with me was the memory of the way things look as time passes through them. Some objects and houses have a power that can be felt from the day they are created. Antiques can claim this quality, but along the way they pick up something else that defines their character. With their marks and scars, they magically absorb the energy of the people who once owned them. There is something soothing in the familiar. When I open an old drawer, the smell of wood imbued with the scent of floral sachets can instantly propel me back to my childhood home.

CHAPTER THREE

A Hands-On Education

I have always relied on my own sensibilities when it comes to appreciating art and antiques. But if I wanted to work in the field, I needed experience. In the 1970s, as New York City tilted on the verge of bankruptcy, I moved to the Upper East Side, anxious to land my first real job. The fast-paced turnover of an auction gallery seemed the perfect setting to learn about antique furniture and art from every period. Christie's, which was headquartered in London, had not yet opened a showroom in New York City. Parke Bernet (Sotheby's) was the only game in town. I soon found out that high-end auction houses had a preference for interns from wealthy families, with connections to potential clientele: mainly those who owned expensive collections they might wish to part with someday. I could not argue the fact that I did not have the right background. Few of those people were in my social circle.

In that same year, William Doyle opened his auction house on the Upper East Side. He was a very personable man, passionate about antiques, and liked the idea of helping young people get started in the business. At William Doyle Galleries, I got a minor job working on weekends on the preview floor. The idea of becoming a decorative arts specialist, which had once seemed so glamorous, faded away when I saw how much of a sales job it really was. I was not cut out to deal with the public. I had a way of not mincing words and was often less than tactful. Working as an antiques restorer, in a quiet studio, under less pressure, appealed to me more.

Throughout my life, I have attended art schools but never longer than a semester or two. I concluded the classroom was no match for hands-on experience. Apprenticing to masters of the trade seemed the best way for me to learn.

An antiques restorer's job begins with having a vision for what a piece should look like when completed. Experience comes from examining period items, talking with other people in the field, and reading about the subject. A basic knowledge of chemistry is essential. We try to employ the same methods and materials used by the creator. This applies to joinery, adhesives, and the various finishes used when the pieces were made. The goal is to make repairs and touch-ups undetectable and reversible. The golden rule is to do as little as possible, and attend to only what needs to be done to make a piece last a little longer. Antique furniture should leave our shops looking old but cared for.

Restorers are great recyclers. Their shops are filled with odd things like seasoned wood, figured veneers, tortoiseshell, mother-of-pearl, ivory, keys, locks, screws, nails, knobs, escutcheons, bails, pulls, and casters, all of which have been salvaged from period furniture, as well as solid wood paneling found in a state beyond the point of resurrection. All these are stored on racks and in drawers and cubbyholes to use on future projects.

It had not been easy to find a weekday job. I had knocked on a lot of doors seeking a position with a restorer but was repeatedly told by the men who owned the shops that it was their policy not to hire women. At last I was hired at Thorp Brothers, then the leading firm for restoration of antique European furniture in New York. Women were allowed to hold a brush but, as in every other place I observed, never a cabinetmaker's tool. At Thorp's I learned about conservation materials, finishing techniques, and the exotic veneers used in marquetry furniture. There I was introduced to the art of gilding.

Two years later I was living in Savannah, Georgia. I shared a woodworking shop with a talented furniture designer and cabinetmaker named Bud, and his all-male, mostly gay staff. In addition to building furniture, we restored antiques. Then, after five fun years on the Georgia coast, it was time for me to go home, back to New England.

My brother Bobby was married and lived in Newport, Rhode Island. He liked living there for the same reasons I had been drawn to Savannah: the ocean and a general nostalgia for historic architecture. In 1982, when I drove north, Bobby's house was my first destination. I began to do freelance restoration projects for the Preservation Society of Newport County. I was soon offered a full-time position as the head of the furniture conservation department. The society had never had a full-time restorer before. At first, the curator did not quite know where to put me and my flammable materials. My initial shop was in the basement of Rosecliff, a white mansion designed by McKim, Mead, and White, inspired by Louis XIV's Grand Trianon at Versailles. Two months later, a trustee offered an alternative workshop: a heated barn near the Cliff Walk. In my new studio, I worked alone. The collections at the ten mansions the society owned were in rough shape. Daunting projects were dropped off at the "barn" from behemoths such as The Breakers, Marble House, Kingscote, The Elms, Chateau-sur-Mer, and Rosecliff.

Some problems were not visible at first. Powder-post beetles, which thrive in damp woodwork, were posing a serious threat to the mansions. Luckily, there were no tourists standing under the coffered ceiling at Chateau-sur-Mer when, during the last beetle's snack, it collapsed to the floor. The culprits had helped themselves to a century's fine dining. Not only had they munched through the walnut ornamental work overhead but they had also been noshing on the furniture, wall paneling, and mirror and picture frames of every building. I spent a lot of time on the highway, carting pieces to the fumigation chamber in Providence.

Although my job was varied and interesting, it was lonely working by myself. I lived in an apartment of a mansion, but my salary was barely enough to subsist on, which is pretty much the way things go working in any museum environment. It was rewarding to help preserve, but the joy was beginning to fizzle with each meager paycheck. I wanted to be where I could make a better wage, a place with voracious collectors. One city fit that bill: Manhattan.

With solid experience behind me, and having worked on Newport furniture, I was hired by Israel Sack, then known as the best American antiques firm in the country. The shop was named for the founder, who in 1903 had immigrated to America from Lithuania, where he had trained as a cabinetmaker. Settling in Boston, he made reproductions of American furniture and worked as an antiques restorer. After two years of dabbling on the side as a dealer, he set up an antiques shop on Charles Street, and eventually opened up another in New York City.

Crazy Sack, as he was called, had a great eye for and knowledge of American furniture. Many credit him as the founder of the American market. Gifted with savvy business skills, he soon attracted the notice of pioneering early-twentieth-century collectors. With his clutch of industrialist clients, such as Henry Ford, Henry Francis du Pont, Francis and Mabel Garvan, and Ima Hogg, his firm took off. Israel's oldest son, Harold, took over the reins of the business in 1933, after graduating from Dartmouth, and named his shop in New York after his father. Brothers Albert and Robert soon joined, and the family team moved forward as the leading authorities.

Harold accurately prophesied that antique furniture would eventually bring the same prices paid for fine art. He continuously broke records paid for American antiques, especially early Newport pieces. *The New York Times* summed up the extent of Harold's activities in his obituary, noting that he "bought for and sold to the Metropolitan Museum of Art, the Art Institute of Chicago, the Museum of Fine Arts in Boston, Colonial Williamsburg and the Henry Francis du Pont Winterthur Museum." As a result of family contributions, three Federal period galleries in the Metropolitan Museum's American Wing bear the Sack name.

At Sack's showroom on Fifty-seventh Street, I was hired as a restorer even though Albert found it peculiar for a "girl" to want to get her hands dirty. At their workshop in Long Island City, I was under the supervision of their head restorer, a guy named Sal, who I observed spent most of his time on Sack's clock watching television in his office while I gilded and made repairs on all the mirrors.

As I was not learning anything new from Sal, I grew anxious to break away and start my own company. My sister, Susan, lived in New York, too. She was working as an illustrator for books and movie posters, but the decorative arts had always appealed to her, so the two of us decided to open a studio together. She would paint murals and specialize in decorative painting, while I would continue to restore antique furniture and gild seating and mirrors. I named my company Antique Conservation Inc., and we rented a loft in the meatpacking district, on Fourteenth Street. Soon, trucks delivering precious eighteenth-century furniture began to pull up alongside those picking up animal fat and bones. I hired a staff of mostly women. Some had conservation backgrounds, and we all learned from each other. We soon developed a reputation for doing high-end work and got a lot of publicity; as a result, we were making money. In the decorative arts world, we were known as "The Sisters." The Sacks still sent me mirrors and referred their clients to me. And in time, Christie's opened a showroom in New York, and I was introduced to specialists in the American and English Decorative Arts departments who would call me in to do minor repairs on furniture before auction previews. They also sent me their best collector clients.

It seemed I had a golden touch with mirror frames. Every type of vintage mirror came my way. English Georgian walnut veneered and parcel gilt frames were sent over to have parts replaced, and prior bad repairs reworked. American Federal reverse-painted glass mirrors showed up on a regular basis for a while. Where sprays of wheat and flowers extending onto delicate wires were missing, replacements were cast from originals.

Convex mirrors, similar in shape to the one in the background of Jan van Eyck's famous 1434 marriage painting, arrived wrapped in blankets and tape, while tall, narrow pier mirrors that had fallen off walls were sometimes delivered in pieces filling shopping bags and boxes. American girandole mirrors with bracketed candleholders were sent over for more gold, more leaves, extra decorative balls. An eagle perched on the crest of a rocky crag might call for a new beak or a replacement tip to a feather on an outstretched wing.

French and Italian mirrors, six to seven feet high and four feet across, were laid flat on plywood tables. Nothing can beat the artful workmanship on French pieces carved in dense walnut. Low-relief carving is the true test of a master carver. Here there is no room for mistakes. Once the wood is chipped away, there is no putting it back without a trace.

My favorite mirrors were those where life-size masks of women's faces appeared on the upper center crests. Sculpting hair gave carvers a chance to show off their skills at creating movement and lightness. Wavy locks are windswept back but for two twisted, thick strands framing the cheeks and tied in a bow under the chin, the ends then flowing from side to side. And the gilded coiffures were intertwined with ornaments in the shapes of feathers, shells, wreaths of flowers, and strands of pearls, all symbols of nature, love, and wealth.

Few people own such valuable things. My collector clients were respectful and never rushed me. With no real deadlines to complete my work, I sometimes kept pieces longer than necessary. A chaise longue made for Marie Antoinette was thrilling to have around, for example. We all took turns stretched out on the red velvet cushions encased in a gilded frame with bowed ends in the shape of a Viking ship, the pleated fabric trimmed in silk tassels.

In New York City, artists pioneer neighborhoods where the rent is low, after which moneyed professionals move in, displacing those who made the neighborhood interesting. Around 1990, we were evicted from our building on Fourteenth Street so our studio could be converted into a luxury loft. My next address was in a grungy building in New York's congested garment district, near Penn Station. This is where my clients assumed I was diligently working on their antiques on the day I went to the auction at the Miller farm.

It was not easy finding movers to haul the enormous mirrors

from Clayville, Rhode Island, to my studio. Most transport companies would not be held liable for goods within crates they did not build themselves. Mirrors must be transported standing, strapped onto an interior truck wall, and ten-foot crates would take a tall rig. I finally found and hired two uninsured, hefty guys from New Bedford, Massachusetts, who were willing to wing it.

Shortly after the shipment arrived, I got a 2:00 a.m. phone call. The burglar alarm had gone off in my studio. In minutes, I was headed for midtown in a yellow cab. Two officers in a squad car were waiting in front. Fumbling through a weighty bouquet of keys, I ushered them through the lobby door.

The three of us rode the passenger elevator to my floor.

"Don't turn on the lights," one officer said as I turned the key of the loft's barred metal door. "We'll take a look around with our flashlights."

In the studio, the officers crisscrossed beams. "Wow!" one said. "What goes on here anyway?"

As I explained I was in the antiques business, his light illumined the mirrors leaning against the wall, then flashed to the floor, which was strewn with old newspaper padding I had just hours before pulled from the casings. Other restoration projects lay in various stages of disrepair on tables and sawhorses.

One policeman stood by me while his buddy headed through the loft to the back door. "I don't see anything. The alarm must have been tripped by a loud noise," he said. "Now you can turn on the overheads."

The two officers roamed around in their blue uniforms, fascinated by the furniture and objects that filled the shop.

"Hey, Frank, look at this. It's a couch with a big fish! Neat! Get a load of those gold mirrors. Now, *they* look expensive!" one said.

"Nice. Real nice," the other noted appreciatively. "Is that paint or real gold on them? Boy, look at that carving! Now that must have been a lot of work. They are something." He moved in for a closer look much in the manner of an art expert, using his flashlight to supplement the fluorescent tubes above.

I gave the officers a tour of the studio, explaining briefly what some of the things were and how they would look after restoration. The policemen seemed captivated and were having a good time. "Hey, let me ask you something," Frank said, readjusting his cap. "I have this old refrigerator. It's real wood. Oak, I think. Bought it for next to nothing." He smiled as he recalled the bargain he felt he had scored. "Only thirty-five dollars! You should see this thing." Frank extended his arms horizontally and vertically to give me an idea of the icebox's dimensions. "Chrome handles, in great shape. It's going to look great in my house." Frank's dream for the refrigerator was to incorporate it into the bar he planned to build himself in his Brooklyn basement. "Ms. Huggins," he said, "would you mind telling me how I should refinish it?" His confidence in my expertise was likely inspired by the shelves lined in bottles bearing French labels, jars containing an array of pigments, tin cans filled with assorted brushes, and rows of wooden-handled tools.

It was three-thirty by the time we left the building. "We're not supposed to do this, but we're going to give you a ride home," Frank volunteered.

Outside, the wind lifted and spun paper debris off the sidewalk, hurling empty coffee cups and newspapers into the metal gates of closed storefronts and over the hoods of parked cars. In the cruiser, the three of us whizzed past the neon lights of Times Square and continued our conversation about antiques until, twenty blocks later, I was deposited in front of my apartment building.

After so many outstanding pieces have passed through my hands, my tastes have evolved to recognize the qualities that make a piece "good." But there is a tight cabal of authorities who control the market. Worth depends on their assessments, evaluations, and opinions. Selling the mirrors and the dolphin sofa would require their blessing.

I began by talking to experts and reading published material for a better handle on what I was about to face. There are five basic qualities collectors look for in antiques. The standards are (1) market freshness; (2) whether the piece is a superior example of a popular design of the given period; (3) provenance; (4) rarity; and (5) the quality of materials and craftsmanship. I felt the sofa promised a blue-ribbon rating in all categories. By contrast, the fable mirror broke all the rules. The biggest bugaboo was number 4, rarity. I soon discovered that not even one American-made Aesop mirror inspired by a Thomas Johnson–engraved plate had ever appeared. That was not good.

Hitting the bell on all counts with the dolphin sofa and needing to square up with my brother, I called Christie's. I hoped to be able to place the sofa in January's Important American Decorative Arts sale. With the catalogs already printed and the sale to take place in two months' time, I knew I was cutting it close. I had an allegiance to Christie's. I liked just about every specialist I had gotten to know there. Their American and English departments were my sources of referrals to top collectors. And the staff, who in general still fit the profile of coming from the "right families," are knowledgeable, courteous, attractive, and well turned out.

I sent John Hays in American Decorative Arts a photograph of the sofa in its found state. When I called him, I was surprised to hear him say, "There are a lot of American Classical sofas around, and they don't bring that much."

Huh?

Even if the market were flooded, I did not recall seeing any as good as the one I had in my shop. If rarity, furthermore, were a handicap, as in the case of the Fox and Grapes mirror, just how many made for "a lot" of dolphin sofas?

I argued the Classical sofa's merits, mentioning the fins and the continuous arms finished with verdigris scales, as well as the acorn relief pattern on the back seat rail. The sofa was rare, in the sense of being one of the best in its class compared with others made in the same period, the first quarter of the nineteenth century. I thought I understood the models John was referring to. They were the squattier, clunky renditions with cornucopia carvings on the foot brackets. If those were what John meant by "a lot," he was right. There were plenty around, and I did not particularly care for them either. But I was certain the one I owned was uncommon for its design and quality.

I still could not persuade John. His lowball estimate of $20,000 was disappointing. The sofa, I thought, just had to be worth more. I was convinced that if John could see it in person, he would agree with me. He mentioned the present condition he had seen in the photograph I sent him as a possible deterrent. I assured him that most of the original finishes could be salvaged from underneath the paint. Still he remained unconvinced.

If I could not get this specialist to rally enthusiasm for the piece, it did not make much sense to give it to Christie's. Entering the sale without its being listed and pictured in the catalog seemed imprudent, too.

I decided to seek a private buyer. Such a client could be found through an independent art adviser. Good advisers have solid backgrounds in their fields, have held positions as top specialists at auction galleries, or have worked for museums or other preservation institutions. They know the market and how to spend their clients' money wisely.

After an initial discussion, I sent photographs of the sofa to Ron De Silva, someone I had known for years from restoring antiques for his clients, almost exclusively nineteenth-century furniture collectors. He is a former head of Sotheby's American Furniture and Decorative Arts Department. Besides being consultant to this small group, Ron is a private dealer and adviser, and runs an appraisal business from his home office in Garrison, New York.

Ron called me back a nanosecond after he received the pictures. "Fabulous! Gorgeous!" he proclaimed in his thick Providence, Rhode Island, accent. I told him about Christie's discouraging estimate, and he agreed that the price seemed low. I proposed paying him a commission, the amount of which was not discussed, if he could find a private buyer.

The apex players in the world of high-end American furniture were a relatively small group at the time, perhaps twenty. The most coveted American pieces are from the mid-1700s to 1800.

Fewer still were nineteenth-century collectors. This was Ron's niche. Bearing in mind that market freshness increases value, a quiet, discreetly managed sale was my preference. An American specialist once told me that antiques passed around too much, even if lovely, lose their desirability. She made the analogy of an attractive young woman with a reputation damaged by taking too many lovers. The more people talked about something, the more they would embellish its flaws, running it down, until no one dared get near it. I had heard stories of experts publicly arguing over a piece until the issues surrounding it were so unsettling that buyers were scared off. Once the piece hit the auction floor, the same dealers and museum buyers who shortly before were beset with reservations would purchase it, a technique useful in acquiring perfect period furniture and other masterworks at bargain prices.

Several days later, I was astonished when Ron called and sheepishly suggested Leigh Keno as a contender for the sofa. Keno was not a fresh source for me. I knew him from his time on staff at Christie's. After he had gone out on his own, I gave him a lead on an eighteenth-century Newport Goddard card table in what appeared to be original condition. The table showed up at my shop and was destined for Sotheby's. The Rhode Island table, with ball-and-claw feet with open talons, was a prize. Leigh sold it to a famous collector and had to pay me handsomely for the tip. After that, every time I spoke to him, he grumbled that I had made all the money on that transaction.

By 1995, Leigh had a flourishing reputation as an upstart in the American decorative arts field. From networking on the staff at Christie's, he knew who to call when the right things came his way. The Sacks were growing old. Leigh, ferociously ambitious, was anxious to step into their place. Years later he was further promoted by his TV exposure on *Antiques Roadshow*, where he and his identical twin brother, Leslie, are regular guests. The twins have risen to stardom by quoting mind-boggling prices for American furniture to presumably clueless guests, who, upon hearing the dollar amounts of their antiques or memorabilia, feel like lottery winners. But the chance that a common citizen owns a piece of American furniture of any great value is about the same as the chance of having the winning lottery ticket. Prices quoted on TV are not close to what a seller will receive. These are dealers' prices, which take into account the best market circumstances, including timing and knowing the right client.

Nevertheless, I owed my brother Bill and was under self-imposed duress to pay him back. Ron De Silva understood when I expressed my apprehension concerning Leigh, mostly because he was a dealer, not a collector, and not a fresh source for me. Ron said if I preferred he not contact Leigh, he would seek another buyer. I also knew, though, that when dealers want something, they pay immediately. I agreed to have Ron speak to Leigh and to have him come look at the sofa. In the meantime, I would try getting one more estimate.

I decided to see if Sotheby's might be interested. I still might be better off, I thought, with an auction house, where the sofa would have more exposure. There was one problem for me. The head of the American Furniture department at Sotheby's was Leslie Keno. The twins were in constant communication. Nevertheless, I sent Leslie the pictures. When I called him, the first thing I asked was whether Leigh had spoken to him about the sofa. Leslie admitted he had but added it did not matter if his brother were a contender for the same piece. If I wanted, he would take it in the Sotheby's next sale. The two big houses held simultaneous sales in January. Again, it was too late to make their catalog, and, like John Hays at Christie's, Leslie did not offer to come by to see the sofa. His estimate of $20,000 or "possibly $25,000" sounded so familiar I wondered if he'd had wind of my conversation with Christie's. My field is a small world, and talk of very good things about to come on the market spreads like wildfire.

After a short pause, Leslie, covering his tracks, ventured that the sofa might bring more if restored. The potential figure was withheld. From his unenthusiastic tone, I assumed "more" would not make a big difference. The sofa could also be torn apart on the auction floor for having been restored. I computed what I'd fetch after the commission to the auction house—assuming they were right about the price—and figured I would be better off selling it to a dealer after all and should wait to hear what Leigh had to say.

With an appointment set up, Leigh arrived at my studio midday. As he passed through the door, he glanced at the sofa, smiled, and kept walking until he stood in front of the Fox and Grapes mirror. It lay on a long worktable, in the first stages of being restored.

"What's this?" he asked. His arms were braced on the table's edge, his bleached blond head parallel to a basket of gilded grapes.

"No . . . it can't be." Perplexed, he fell silent. Then, leaning on one arm, he looked up. "If this is what I think it might be, it is the best American mirror ever found!"

Leigh's instincts are mostly sound, so I was elated. "It feels American to me, too," I said, gratified that he was responding to the frame as I had upon first seeing it. "By the way, if you had spotted it at a country auction, would you have bought it based on nothing more than intuition?"

"Yeah," he replied, laughingly turning his head sideways to look at me while he hunched over the mirror. Second-guessing his initial instincts, though, he asked if I would mind an investigation of his own, rather than an assessment based on gut feeling. An outright proclamation of something being "the best," when he so recently had come to be regarded as a top dealer in American furniture, could prove a liability if he was wrong.

Even Leigh Keno knew that he needed the blessing of the small contingent of players in the field, "experts" who might collectively back him up and agree on a time frame while sanctifying every other finicky facet on their exhaustive list of criteria. If comparative examples could not be found—the method of going about this sort of thing—the process could take years or, worse, never be resolved. Anything deemed "the best" would be scrutinized and challenged; it would not be warmly regarded if not in the hands of the cabal.

"Would you mind if I take some of the hardware with me to be analyzed?" he asked. "That might tell us something," he went on, speaking like we were a team.

Both of us were puzzled about the mirror's age, so I agreed to let Leigh initiate an investigation. Together we got out screw-drivers and pliers to extract from the frame oxidized nails and other fasteners to be sent off to Luke Beckerdite, then the executive director of the Chipstone Foundation in Wisconsin, which is dedicated to preserving the founders' American collection and to promoting education and research in the decorative arts.

Turning to the sofa, Leigh seemed delighted. "I think I may have a buyer in the Midwest looking for something like this. I'll call them. I'm pretty sure I'd like to have it. How would you like to proceed? Do you want me to speak with Ron, and he and I can negotiate the sale?"

"Yes. I guess that's right," I said, miffed with myself now that I had gotten two dealers involved.

Sofa discussions out of the way, Leigh sat on a stool near my workbench and we chatted about the business. He was glad to get something privately, he said—doing so was becoming increasingly difficult. With the stratospheric prices auctions were commanding for American furniture, sellers now preferred that route rather than selling directly to dealers, whom they distrusted. Leigh thanked me for offering the sofa to him first and said he would be in touch soon.

Ron De Silva called me the next day with an offer from Leigh for $50,000, a figure he thought worth considering. I would have more than covered my outlay, combining the purchase and restoration fees. What I did not have were comparative sales figures for other such sofas. I didn't have time to pore over years of auction catalogs at the New York Public Library, so feeling pressured to recoup what I had spent, I agreed to have Leigh call me with the offer.

Almost as soon as I had hung up with Ron, Leigh, his soft side in remission, was on the line. "Fifty thousand is all I will pay for it," he said. "Restored. That's my final offer. Ron's three-thousand-dollar commission will be deducted from my payment to you." Without much hesitation (and no counteroffer), I accepted the price, which I think surprised him. Given his tone, I had sensed he was prepared to haggle if need be. Assuming the market cornered, he voiced his regrets. "I cannot believe we did not see that sofa. You know I have someone in Rhode Island, scouting for things."

I said something whiny. He countered that he had called Mike Corcoran to find out how much I had paid. "You did all right," he said. "You made enough."

It seemed true enough, but I had hoped for more than "all right," considering how fine the piece was. Before we hung up, Leigh told me the fasteners he had borrowed from the Fox and Grapes mirror would be mailed back to me. Whatever Luke Beckerdite had said to him was enough to smother his interest.

As I began to restore the sofa, I was struck by the incongruity between my trade and the pace of twentieth-century life. The process I followed to gild had not changed much for the last five hundred years. To make gesso, which would be used as the primer coat, I sifted whiting (a caltrite powder) into a container with water and melted rabbit-skin glue. The bole (blue, black, Venetian red, or yellow ochre pigment) was still hand-ground from dry clay bricks imported from France. And I sharpened my chisels on an oiled stone.

In the time it took me to touch up the dolphin's scales and replace one missing maple stretcher to the sofa seat, the frame of a residential skyscraper was erected across from my studio's south window, blocking my view of Twenty-third Street. As the neighborhood transformed from brick to steel, I was literally waiting for the paint to dry.

Through Leigh, I learned there was a sofa similar to ours in the American Wing of the Metropolitan Museum of Art. The fishtails on mine were missing, and we needed a reference. I was asked to copy the tails of the Met's Classical sofa since the dimensions of both pieces were precisely the same. I knew just who to call for the job. Bill Sullivan lives in New York City, had worked for the Met, and is regarded by many as one of the best woodcarvers in the country. Leigh set up an appointment to have Bill and me meet him at the museum on a Monday, the day it is closed to the public.

On a cold November morning, Leigh and I shivered in our winter coats waiting for Bill. From the top stair at the entrance, we looked down upon pedestrians bundled, hatted, and gloved, trotting off to work at the fast clip New Yorkers are known for. When Bill proved late, we decided to proceed. We were let in through the glass doors by a security guard. Leigh announced our appointment with Peter Kenney to the front desk. Kenney, curator of the museum's nineteenth-century American Decorative Arts collection, soon appeared to escort us to the American Wing.

We passed through long corridors of artifacts. Within glass cases and at eye level, the museum's vast collection of ancient religious articles peeked back at us: silver chalices decorated with elaborate enameling, Byzantine crosses embedded with precious cabochon jewels, carved ivory caskets from Constantinople.

Approaching our destination, we entered the dimly lit medieval room. Tapestries of hunting scenes hung on blocked limestone walls. Stained-glass windows were lit from behind. In the center of the room, statues of saints made of wood, marble, and limestone displayed decay and age where worms and time had worn off gold and polychrome finishes. Painted panels told of posthumous miracles performed by martyred saints come back to earth to answer prayers. Virgin saints, crafted in A.D. 1100, had made the pilgrimage from churches in Auvergne, France, to rest in these galleries.

When I saw sundry sculptures of the Virgin Mary and her child, my thoughts again turned to mirrors. In medieval times, the practice of bringing mirrors into Catholic churches was instigated with the Madonna in mind. Mirrors were held to be symbols of purity and spiritual illumination.

Entering the American Wing, we could peer through the wall of glass facing Central Park at a parade of joggers passing through the trees. In the inner courtyard, a bronze Diana's raised bow pointed us toward the American furniture wing.

The Israel Sack American galleries greeted us with portraits of the founding fathers. We strode by tall case clocks, chairs, and Philadelphia highboys. I noticed the lower panel on a Philadelphia eighteenth-century high chest of drawers was carved with a swan and a serpent spewing water, a fable that referenced a

Thomas Johnson design. I paused to inspect the narrative's animals as well as those on a nearby card table for any carving similarity to my Fox and Grapes frame, but no luck. It was going to take more than walking through a major museum to determine my mirror's whittler.

Kenney and Keno walked close together. As I trailed behind them, I overheard their conversation. "Leigh," asked Kenney patronizingly, "where did you ever find that sofa? You're amazing being able to find things like this. How do you do it? It's fabulous!" Without breaking pace, Leigh turned his head in my direction.

"Maryalice found it," he replied. Kenney glanced back at me. He looked perplexed, and I understood why.

American Decorative Arts, especially furniture, has always been a boys' club. The real barrier is the staggering amount of money American furniture continues to bring. Things can turn ugly when the stakes get high, with a lot of shoving going on behind the genteel façade. Women play important roles in the field. They hold curatorial positions, research, write dissertations, and author books on the subject, but they seldom reap significant financial rewards compared to their male colleagues.

"I wish we could have bought your Classical sofa for the Met," Kenney went on, "but the trouble is ours was a gift and we cannot deaccession it. I prefer yours, though."

I silently concurred with Kenney, who had not seen my sofa in person but could tell from the photographs that it was as fine an example as they come. The pieces were on par, just different.

I found the wide inlaid brass Greek key design on the front rail of the Met's model garish and cluttered. The collision of so many materials, curves, and lines intersecting in one place brought one's eye straight to the floor. On my sofa, the front rail was made of plain rosewood veneer, devoid of additional decoration. The exotic rosewood was statement enough, making the space clean and elegant.

I compared the back rails of both sofas. The Met's, I was told, was made by one of New York's most prestigious furniture makers. However dangerous it is to throw stones at gods—especially when their gifts are displayed on museum platforms—I could not help but prefer mine.

On the Met's sofa, the plain, half-round back seat rail seemed out of balance with all that went on in front. On mine, the back rail was carved. By placing the decoration there rather than in the front, the maker encouraged your eye to sweep from the fantastic dolphin heads below and follow the loops and twists on the sides to arrive merrily on the curved rail above the seat back, which was embellished with oak leaves and acorns.

I also preferred the materials used on mine. Real gold lay underneath the verdigris on the dolphin scales (a French technique). Being a pure metal that never tarnishes, gold gave the scales extra shimmer. The Met's bronze powder version had dulled over time. Our maker's higher-quality finish materials made the overall design more pleasing to behold.

Bill, the carver, finally showed up with his tape measure and sketch pad. He and I began to take photographs and trace the outlines of dolphin tails onto paper. Kenney confided that the Met model's tails were not originals, that there were few such sofas around of this quality, and all of them on record—again, a rare occurrence—were missing tails. As a result, the museum had created a design they felt worked. To be on the safe side, we were given orders to copy theirs.

It took two weeks for me, and the three conservators I hired, to restore the sofa. We had a deadline to meet. Leigh dropped in once in a while to check on the progress. At the same time, he and I discussed how the new upholstery should look.

Shortly after the Classical sofa left my studio, it was exhibited in Keno's booth at the prestigious January American Antiques Show held at the Armory on Park Avenue. In his catalog, the sticker price for the sofa was $190,000. A red dot indicated that it was sold. The buyer from the Midwest whom Leigh mentioned to me did in fact purchase it, maybe even before the ink had dried on the check he wrote to me. The new owner of my dolphin sofa was the Detroit Institute of Arts in Michigan.

When I had finished restoring the sofa for Leigh, I made him a folder that contained pictures and written descriptions of the restoration process. Yet I was in such a rush to complete the work on time for the show that I neglected to make myself a copy. I called his shop to see if he would be willing to reproduce the photographs and mail them to me so I could have them for my portfolio. This request seemed to rankle Leigh. He asserted the reason for my request, and for the fact that I had not been returning his phone calls promptly, was simple: I resented the sofa's Armory price tag.

There was no getting around my displeasure with the outcome, given the low quotes I'd received. Since I hadn't complained, I was under the impression I was being a pretty good sport when it turned out that something viewed as "common" by the highest echelon of specialists now stood on the floor of a famous museum. Adding to my frustration was that I also knew that an institution most often pays far below the price something would bring in the public marketplace.

Picking up on my disgruntled tone, Leigh spewed. He suggested I try opening a shop of my own in the high-rent district of New York like he had if I thought being a dealer was so easy. He had other recommendations for me of a more personal nature. Apparently he had found some fissures in my personality, because at the end of our conversation he recommended I check in with a psychiatrist.

I thought about Leigh's advice for a moment and concluded I wasn't inclined to follow through with his prescription. Analysts' couches are usually modern, not my taste. What would be the point of my spending sessions staring at the ceiling thinking about how the doctor's sterile office could be redecorated with antiques? I had other things to figure out. The Fox and Grapes mirror had taken hold of my mind. So, undiagnosed and unmedicated, I set out to learn everything I could about it.

CHAPTER FOUR

The Fox and Grapes Mirror

One day a vixen passed a lioness in her den. "You're not as mighty as you think," said the vixen. "You never manage to give birth to more than one cub at a time."

"True," the lioness quietly replied, "but that one cub is always a lion."

The lion lesson on one-of-a-kind value does not apply to the world of antiques. According to the expert Myrna Kaye, author of the book *Fake, Fraud, or Genuine? Identifying Authentic American Antique Furniture*, "Rare is an offensive four-letter word. Unique is an abomination."

This is confusing because the same term was used as a badge where the Classical sofa was concerned. But what Kaye means when she uses the word *rare* is different. She is referring to the "strange," the out of the ordinary, the unique. *One of a kind* serves as a prevailing disqualifier for period furniture. With such published opinion, I knew trouble lay ahead in getting American decorative arts experts to help me out with the Fox and Grapes frame. Unless another showed up to compare it with, I would have a problem generating interest in my quest to find out who the maker was and where he worked. I began sending photographs around to experts and waited to hear back.

While reassembling and restoring the Fox and Grapes frame in my shop, I received a serendipitous call from a man regarded as one of the top experts on American carving. His name is Alan Miller. His restoration of early American pieces is considered unmatched, and his opinions have been published in periodicals and books. Museums and top collectors hire Miller to bid on their behalf at important American auctions. I had heard that both he and Luke Beckerdite were able to identify Philadelphia carvers by their distinctive chisel marks. Miller, speaking at a wood-carving symposium given at the Peabody Essex Museum in Salem, Massachusetts, said, "The art of carving can be equated to the quality of dancing in space. Carving adds rhythm to the line . . . Good doesn't have to be fancy or complicated . . . It is clear, powerful, unified, and expressive."

On the phone, Alan explained that his gilder in Pennsylvania, where he lived and worked, was not getting to projects as fast as he wanted. He asked if I would be interested in doing a small gilding job on a Federal mirror. I said yes immediately, and was excited at the prospect of his dropping by my studio. I could show him my mirror and get a professional opinion.

The following week Alan arrived dressed in jeans and a perfectly creased and faded leather jacket, a small golden hoop through one earlobe. Under his arm he carried an antique mirror of a type I had worked on dozens of times for Sack's. As we discussed the project, it was at once evident that this man took his career and himself very seriously. But that is the nature of the beast. I have yet to meet a carver who doesn't have an ego. Working in that field in our era of technology is an anachronism, so I am not too bothered by this slightly annoying trait.

Having established how Alan wanted the gilding to look, which I already knew from experience, I asked for his thoughts on my mirror. He glanced over his shoulder to where it was laid out. It seemed he felt safer looking at it from a distance, as if the frame might harbor a virus. I was disappointed at what he had to say, which was to pronounce with assurance that the mirror was made in England in the 1890s. That he had never before seen one like it in this country was given as the reason.

I nonetheless ventured that I thought it was American, and earlier. Alan asked what type of wood it was made of, with no comment on the carvings. I said that it appeared the wood was American white pine but that I had not yet confirmed this with a lab. Alan huffed that American wood was exported all the time to England for use there in shipbuilding. I knew pine was commonly used for ship spars and had heard of the wood being called "mast pine" but had never heard of this species used in furniture or frames in Britain. Limewood or bass would be more expected for carved frames made in England.

As far as I had been told, the use of white pine in the secondary construction of furniture and frames was determining and conclusive evidence of American manufacture. Furthermore, if someone in England had the money to commission a mirror of this size and cover it in expensive gold leaf, wouldn't they expect something that was, well, more typically sophisticated and English-looking? And what were the chances an American would call for a mirror to be made in England and it just so happen to be made of an American wood?

Alan remained unmoved by my logic. When I challenged his date of manufacture, he responded that mirrors as large as mine did not exist in America at the end of the eighteenth or generally during the first half of the nineteenth century. For one thing, he led me to believe such large plates of glass were not available here at that time. I had always assumed this, too, based on what I had seen and heard, but I also knew that very few mirrors had retained their original glass. I now questioned those very expert theories and assumptions I had so readily accepted. I was moved to bone up.

During Alan's second visit, to pick up his common Federal mirror, he took a few minutes to take a closer look at mine. This time he rolled the production date back to the 1860s. He was positive it could not be earlier. I asked for an explanation for his refreshed assessment. He wearily reiterated that the mirror's size was evidence enough.

Indeed, the house it came from in Providence was built in 1860. But I still thought the frame was earlier. I did not think a frame of this size would have been moved too often and suspected it had once been placed in another house nearby. I told him I planned to trace the mirror back to the original family who had owned it in Rhode Island. If archival family papers existed in the Rhode Island Historical Society, I ventured, the mirror might be described in correspondence or in a household inventory, leading me to the maker.

"You will never find it," he scoffed. "Never. It's almost impossible to find that kind of documentation."

I was determined to take up the challenge.

Like everyone else, I had lived with mirrors my entire life. The Fox and Grapes mirror made me start to think about them in a new way.

Some mirrors are pure function. They hang over a sink or on a doorway so that we can check our fronts or determine if anything untoward is occurring in the rear. As for decor, glass and frame are chosen because they go above a couch or bring light into a dark corner or hallway. Others serve as part of the interior architecture; for example, those placed behind fixed moldings above fireplace mantels and even on ceilings. Feng shui experts suggest strategic placement of mirrors to improve the circulation of energy, chi. My own determination to learn about one mirror—grand in scale and rich in narrative—would yield me some fresh enlightenment.

It appears that ever since man gazed into a pool of water and fell for his own image, he has felt the yen for a portable mirror—a preoccupation for every succeeding civilization. The earliest mirrors from the Stone Age, around 6200 B.C.E., were made of polished obsidian, a natural black glass created out of volcanic eruptions. In the Bronze Age, and for centuries after, man blended, flattened, polished, and adorned all manner of metals—copper, bronze, tin, lead, silver, and other malleable types—in his quest to observe his face. In addition to providing this vision, mirrors were believed imbued with mystic significance.

In Egypt in 4500 B.C.E., kings were buried with their mica and selenite mirrors symbolic of life, eternity, and truth. Mirrors represented the sun god, Ra, as well as Hathor, the goddess of love, fertility, beauty, and dance, and were put to practical use during construction of kingly tombs. Outside the pyramids, mirrors were positioned to catch the sun's rays and shine light inside rooms where muralists and laborers prepared the setting for the transfer of their rulers into the next world.

When Pharaoh Ramses suspected Moses of causing plagues, he released the Jews from slavery. Old Testament scholars have speculated that Jews at this time were engaged in the art of mirror making. When they were permitted to take anything with them as they departed Egypt, one of their requests was mirrors.

In 1000 B.C.E., both Etruscans and Phoenicians traded in mirrors. Their word for soul, *hinthial*, means "image reflected in a mirror." The ancient Greeks created elaborate cases for their small mirrors, decorated with flowers, fruit, and birds—all Aphroditian symbols. Like the earlier Egyptians, the Greeks offered these objects in their burial sites as gifts to the gods.

Mirrors were used during military campaigns. Sunlight reflecting off mirrors blinded both horses and riders. Around 210 B.C.E., Archimedes began experimenting with mirrors. Among other feats of military engineering, he applied his geometric theories to mirrors in the defense of Syracuse against the Roman fleet. Archimedes allegedly arranged multiple mirrors on the peaks of hills to catch the sun, directing the concentrated light onto enemy ships in the harbor to set them on fire.

The Romans invented the glass mirror. Pliny the Elder wrote of a huge glass manufactory in the ancient coastal city of Sidon (now in Lebanon). From a British catalog, *Reflections of the Past*, I learned that, according to Seneca, a large "full length mirror cost more than the dowry of a general's daughter." Secular usage is illustrated in Pompeian murals, where women wield mirrors as everyday accessories. Round compact mirrors of lesser quality were mass-produced and available to a general public, including slaves, and "were used as amulets which were thought to have magical powers." These examples consisted of blown, convex shapes of discolored and uneven glass backed by metals, which easily tarnished. The aristocracy possessed larger mirrors, backed by the more expensive and reflective silver, and set into panels that moved up and down in the manner of a window sash. Mirrors made quite a hit at feasts and orgies, where people could watch themselves and others gorge.

From 206 B.C.E. and for the next two thousand years, as the writer Mark Pendergrast put it, the Chinese were "the masters of mirror making." Cosmic mirrors were round to represent the moon and the sun. The backs, made of jade, iron, and bronze, were decorated with symbols of the universe, such as dragons, plants, and insects. Mirrors in China were valued for their magical powers and their communication with the supernatural world. The Chinese carried personal mirrors, about two inches in size, as means to ward off evil spirits as well as to check appearance. Mirrors were attached to clothing by cords. When someone was on the verge of death, the mirrored garment was draped on a bamboo stick to encourage the fleeing soul to linger. Even broken mirrors were believed to retain mystic potency; the shards were ground and ingested for medicinal purposes.

In Japan, mirrors were associated with the souls of women "just as the samurai sword was representative to that of the man." They were presented as wedding gifts to daughters and intended as heirloom means to communicate with ancestral spirits.

Meanwhile, in South America, the Aztecs constructed mirrors out of polished pyrite, slate, hematite, and jet, and used them to light sacrificial fires. When Hernán Cortés appeared before the Indians dressed in glittering armor, he was perceived to be their predicted god. As late as 1883, it was recorded that in Mexico certain designated mirrors could reflect both future and past.

To create a mirror that would reflect one's image clearly and in its entirety had been the centuries-long goal of artisans. The first relatively clear mirror appeared in Venice in 1507. Two Muranese artisans claimed a secret formula for creating perfect mirrors of blown glass. Thus began the lucrative trade in Venice, a market that the Italians managed to monopolize for almost two hundred years. Molten glass was removed from high-temperature furnaces, then flattened on stones. When cooled, the almost colorless product was highly polished and its back was covered in tin.

Having the necessary furnaces so close to the moated city's

celebrated architecture was hazardous, so the operation was moved to the nearby island of Murano. The mirrors produced here were reputed to be the best in the world. They remained relatively small, but their quality was still better than anything seen before. Throughout Europe, demand for the Venetian product soared.

The Italian formula was a state secret, and, while glassmakers were indulged by the doges in exchange for their skilled contributions, workers and their families were strictly forbidden to leave the compounds where their lucrative activity took place. Anyone who tried to escape with the Venetian recipe risked being hunted down and killed by Italian state emissaries. Families left behind, serving in place of the traitorous relative, were imprisoned indefinitely.

In 1664, the French minister of finance under Louis XIV, Jean-Baptiste Colbert, ignoring the Italian statute and shunning the advice of his close friend the Bishop of Béziers, was determined to draw Venetian mirror makers onto French soil. Imported mirrors were so expensive that Colbert could not resist the opportunity to capture the market for France. This he accomplished. In 1665 twenty Venetian artisans arrived to establish France's first glassworks in Paris, on the Faubourg St.-Antoine. As fire and air pollution became a concern, the entire operation was sensibly moved to St.-Gobain, on the Parisian outskirts. There, the French worked ambitiously to improve their product. Soon the mirrors made in France surpassed any from Venice.

Even before Colbert got the idea of stealing the market from Italy, Elizabeth I was struck with the mirror fever that had seized the rest of Europe. She was able to smuggle the glassmaker Giacomo Verzelini out of Venice and set up a major glass house in England. Under her sponsorship, the first large-scale furnace in London was opened. The industry thrived until 1615, when King James I, who valued trees over mirrors, became alarmed by the immense deforestation taking place to feed the furnaces. He forbade the use of wood fuel for glass manufacturing and at the same time declared an embargo on imported glasses. The switch from wood to coal produced a disfigured product no one particularly cared for. In 1662 George Villiers, the second Duke of Buckingham, began buying up all the glassmaking patents he could get his hands on. With the assistance of John Bellingham, who had gotten hold of formulas from the Netherlands, the Vauxhall Glassworks in London was inaugurated. Even though critics called the fiddle-playing duke a "buffoon," he managed to monopolize the looking-glass market in England and made a bloody fortune.

In 1665, during the reign of the Sun King, Louis XIV, the Hall of Mirrors was completed at Versailles, where 357 dazzling mirrors were displayed. For the first time in world history, people were able to see themselves clearly, relatively undistorted, and in their entirety, compounding demand.

By 1676, both the French and the English were able to produce blown plates with the clearest glass the world had ever seen. Noting their popularity and the huge prices paid for such mirrors, Parliament was determined to seize a piece of the action. The British government imposed high luxury taxes on looking glasses, with the rate calculated according to size. This situation continued into the eighteenth century, quelling desire to develop mirror manufacturing in Britain further. Regardless of cost, the rich were still eager to purchase mirrors in France.

Throughout Europe, mirrors were among the most prized and expensive items a person could own. As the competition continued to produce the clearest glass and the most fantastic frames to surround the plates, the goal was still fixed on size: the bigger the better. In France, the price of a mirror of considerable dimension was level with the cost of a moderate château. An example of seventeenth-century value is illuminated in Colbert's inventory at his death in 1683: "A Venetian mirror, 46 by 26 inches, in a silver frame, was valued at 8016 livers, while a picture by the painter Raphael is put down at 3000 livers."

Even though France had the mirror market cornered, the French raced to make improvements. Blown glass was still the method used, but it had never proven successful for the large panels the rich craved and were willing to pay for. The largest blown example in the latter seventeenth century measured only seventy inches high.

Experiments to cast large sheets of glass by pouring molten sand into flat iron molds set on tables yielded mixed results. Then, in 1691, Louis Lucas of Néhou developed a method for casting plate glass at the St.-Gobain Glass Company that created a more predictable product. By early 1700, mirrors were measuring eighty-eight by forty-four inches, one quarter inch thick. For the next eighty years, France dominated the market.

The human cost of mirror production was well known but of minor concern for those who had the urge and means to decorate. Workers in the manufactories dropped like flies. Exposure to intolerably hot furnaces combined with deadly mercury fumes ensured a short career. The term *quicksilver* comes from the process of coating the backs of mirrors for reflective purposes, but it is misleading. Silver was not used until 1835, when the German chemist Justus Von Liebig introduced his method. Until then the backs of mirrors were coated in mercury.

The call for a grand-scale mirror continues, although today the largest sought are for scientific rather than decorative purposes. We have come a long way since Sir Isaac Newton presented his reflecting telescope to the Royal Society in 1671. Beneath the University of Arizona football stadium in Tucson, the Steward Observatory Mirror laboratory labors over the "Giant Magellan." If the half-billion-dollar experiment goes the way scientists hope, the Magellan will be the largest telescope in the world. Due for completion in 2016, the celestial sweeping instrument will be installed in Chile, where the night sky is the clearest. The man in charge of the lab is Professor J. Roger P. Angel, a physicist, astronomer, and mirror maker.

"Bigger is better in a big way to see faint objects around bright ones," according to Dr. Angel. The rotating furnace in the Steward laboratory, thirty feet by ten feet high, generates 2 million watts capable of heating eighteen tons of molten glass to 2,100 degrees Fahrenheit. After the mirror has cooled, it will be polished "to within a millionth of an inch of the desired curve." "Combined with so-called adaptive optics to reduce the blurring from the atmosphere," each of the seven mirrors, measuring 27.6 feet in diameter, will be part of the same giant parabola "blending their light at a common focus." Once completed, the telescope will be able to sweep up "starlight dispersed into foggy invisibility over billions of light-years and compress it into crisp bright dots astronomers [can] read like a newspaper to learn what was happening around a distant sun or when the universe was born." Astronomers are hoping the telescope will shed light on "the so-called dark energy that seems to be splitting the universe apart."

Challenged by the assumption that there were no large mirrors in eighteenth- and early-nineteenth-century America and that I would never find where mine had been made, I was compelled to undertake my own research.

I knew Alan was correct in one sense. There were no glass plate manufactories in the United States until the second quarter of the nineteenth century. Before this time, large glasses were often resurfaced here, but mirror plates were always imported from France and England. Although few still exist from that era (because of climate, breakage, and "reconditioning"), I soon learned that many colonial families were recorded as having owned very large mirrors indeed. The decorative arts historian Elisabeth Donaghy Garrett gives an example of "a pair of eight-foot mirrors [that] were up for sale at a public auction in Boston in 1762." Referring to "pier-glasses," the author writes, "A wide diversity of this type and size was readily available throughout the eighteenth century, with the most coveted and highly esteemed being the largest. The eighteenth-century regard for symmetry implies that pairs of such glasses were displayed between windows."

These dimensions were similar to those of my mirror. That blew Alan's alleged theory about glass size.

According to Garrett, "Large expanses of plate glass became popular in the reception rooms of the upper classes. The more elegant the interior, the larger and more numerous the glasses. Alone or in pairs, large glasses compare favorably in value with other expensive items in household inventories; often more than a desk and bookcase, equal to a dozen or more chairs, and something less than a tall case clock or the best bed resplendent with hangings."

One theory that may explain the bolder American carving style seen on my mirror versus the more delicate English style can be pinned on the American obsession with housekeeping. In the annual onset of spring cleaning, things were moved, taken down, and rolled up so that waxing, polishing, and washing could commence. Chunkier carved elements were less apt to be broken off and lost to careless feather dusting. In 1774, Charles Carroll contacted his London agent and ordered a pair each of pier mirrors and gilded girandoles (convex mirrors with candleholders on the sides) for his Maryland home. In the letter he specified that the carvings "be of the solid kind; it has been found by experience that slight carving will neither endure the extremes of Heat & cold nor the rough treatment of the negro servants."

In the eighteenth century, a certain instructiveness often informed the narrative of a mirror's frame. Carvers assumed viewers were familiar with their iconography and able to contemplate its message. As David Stockwell explained in his article "Aesop's Fables on Philadelphia Furniture," fables were extremely popular in eighteenth- and nineteenth-century America for teaching ethics and values to children. During the American Revolution, several editions of these ancient Greek morality tales were published in three languages, followed by nine more before 1800.

The popularity of designs favoring fables soared with the publication of Thomas Johnson's pattern books for carvers. The Fox and Grapes design on my mirror was issued in 1758 as plate number 6 in *Collection of Designs* and reissued in *One Hundred and Fifty New Designs* in 1761 as plate number 22. In 1824, a publisher in London reissued Thomas Chippendale's designs and falsely attributed Johnson's work to him. Since that time, there has been confusion over authorship. To confound matters further, it is said that Chippendale lifted a few designs not only from the earlier French designers but, according to one twentieth-century author, from Irish ones, too.

Johnson's exuberant engraved plates inspired by Aesop served as some of the most important sets of designs of his time. The talent of the carver was critical to the piece's success. Johnson's complex schemes, with their severe undercuts, scrolling foliage, extreme volutes, cascading flowers, branches, and fruit, as well as human figures and animals, were daunting to execute, although he didn't think so. "Tho' these designs were meant as assistants to young artists," Johnson wrote, "yet I hope I shall not incur the censure of any superior genius by declaring them use to all."

Johnson's influence was widespread. In America, especially Philadelphia, his designs in the second half of the eighteenth century were incorporated into the bases of tea tables, chimney-pieces, wall brackets, and mirror frames.

Only seven pieces of eighteenth-century Philadelphia furniture illustrating Aesop's tales and inspired by Johnson's motifs have survived. Crows, swans, dogs, foxes, and grapes are carved into the drawers of dressing tables and highboys. Since there were so few known fable-inspired pieces still in existence, I felt it best to compare what had survived with my mirror for any carving similarities, inspecting texts with the aid of a magnifying glass. Two Aesop examples as reinterpreted in the Johnson plates were in the Philadelphia Museum of Art. On one drawer of the Howe highboy there was a relief of the fox and the grapes. The central frieze of a fireplace mantel taken out of the eighteenth-century Powel ballroom in Philadelphia featured another popular theme, "The Dog and the Meat."

Fables were also incorporated into architectural plasterwork. At Kenmore, in Virginia, home of George Washington's sister, Betty, and her husband, Colonel Fielding Lewis, a compilation of allegorical themes was crammed into one panel of the fireplace mantel: *Beware of flattery . . . Pride cometh before a fall . . . Spite will act like a boomerang . . . Where force fails, patience will often succeed.* These sayings decorously prodded the Lewises and their guests to mull life's lessons as they sipped sherry by the fireside.

None of these examples smacked of my carver. The work on the mahogany highboy was much more refined; the same was true of the Powel mantel. However, this work has been attributed to immigrant carvers who learned their craft in England. Perhaps my carver was a disciple of a more accomplished and better-trained carver.

Carvers and gilders in eighteenth-century Philadelphia were kept very busy supplying frames for pier mirrors, chimneypieces, and dressing mirrors for wealthy patrons. In "Documented Philadelphia Looking Glasses, 1800–1850," Peter L. L. Strickland notes, "The 1794 Philadelphia directory lists only five men under the headings carvers and gilders and picture-frame makers. In 1800 there were at least eight of these men listed in these categories, by 1805 the number had risen to fourteen, in 1820 to thirty-three." By 1850 the number exceeded one hundred.

As in England, it was not the general practice for American carvers to sign their pieces. Therefore attribution serves as the closest scholars can come to placing an anonymous artisan's work. Account receipt books, however, and advertisements in newspapers have brought to light a few of Philadelphia's most esteemed carvers. Two in particular are believed to have promoted Johnson's designs in America: James Reynolds and Hercules Courtney. I did not imagine that my mirror was made by either of these men but wanted to find out as much as I could about these Aesop carvers, thinking that information might lead me to who might have carved the Fox and Grapes. Could the carver have apprenticed with one of these craftsmen?

James Reynolds, a carver and gilder from London, arrived in Philadelphia with his wife in August 1766. In September of that year, he placed an advertisement in the *Pennsylvania Gazette* announcing the opening of his new shop. Luke Beckerdite, again, in his *Antiques* magazine article "Philadelphia Carving Shops: James Reynolds," reproduced the ad:

James Reynolds, Carver and gilder, Just arrived from London (by Captain Sparks) at his house in dock-Street opposite Lodge Alley . . . UNDERTAKES to execute all the various Branches of Carving and Gilding in the newest, neatest, and genteelist Taste, such as Capitals, Mouldings, and other House Work, chair and Cabinet Ditto, Glass and Picture Frames, Slab and Table Ditto, girandoles, Chandiliers, &c. and Ship Work in general.

The following year Reynolds opened a shop at a new address, where he sold imported goods listed as looking glasses, wallpaper, and general artists' supplies. He manufactured gilded and painted mirrors, picture frames, and wall brackets of his own design, partly based on the plates of Thomas Johnson and another English designer, John Linnell. In 1784, Reynolds placed an advertisement in another Philadelphia newspaper. The Golden Boy, named after Johnson's business in Westminster, was located near the Bunch of Grapes Tavern on Third Street, where "he offered 'a very large and genteel assortment' of imported looking glasses 'in carved and white, or carved and gilt frames.' "

In addition to selling imported mirrors, and frames he made himself, Reynolds took on commissioned carving work from local cabinetmakers. Receipts from 1770 show that he was employed with other artisans to carve architectural elements in spectacular houses owned by merchants and politicians. When the mayor of Philadelphia Samuel Powel bought his town house, he called on Reynolds and other émigrés as well as native-born artisans to carve the architectural work. A Powel room is now installed in the Metropolitan Museum in New York.

Reynolds's other prominent clients included George Washington and a close associate of the president, John Cadwalader. Apparently Cadwalader's propensity for dueling had no effect on his military career or social standing. In his short lifetime, he turned down political promotions to pursue a career in business. He became a wealthy merchant, had a taste for luxury and an eye for quality. Cadwalader commissioned Charles Willson Peale to paint the portraits of his family, and Reynolds was commissioned to create the frames.

I had often worked on early Philadelphia mahogany floor furniture. After a while it is easy to identify carved pieces produced there. My first hunch upon seeing the Fox and Grapes mirror was that it may have been manufactured in that city. I needed to take a refreshing look at Philadelphia frames in person. The best examples were owned by museums.

My trip to the small American portrait gallery in the Metropolitan Museum did not offer further clues. On the crest of a frame that surrounds a portrait of Richard Dana painted by John Singleton Copley slinks a hairy little creature. It looks somewhat like a fox but in other ways like a bushy-tailed dog. The animal's strangely carved body is the only aspect it has in common with the figure on my mirror; people often had mistaken the awkward fox at the bottom of my frame for a dog.

In another gallery was a mirror with a frame attributed to Reynolds. It bore an Elliot label on the back. The glass was not original. The Rococo design featured the expected garlands of flowers, leaves, and clusters of bold fruit that intertwined with C-scrolls. The shape and details of the pears on the Reynolds frame looked strikingly similar to the Fox and Grapes. The way the flower petals were carved did, too. The placard below the Reynolds mirror stated, "It is the only mirror frame from the period which is fully carved in the rococo manner." The wood was American white pine. The frame was not gilded. It was painted white, a popular finish in Philadelphia in the 1700s. But my mirror was three times the scale, which meant all the carvings had greater volume, too. The Reynolds mirror was a perfect American example of the period, and therefore it was much more valuable than mine would ever be. No question the Reynolds mirror was earlier. But it seemed to me that James Reynolds may have had an influence on the carver of the Fox and Grapes.

Another notable carver of the period was Hercules Courtney, who with Reynolds helped establish the Rococo style in America. Originally from Ireland, Courtney claimed that he had worked for Thomas Johnson in London. He arrived in Philadelphia in 1766 (the same year as Reynolds). For three years he was employed by the cabinetmaker Benjamin Randolph, assumed to have sponsored the Irishman's voyage. In the third part of his study of Philadelphia carving in *Antiques*, Luke Beckerdite focused on Courtney and his school, noting that in 1769, Courtney opened his own shop, which he advertised in the *Pennsylvania Gazette.*

HERCULES COURTNEY, Carver and gilder, from London, Informs his friends and the Public, that he undertakes all manner of Carving and Gilding, in the newest Taste, at his house between Chestnut and Walnut on Front Street.

Receipts show that Courtney was highly paid for his magic touch with chisels. He has been credited with reproducing Johnson's work on one of the fireplace mantel appliqués in Powel's fancy town house. Although most carvers remain unknown, those ascribed to the "Courtney school" are believed responsible for particular Johnson-inspired mahogany dressing tables and highboys. In his time, Courtney was recognized as one of Philadelphia's most gifted carvers. Despite his celebrity, he set his woodworking tools aside in 1779 to become a tavern keeper.

Courtney had been carving during the first wave of Rococo, which lasted in England and America from around the time of Johnson's first pattern book publication until about 1800. But it wasn't long before Rococo experienced an Anglo-American revival, starting around the time of the 1824 reissue of Thomas Johnson's *One Hundred and Fifty New Designs.* Once again, another generation of carvers took a crack at replicating the taskmaster's incongruous designs. As the years advanced, the early Victorians cast their eyes upon and opened their purses for French designs, France having been the country of Rococo's birth. This would have displeased Johnson, who was a member of the Anti-Gallican society, a group that opposed "the insidious arts of the French nation."

Victorian designers chose to "update" classic Rococo with their own interpretations, resulting in overwrought and out-of-scale proportions, on the whole bringing no improvement to the first Rococo period. My mirror was overscaled, a definite revival characteristic, which deflated—though it did not entirely over-rule—hope of even a late-eighteenth-century manufacture. The carver, I reckoned, could have been employed as an apprentice, say in 1800, and continued to work at his craft into the first half of the nineteenth century.

From the vantage of scale, the frame could have been categorized a revival piece of the 1830s. A cluster of ivy gathered in the center of the upper divided glass panel lent a peculiar Irish twist. It was so out of keeping with the rest of the frame it seemed a possible replacement for an element lost during one of the mirror's restorations.

I wished my frame was earlier, but evidence was beginning to mount that it was not, and I was a little sour about having to face that fact. But falling into the second revival wasn't too bad either—especially if it proved to be American.

Once, it was believed that mirrors could steal a soul or form its content; in colonial America, such ideas persisted, Elisabeth Garrett said. When a person died at home before the mirrors could be turned to the wall or shrouded in cloth, it was believed "the soul of the departed would get locked in the mirror and never get out." Trapped on earth, the spirit would haunt the household through the glass. As much as I try to squelch my superstitious tendencies, I must admit this notion is something I can't shake. If there were souls locked in the mirror, they had definitely captured me, a fellow Rhode Islander, and I looked forward to getting to know them. I needed to see the house in Providence where the mirror had come from.

I invited myself to stay with my friend Susan Vander Closter, an English professor at Rhode Island School of Design. With map in hand, I walked from her house through a neighborhood dense with landmark Victorian buildings and mature trees until I reached my destination, 62 Prospect Street.

The Woods-Gerry Mansion stood on a corner. Set far back from the street, it was surrounded by a high wrought-iron fence. The brick façade looked stark without its original shutters to mimic the curved tops of the huge Italianate windows. The main entrance, off to the side, led to an arched portico. Curved, shallow brownstone steps lay before a pair of soaring walnut doors set on formidable bronze hinges. The house had an unusual sense of privacy for a city setting. Like its furnishings, it was stamped with the impeccable taste of the original owners. No matter how defiled the building had become as it changed hands, the Woods aura pervaded.

When I got back to Susan's house, I told her how eager I was to find out about the family who owned the mirror, especially after seeing their house. She volunteered to help me with the initial research toward determining provenance. Soon she, too, was caught up in the story of the Woodses' lives and the building of the mansion in 1860. Personal journals stored at the Rhode Island Historical Society beguiled Susan.

"The Woodses," she said, "lived in Providence, as well as part-time in Italy and France. They are pure Henry James." The diaries and letters documented a wealthy, well-traveled nineteenth-century American family. "Marshall Woods's wife was named Anne Brown Francis," Susan said, "which, I suppose, must mean she's a Brown."

This struck a chord with me. The Browns were major figures in Rhode Island history. At that point, however, I did not know much about them except that the four Brown brothers were sea merchants and the founders of Brown University, and that successive generations had been in the textile industry. Antique furniture associated with the surname had set records in American decorative arts auction rooms of New York. Associated with Anne Brown Francis's name, the high quality of the furnishings from her home in Providence seemed to fall into place.

I was happy to find that the historical society had reams of letters and diaries from the Brown, Francis, and Woods families. The building of the house seemed a good place to start. In the best circumstances, a diary, letter, will, or even an inventory of purchases from the 1860s would refer to the sofa and the one mirror I liked so much, where they had been made, and how they had come into the Woodses' home. If I were lucky, archival photographs of the house's interior might highlight its furnishings.

From records held in the RISD archives, Susan discovered

that the Millers had purchased the Woods-Gerry Mansion in 1959 from Edith Gerry's estate, which jibed with what Tracy told me. The Millers owned the mansion for six months before selling it to RISD. Mentioned with the bill of sale from the Gerry estate to the Millers were two Chippendale mirrors, some Italian garden statuary, a highboy, and murals from the dining room. Mrs. Miller offered the murals to RISD, but the president of the school, John Frazier, turned them down, stating that the school did not have ample storage space.

Hearing this, I recalled the canvases displayed on the lawn at the Clayville auction. Like the mirrors, the paintings had been stored in the barn. Deteriorated almost beyond recognition, their once-vibrant colors had oxidized from dampness and neglect. No one had bid on the paintings, not even at the opening figure of $50. A year after the auction, Tracy started to do her own research. An expert from Christie's went to Clayville and identified the artist. These unsalvageable canvases, some sections twenty feet in length and ten feet high, were the work of Giovanni Battista Piazzetta (1682–1754), one of the most famous Italian Rococo artists of the eighteenth century, a Venetian genre painter who taught Tiepolo and has been credited with elevating drawing to the status of painting in his time. Few of his paintings still exist. The ones that do are owned by museums such as the Louvre, the Uffizi, and the National Gallery in London.

The Italian master's loose, bold brushstrokes of horses and riders, once alive with action and color, are now lost to the world. How unfortunate the paintings were taken from their Naples or Venice homes in the first place. It is easy to understand the recent uproar among curators when national treasures leave their countries and fall into private hands.

The college intended to raze the mansion and erect modern student housing in its place, but one Antoinette Downing from the Rhode Island Historic Preservation Commission in Providence can be credited with saving the structure from the wrecking ball. Downing argued that the Italianate building, designed by Richard Upjohn, one of America's preeminent nineteenth-century architects, should receive landmark status.

Although RISD claimed a department of architecture, the administration's plans were not focused on saving historic property, and they fought the preservation commission. But with a community effort then under way to save what was left of Providence's historic buildings, especially on College Hill, the school of design lost its case. Today RISD still owns the Woods-Gerry Mansion. Such domestic structures conflict with the needs of institutions, and some unfortunate alterations to the building have resulted to accommodate the school's functions. However, two lofty rooms on the first floor happily serve as the art school's gallery. The building is dear to graduating students, who in June gather for the last time and show their work in Upjohn's perfectly scaled rooms.

While looking into the Rhode Island angle, I also had opportunities to continue research in New York. One day, for example, I ran into John Hays during a preview at Christie's and confronted him about the low estimate he had given me on the dolphin sofa, now hailed as one of the best extant examples of American Classical furniture to have come on the market in a long time. John was contrite.

He asked if he could take me to lunch. I suspected the invitation was made to appease any hard feelings I might harbor over my loss of at least $160,000 I might have had in my pocket if the sofa had gone to auction. There was no sense dwelling on a missed profit. I still liked John, and everyone, myself included, makes mistakes in our business. If John wanted to make it up to me, I suggested he come to my studio in Chelsea to look at the Fox and Grapes mirror and give his opinion in person this time.

When John arrived and looked down on the mirror in the midst of restoration, he was unimpressed. I was beginning to grasp that the mirror, being unique and hard to place, was one of those objects people either fell for fast or did not take to at all. Reaction was never placid.

"Maryalice," John said, "most mirrors aren't worth that much."

I interpreted this, too, as subjective. Mirrors were not a category that particularly interested John, or many other specialists for that matter. But "worth" was a relative—and changeable—concept. What John said may have been true, at the time. Fine examples of antique hand-carved looking-glass frames never fetched close to the amounts paid for furniture from the same period, but this was subject to change any day. American folk art, for instance, had not been a particularly popular field for a long time. Prices were once low enough that even someone on a schoolteacher's salary could afford to collect good things. This was no longer the case in 2005, when the category's prices began to spike.

Who could have foreseen the day in 1995 when a man named Thomas K. Figge would be willing to pay $801,500 at Sotheby's for a pintail drake decoy from the estate of Russell Aitken, a world-renowned big-game hunter and gun collector from Newport, Rhode Island? In New York, Jerry and Susan Lauren set a new record for American weather vanes. At Sotheby's in October 2006, they paid $5.84 million for a nineteenth-century Indian weather vane of molded copper. American frames are apt to follow suit. I just needed to find out where my frame originated. And I knew where I had to start.

I told John that I planned to look into the Brown family papers at the Rhode Island Historical Society archives for reference to my fable mirror. John could not comprehend how I, with a background of handling the highest caliber of antiques, had become so engaged with a giant mirror he found unremarkable. He tried to steer me back on track.

"Maryalice," he said softly, "people have pored over those Brown records for years. There is nothing more to be discovered."

CHAPTER FIVE

Provenance in the Marketplace

What does provenance contribute to the price of a piece of art or furniture? Why would people pay more for work with a prominent name latterly attached? Market security is one answer.

Celebrity is a desirable component when it comes to selling objects. There is an inclination to trust the judgment of people known in the past as great collectors, who made fortunes as industrial giants, held prestigious political positions, or otherwise served as romantic figures in history. There is also the idea that preowned objects have a talismanic quality, as if the original owners' reputation for taste could be transferred with ownership, the affiliation with a past luminary would bequeath privilege.

Furniture belonging to the famous Brown family from Providence has a history of bringing record amounts at auctions. A provenance with the Brown name attached is held among the most desirable pedigrees a collector could seek in American furniture.

The Browns, colonial sea merchants from Providence, represent the inception of American business. The brothers Nicholas, Moses, Joseph, and John—along with their daughters, wives, and sisters—formed some of the earliest corporations in the country—some of which continue today, three hundred years later. In the eighteenth century, the Browns owned vast farms, a spermaceti candle factory, a chocolate factory, and spirit distilleries.

Hope Furnace, a pig iron manufactory, ultimately supplied most of the material for cannons for the Revolutionary War. The Browns and their partners founded banks and insurance companies, constructed canals and roads, became land speculators. They and their descendants were pioneers in the industrial revolution. Though they were briefly involved in the slave trade, three out of the four Brown brothers became abolitionists and are credited with making Rhode Island the first state in the Union to outlaw trafficking.

The four Brown brothers were the sons of Captain James Brown. Orphaned in youth, they were adopted by their uncle Obadiah, who, like their father, was involved in the sea trade. Obadiah taught his nephews about business while instilling in them a sense of civic responsibility. The Browns established schools, hospitals, a church/meeting house, and a library. To each endeavor they generously subscribed their time and resources, rallying others in similar circumstances to follow suit. Perhaps the Browns' most enduring legacy was their success in removing Rhode Island College (later renamed Brown University) from Warren to Providence. They purchased the land for the university, and the four brothers ceremoniously laid the first stones of the building's foundation. Once the college was thriving, with all of the Browns appointed as officers, they advocated a state library. In 1753, the Providence Athenaeum, a charming library on Benefit Street still open to the public, was established. Brown philanthropy was a hands-on affair. Obadiah ordered the books through his London agents, while Nicholas became head librarian, squeezing time from his grueling countinghouse schedule to volunteer at the front desk "every Saturday, from two to Five of the Clock in the Afternoon."

The brothers, each endowed with his own temperament, ideas, and abilities, eventually went their separate ways. New partnerships formed, and new ventures were established.

Nicholas, a model of steadfast intelligence, was perfectly suited to commerce and had amassed a fortune by the time he died in 1791.

Joseph was more suited to academia and taught mathematics

and physics at Rhode Island College. On the side he dabbled in architecture. Several of his buildings still stand in Providence.

Moses, raised a Baptist, converted to Quakerism and became a major force in the abolitionist movement. In middle age, he excused himself from the family business, traveling south to expound upon his social reformist views. Returning to Providence almost a decade later, Moses began to think of an enterprise that could create jobs for his adopted Quaker community. He and a young partner from England, Samuel Slater, were among the first successfully to operate a cotton-spinning mill in the United States. Moses had not anticipated the human suffering technology would bring along with his well-intentioned plan.

Quakers never worked in the spinning factory. Slater Mill in Pawtucket was so successful that it increased the demand for cotton, thus accelerating the need for more slaves to be transported from Africa to the South to plant and pick the cotton. In the North, women and children as young as seven labored at spinning frames for up to fourteen hours a day, six days a week. Farmers and fishermen, dependent on the Blackstone River for their livelihood, were devastated as the chemicals and dyes from the factory polluted the water.

Of all the Brown brothers, John (1736–1803) was the most eccentric. On the night of June 9, 1772, he and a band of Providence men who called themselves the "Sons of Liberty" instigated an assault on the British revenue ship *Gaspee*. After luring the vessel into the shallow waters of Narragansett Bay, Brown, acting as ringleader, and his smuggler cronies boarded. They shot the lieutenant, looted the cargo, and set the vessel on fire.

Called "a man of magnificent projects and extraordinary enterprises," John had a mind that percolated with innovative ideas. In 1795, the Duke de La Rochefoucauld-Liancourt was in Providence and was astonished by the magnitude and diversity of John Brown's enterprises. In his *Travels through the United States of North America . . . in 1795, 1796, and 1797*, the duke wrote that, although he regretted leaving town without having made John Brown's acquaintance, he judged from what he had seen all around him that Brown was "a person of extraordinary intelligence and enlargement of mind. He has accomplished things that, even in Europe, would appear considerable."

The Browns, acting as agents for colonial craftsmen along the East Coast (mainly Philadelphia, Newport, and New York), saw the best of the decorative arts produced at the time. From wharf to warehouse, they recorded and inspected shipping orders from the premiere upholsterers and furniture makers. Naturally they could not resist the temptation to acquire pieces for themselves, and they became accustomed to ordering specific items directly from the source and on a fairly regular basis. I was hoping to find evidence in the Nicholas Brown and Company cargo logs that a Brown had purchased a mirror such as mine for one of the family's many Rhode Island homes. But I had no such luck—there weren't any elaborate descriptions of the cargo.

After the Revolutionary War, when money was scarce, Americans had to deal with the nearly unfathomable foreign currency being circulated. Bartering became the preferred method of exchange. Cabinetmakers such as John Goddard of Newport traded mahogany handcrafted furniture for quantities of the fresh butter in ready supply at the Browns' sprawling Rhode Island countryside farms.

There have been numerous studies on the Brown brothers and on the cabinetmakers they employed in the eighteenth century. While they ordered some of their furnishings from their agents in Philadelphia, it is the furniture they commissioned in their native state, from the shop of Townsend and Goddard in Newport, that has stirred so much interest among Americana scholars and collectors. Identifying a maker with certainty is rare in American furniture, but unlike most furniture makers, this Rhode Island group sometimes signed their pieces.

Evidence of Brown family provenance is particularly valuable—it's helped to break two world records at auction. These sales mark the point where American furniture really took off. The first groundbreaker was an eighteenth-century Newport kneehole desk with carved shells, which sold in 1983 at Sotheby's, New York, for $687,500 and belonged to John Brown. In 1989 at Christie's, an eighteenth-century nine-foot-high bonnet-top Newport secretary that had come down through the heirs of Nicholas Brown from Providence fetched $12.1 million.

This latter price has never been eclipsed for a piece of American furniture. The price for the kneehole desk, however, has been beaten many times, once by the aforementioned duck decoy. The buyer for both Newport desks was Harold Sack of Israel Sack Antiques, buying on behalf of two Texas clients.

These world record–breaking desks bear two important Rhode Island titles: the Newport cabinetmakers and their distinguished clients, the Browns of Providence. Establishing provenance, however, is notoriously tricky. Actual bills of sale and labels serve as the best documentation, but these seldom survive. Moreover, cabinetmakers rarely signed their work, nor were original owners apt to detail their furniture in wills.

When perusing articles and papers pertaining to decorative arts, one needs to pay strict attention. For these reasons, experts seldom make a commitment about provenance. Readers should note the overabundance of qualifying language such as "most probably," "possibly," "most likely," "perhaps," "probably," or "it seems as though." Although comparative studies attempt honestly to confirm creators, unless an object is signed or bears the mark of the maker, expert opinions are mainly educated guesses. Style, construction, and the type of wood used are certainly indicators of region and, in most cases, time lines, but there will always be exceptions. It is not unusual for a once-coveted object to be carried off the museum floor when new information casts a different light on it. Descriptions in letters and such documents count, too, but most often they do not disclose enough to allow experts to draw conclusions with absolute certainty.

I went to the New York Public Library to hunt for the auction catalog with the $12.1 million secretary, to see the kind of documentation found to trace it to its original owner. Christie's sale was held on June 3, 1989. The catalog's title, *The Magnificent Nicholas Brown Desk and Bookcase*, announces the provenance with certitude. The next page is a picture of the stately desk with the familiar Goddard shell carvings on the lid above the drawers and carved shells on the upper three doors in the bookcase section.

After the page listing specialists comes Christie's "Limited Warranty" disclaimer.

From the date of sale, the auction house provides a six-year guarantee

> that any article described in headings printed in UPPERCASE TYPE . . . which is unqualifiedly stated to be the work of a named author or authorship is authentic and not counterfeit. The term "author" or "authorship" refers to the creator of the article or to the period, culture, source or origin . . . Only UPPER CASE TYPE headings . . . indicate the degree of authenticity of authorship warranted by Christie's . . . ANY HEADING WHICH IS STATED IN THE "GLOSSARY" TO REPRESENT A QUALIFIED OPINION IS NOT SUBJECT TO THE WARRANTY CONTAINED HEREIN. Christie's warranty does not apply to supplemental material which appears below the UPPER CASE TYPE heading of each lot in this catalogue and Christie's is not responsible for any errors or omissions in such supplemental material.

The lowercase I now surmised to mean embellishment.

Under the heading "Absence of Other Warranties" is another paragraph in bold capital letters:

> ALL PROPERTY IS SOLD "AS IS" AND NEITHER CHRISTIE'S, THE SELLER'S AGENT, NOR THE SELLER MAKES ANY EXPRESS OR IMPLIED WARRANTY OR REPRESENTATION OF ANY KIND OR NATURE WITH RESPECT TO THE PROPERTY. IN NO EVENT SHALL CHRISTIE'S OR THE SELLER BE RESPONSIBLE FOR THE CORRECTNESS OF, OR BE DEEMED TO HAVE MADE, ANY REPRESENTATION OR WARRANTY OF . . . ATTRIBUTION, PROVENANCE . . .

I glanced above and read the bold capital letters at the end of the "Limited Warranty."

CHRISTIE'S LIMITED WARRANTY DOES NOT
APPLY TO THE ATTRIBUTION OF PAINTINGS,
DRAWINGS, GRAPHIC ART OR SCULPTURE
CREATED BEFORE 1870, AS THE ATTRIBUTION
OF SUCH IDENTITY IS BASED ON CURRENT
SCHOLARLY OPINION, WHICH MAY CHANGE.

Page 11 contains a picture of the Nightingale-Brown House,
a wooden mansion built in 1792 for the Nightingale family and
purchased in 1814 by Nicholas Brown II (son of the original desk
owner). The next page provides a description of "The Brown
Family of Providence," a quick read about the Browns' great
legacy in the worlds of politics and early colonial commerce, with
page 14 dedicated to a short biography of Nicholas Brown I and
his son, Nicholas Brown II. Page 15 replicates an eighteenth-
century label bearing the image of a whale and a warranty for the
freshness of the spermaceti candles. The label is bordered by an
ornate motif, a romantic reference to the times of the Brown
brothers.

But what do spermaceti candles have to do with the desk
other than to indicate that the man who presumably owned the
desk owned a candle manufactory?

On page 16, "The Browns and Their Furnishings" briefly
introduces readers to Wendy A. Cooper's articles on John Brown,
published in *Antiques* (February and May 1973). Throughout the
page, words like "probably," "most likely," and "possibly" speak
again to the complexities of attribution and provenance. Citing
Cooper, the text reads, "In 1776, a letter from Goddard to
Nicholas Brown I possibly refers to one of the four block-front
desks and bookcases made for each of the four Brown brothers."
Goddard wonders if the brothers have any interest in "a desk &
bookcase which I have to dispose of."

In all likelihood, Nicholas Brown took up the cabinetmaker's
offer. But this letter does not serve as solid proof the sale took
place. The letter from Goddard was simply a solicitation, with no
documented response from Nicholas Brown (a minor detail
glossed over in the catalog).

Christie's continued to build its case. The footnote refers to the Providence City Archives, which hold the inventory of Nicholas Brown I's estate. "The only certain documentary reference to Nicholas's desk and bookcase" can be found in the inventory of his estate, published after his death in 1791. In the inventory, "The desk and bookcase is described as a 'Bookcase with books,' and very highly valued at L95. The fact that it is more than seven times as expensive as any other furniture and higher in value than his entire inventory of silver emphasizes the extremely high relative quality of this piece of furniture."

The following page reproduces parts of two pages from the "Inventory of the Personal Estate of Nicholas Brown Esquire, Deceased." Nowhere is the word *desk* ever mentioned, only "bookcase with books," which was listed as being in the dining room. The term *secretary* is not used until much later in time, and since *desk* is easily the best word for such a piece, it would be odd to rename it just a bookcase.

On page 19, there is a posthumous portrait of Nicholas Brown II by Thomas Sully. Brown is standing in front of a seascape, with no desk in sight. The caption states that Nicholas Brown II moved the desk and bookcase to the Nightingale-Brown House in 1814. But there is no will or household inventory to back up this assertion with regard to Nicholas II, who, by the way, was not the original owner of the desk.

The next page speaks to the matter of attribution: "The Magnificent Nicholas Brown Chippendale Mahogany Block-and-shell Desk and Bookcase" is attributed to John Goddard, Newport, Rhode Island, 1760–1770. The desk and bookcase are then described in detail. Midpage, we are told again, "It is believed that each of the four Brown brothers owned a blockfront and shell-carved desk and bookcase." In addition to the desk at auction, two are said to survive, one in Yale's Garvan Collection and another in the Rhode Island Historical Society (displayed in the John Brown House Museum on Power Street). These desks and other "six-shell desk and bookcases" are compared in scholarly publications, but, we learn, "None of these scholars provide firm attribution for either group of desks but all refer to the Brown-Goddard correspondence mentioned in the introductory essay."

Comparisons with other desks made in eighteenth-century Newport substantiate that the piece was made in Goddard's shop. It was magnificent, as described, without exception a perfect example of colonial New England craftsmanship. On that basis, the secretary could stand on its own, but proof of provenance was hardly absolute. Wherever and whomever it had come from, it had ended up in the childhood home of J. Carter Brown from Washington, a descendant of the many Nicholas Browns of Providence, Rhode Island. As far back as Carter could remember, the secretary was in the house on Benefit Street in Providence. The fact that it was being sold by Captain Nicholas Brown, the brother of J. Carter Brown, Director of the National Gallery of Art, Washington, D.C., made for a spiffy provenance, with little need for further embellishment. Few would dare question it.

It came down to this: a great Newport, Rhode Island, eighteenth-century secretary was fancifully coupled with a spermaceti candle label, a Sully portrait, some correspondence with John Goddard, a handwritten inventory that referred to a bookcase and books from the dining room, and references to scholarly publications, all of which constructed a link of the furniture to Nicholas Brown. The warranty clauses in the front of the catalog state the facts, which are that in the future, expert opinion "may change." The very bottom of the page noted that an "Estimate" was available "on request." Only very wealthy buyers need ask.

If evidence such as that provided in the Christie's catalog could be woven into provenance, it seemed less a long shot for me to determine that of the Fox and Grapes mirror and its maker. With as much in mind, I tore after the Browns for any mention of mirrors. It was time, too, to stalk not only the dead ones but the living I knew still lingered somewhere around Providence.

The Rhode Island Historical Society was my first destination, in particular the rare manuscripts division. I began with handwritten journals and letters from the Brown collection deposited there by the family over many years and providing an excursion in time. Rick Stattler, the division head, greeted me on my first day and was eager to help out. Before assigning me a desk, he asked what I was looking for and where I wanted to begin.

Fortunately, I knew where I wanted to begin, or rather, with whom. Hers was the name that had seemed most significant, since she was a Brown descendant. "I'm looking for references to a mirror I believe may have belonged to Anne Brown Francis Woods. If you have a genealogy of the Browns, I'd very much like to see it. She was the wife of Marshall Woods. They lived on Prospect Street in Providence."

"Anne Brown Francis, now she's one of those weird ones." Rick laughed.

"What do you mean by that?" I asked.

"Well, for one thing, her great-grandfathers John and Nicholas Brown were brothers. Then her father, John Brown Francis, whose grandfather was John Brown, married Anne Carter Brown, Nicholas II's daughter. Anne Brown Francis was the issue of that marriage."

I froze as it sank in. In retrospect, I guess I knew that, in the past, marrying such close relatives was condoned in most cultures, and often preferred, especially among the aristocracy. On Block Island, even my own humble ancestors had intermarried. It was a practical way to keep assets in the family. But it was terribly confusing.

Rick drew a chart of the Brown family tree to get me started. The whole clan appeared in a maze of marriages to first and second cousins. Each branch used the same names, too, which made necessary a chronological notation beside every John, Nicholas, Moses, Carter, and Anne, Hope, Mary, and Abby. Nicknames became essential.

"I think I might have something for you," Rick said. He brought out a large, musty cardboard box with one noteworthy letter among its contents. It was written by Elisa Goddard of Providence to Abigail Goddard in Baltimore, whom she addressed as "Rosella." Elisa was a bridesmaid at the January 1, 1788, wedding of John Brown's eldest daughter, Abby, to his new young business partner, John Francis from Philadelphia. The wedding was held at John Brown's uncompleted mansion. Even though the building was still under construction, it was finished enough to have the wedding ceremony and the party held there. Elisa begins:

> Last Tuesday evening I witnessed the union of my two friends, John Francis and Abby; I was present and officiated as a bridesmaid. The bride was dressed in an elegant white satin, a very handsome hat, and suite of the most elegant Brussels, I ever beheld. A white ribbon was clasped around her neck with a pearl star, her shoulder was ornamented with the same, together with her hat. Bracelets set in pearl, with fine strings of the same to bind them on her arm, a handsome watch ornamented with a new chain, finished her dress, to which a bouquet of flowers must be added.
>
> She was quite charming, and the most interesting object you can have an idea of. The Bridesmaids, I would inform you, made no despicable appearance, all three of us in white, in pure white, our hats white cane, the crown highly elevated with wire and flowering gauze, finished by a quantity of large white plumes.

Lovely as she looked, Elisa was disappointed "that there were no eligible young bachelors to exhibit ourselves to, that we should care a pin whether we looked well or ill." "This is the second time I have been a bridesmaid," she complained. "I think it ought to be my turn next to be a bride, every dog has his day, as the saying is, if so mine is to come, but if marriage is to make the day I fear it will be without the groom, as there is scarcely such an animal as a man in the town." Elisa ends the letter with a description of a reception party held a few days later to celebrate the marriage:

> On Friday Mr. Brown gave a smart ball at his house on the hill. Indeed it will be a most elegant place. We had four rooms lighted up on the second floor, one for supper, another for cards and two for dancing. We danced in the large chamber of the hall, and continued it through the

door into the next room, which made the whole length of
the house. The rooms are already genteel, but will be elegant when finished and furnished. *Two of the largest and
most elegant mirrors I ever saw ornamented the rooms.* Standing
in the door which is in the middle of the partition, you are
just in line with them, so that at the head of the dance you
can look down through [a] crowd of sprightly dancers, and
if you are a little elevated above the common race of mortals or chance to be made so by high heels, or long feathers, you can then have the pleasure of contemplating your
image and seeing it repeated fifty two feet, so at the foot of
the dance, you may see the same, the effect was charming
to look on, and such a moving multitude. [italics added]

Elisa Goddard's explicitness about the size of the mirrors was
again proof that large mirrors were not so rare in eighteenth-
century America. Whether or not her measurements of the room
were accurate, this much was certain: the mirrors in John
Brown's unfinished mansion at the time of the party were impressive enough to have an arresting visual impact on Elisa. For her,
they captured and expanded the feeling of what was going on in
the room, lending the party atmosphere an even higher drama.
They were—as any good ballroom mirror ought to be—alive in
the most romantic way.

What Elisa was most taken with was the awareness the two
mirrors gave her of herself as they reflected back her image in a
crowd of dancers. The mirrors had to be quite tall and wide to
accomplish this. From what I was beginning to find in newly
published books, I could deduce that those at the wedding, as
described, were most likely a pair of large pier mirrors, which in
wealthy homes were not that uncommon, most often placed
between windows and generally architectural in form. What style
did Elisa indicate by "elegant"? Could her passing assessment
mean an elaborately carved mirror like the one I had, or Neoclassical, in which case less meant more? One thing was certain: The
mirrors mentioned were of extreme dimensions. What was missing was a fuller description of the "elegant" mirrors themselves.

It seemed a long shot that the Fox and Grapes mirror had been made as early as 1788. Still, the Rococo design would have been appropriate, since John Brown's house was one of the last to be built in the waning Georgian style. In 1803, the future president John Quincy Adams called the Brown residence "the most magnificent and elegant private mansion that I have seen on this continent." His mother concurred. Abigail Adams wrote to her sister Mary Cranch in 1789, "The house and everything in it was one of the grandest I have seen in this country. Everything in it bore the marks of magnificence and taste."

CHAPTER SIX

John Brown's Mansion

Through eBay, I found a copy of Antoinette Downing's out-of-print book on early Rhode Island architecture. Pictures of the Brown mansion included interior photographs. In the central first-floor hallway, baskets of fruit and flowers were incorporated in the crown moldings over paneled mahogany doors. I wondered if John Brown had carried the same theme into the room by ordering a Rococo mirror to perpetuate the motif. Inspired by the possibility, I rushed off to Providence.

On a steep hill near Brown University sits a three-story brick Georgian pile with black shutters. It is the John Brown mansion on Power Street. The house, set back on a grass knoll, now belongs to the Rhode Island Historical Society and is open to the public. I let myself in through a wrought-iron gate and walked along a brick path to the front door, where I bought my entry ticket and signed up for the house tour with two other out-of-towners. Led by the guide, we entered a corner room she called the study. Over the fireplace mantel was a carved, painted squirrel munching on an acorn: the Brown family emblem, we were told. This prodded my memory toward the dolphin sofa, where the same motif existed on the back rail. Had attachment to the industrious squirrel enticed the family, after John Brown, to perpetuate the tradition in furniture meant to match this room? To my knowledge, the oak-leaf pattern was highly unusual on Classical sofas, although I had to ask myself if I overreached in attaching an association to everything I saw.

The central doors in the main hall, with their heavy, arched moldings, led to the drawing room. A crest of fruits and flowers in a basket echoed the fable mirror. The carved moldings were original to the house and, although similar, were clearly not executed by the same hand as my frame's. The main characteristic in common was the rather static and chunky early American–style carving. I could hardly wait to reach the second floor and inspect the size of the rooms where Abby Brown and John Francis's 1788 wedding had taken place, my tape measure in my pocket to gauge the distance between the two windows and whether the ceiling height could accommodate an eight- by three-and-a-half-foot mirror.

The rooms were now bedrooms. I made my way to the partition that divided the room described by the bridesmaid. How large would two mirrors need to have been to reflect the dancers' bodies? The frame bases would have had to nearly touch the floor. It seemed likely that, if the mirrors had been meant to be permanently placed there, they were pier mirrors, as I had first thought when I read Elisa's letter. Mine was not one. Nevertheless, I unfolded my measuring tape and set to work, recording the distance between the two windows facing Power Street.

It was obvious that my mirror was a bit wide and would have covered some of the window molding. Vertically, though, it could fit—from my standpoint the most crucial factor if, say, a mirror was not meant to hang there permanently. With plenty to spare in the ceiling height, the width did not rule me out: tables, chairs, and benches covered in green baize had been brought in and set up temporarily for function and festivity; perhaps mirrors had been brought in as well. It made sense that a mirror as ornate as mine would ultimately have been hung in a more public room once the house was finished. Incidentally, the bridesmaid had been accurate about the dimensions of the room. It measured precisely fifty-two feet.

After the tour, I mentioned to the guide that I had a mirror that had once belonged to John Brown's great-granddaughter. I was wondering if it could have come from the mansion at one time. I asked if anyone was available with background knowledge of the house and furnishings. She disappeared, returning a few minutes later trailing a formidable Ms. Eppich, who bore a resemblance to my third-grade schoolteacher. Short and powerfully built, she was primly dressed in a gray wool skirt with a tucked-in, button-down blouse. I launched into the story of my mirror, laced with theories about how it might once have been owned by the Browns. I mentioned the letter written by a bridesmaid in 1788, where she describes a mirror.

Ms. Eppich endured this onslaught of speculation as best she could, but I could tell from her body language that both the subject and my presence made her uncomfortable. As I rattled on, a deadpan expression remained on her face while she glared at me with her head pressed into her shoulder, arms akimbo. She had little patience with a dreamer who had sprouted from a house tour with no academic credentials or scheduled appointment.

"Wendy Cooper, presently the American curator at Winterthur," Ms. Eppich wearily announced, "has documented the mirror mentioned at the wedding reception, and it is in the house now."

At the historical society they had told me that the only furnishings in the Brown house described in any detail when John Brown lived there were the large, ornate mirrors from the "Rosella letter." I had read Cooper's articles from *Antiques* magazine on Brown furnishings, where she did quote the bridesmaid's letter, if not in its entirety. But she had left out the crucial detail of the reported size, which could have been ascertained by standing back fifty-two feet.

Ms. Eppich was determined to relieve me of my delusions by showing me "the" mirror described at the Francis-Brown wedding and identified by Cooper in her 1971 doctoral thesis. We marched into the dining room. "Here it is," she said as she straightened, pointing to a gold mirror bearing flags and war trophies on the crest.

After a brief silence, I said, "I'm afraid it just can't be. It is a very nice early mirror, but I think it is too small to be the one mentioned in the bridesmaid letter." A glass of its size could not have reflected a procession of dancers from their heels to their plumed headgear at a distance of fifty-two feet, as noted two hundred years before, or elicited the wondrous review. I was not persuaded by the trophy mirror, even though an expert had posited it as the most likely candidate. There was no reason for me not to believe it had once belonged to John Brown, but other than its golden provenance, it was just a common trophy mirror.

Ms. Eppich, now acting more hospitable, showed me every mirror in the house. They had all been donated by Brown descendants over the last fifty years. All were good examples of eighteenth- and early-nineteenth-century mirrors of expected style and proportion. But again the glasses were too small to reflect an entire figure, never mind "a crowd of sprightly dancers" at a distance. I was now certain the wedding mirrors had never been found. Had Anne Brown Francis Woods come to possess one of the pair, leading to its present obscurity?

I knew the mansion had been sold at some point in the nineteenth century and asked Ms. Eppich when. "Eighteen fifty-three," she answered. From reading a genealogy chart, I knew Anne Brown Francis by that time had been married to Marshall Woods for five years and was living not far away, in a refurbished house on Waterman Street, with two small children.

"What happened to the furnishings?" I asked. Apparently taken aback that I had failed to glean the obvious, Ms. Eppich drew in a big breath and held it as she stroked the collar of her shirt. Composure regained, she stepped back to deliver the answer. "Well, everything was divided up between the Brown, Francis, and Herreshoff families in 1852."

"Which would be my point," I said. "The woman I believe must certainly have inherited some of the furnishings—and possibly some mirrors—was named Anne Brown Francis Woods." I emphasized the two names in the middle. The correlation had no impact.

As I was leaving, I spotted a painting of two little girls in the dining room. The artist was Chester Harding, and his subjects, painted in the 1830s, were Anne Brown Francis and her older sister, Abby. Their grandfather Nicholas Brown II had commissioned the work for his own mansion on Benefit Street. Beneath the painting was a table with a green dolphin base that I thought likely to have been the companion piece to the Classical sofa I'd bought in Clayville. The placard explained that both painting and table had been donated by a descendant of the Browns and Woodses. Her name was Washburn. I made a note to look into her household inventory sometime down the line.

I decided to contact John Carter Brown. It was 1997, and at the time, he was the director emeritus of the National Gallery in Washington, D.C., the institution he had served for twenty-three years. A populist, he had transformed the museum by presenting blockbuster shows, promoting free admission, increasing attendance, and modernizing the facilities. But his progressive ideas had met with resistance at times. "There is a kind of conservatism in the museum world," he noted in an interview. People, he said, sometimes have a hard time revising opinions.

I wanted to see if Brown, a descendant of Nicholas Brown, knew anything about his distant relatives the Woodses and their furnishings at 62 Prospect Street in Providence. I was hopeful because Carter Brown had expressed a keen interest in architecture, developed from growing up with a father who always kept a drafting table in the house he had inherited on Benefit Street in Providence. His father, Nicholas, had been an advocate for saving the Woods-Gerry Mansion. I wondered if the father might have passed on details of that interior to his son.

With proceeds from the sale of the $12.1 million Nicholas Brown secretary, the family had restored the Nightingale-Brown House in Providence. I wrote to Carter at the Knickerbocker Club, his New York City address, which I had gotten from his former New York decorator, enclosed photographs of the Classical sofa and the Fox and Grapes mirror, and asked if he had ever seen them in the Woods house and, if so, if he had any recollection of where they came from. I knew Nicholas Brown II was Anne Woods's grandfather and wondered if she might have inherited either of these pieces from the Nightingale-Brown House on Benefit Street.

Carter Brown promptly replied and said that he admired the mirror and the sofa, but he did not know much about the Woods side of his family. He suggested I get in touch with Denise Bastion, assistant director of American studies at the Nightingale-Brown House in Providence. He offered to forward the letter I had written him. When I reached Ms. Bastion, she told me that Brown had spoken with her on my behalf and that she would send me any information she could find about a large mirror that at one time might have been in the house. She was good humored on the phone, and she and I had an amusing exchange about the recycling of names in the Brown family. She offered to mail me the will of Nicholas Brown II (1769–1841) and the inventory from his estate.

In September 1997, I received a letter from Denise Bastion. She wrote that nothing about a mirror had materialized during a brief search through the Brown archives but that the only house before 1850 that could have taken a mirror measuring eight feet would have been the Nightingale-Brown House, now the John Nicholas Brown Center, part of Brown University. Enclosed with the letter was the 1841 will and inventory of Nicholas Brown II, a copy of the one on file in the Providence probate court. Ms. Bastion had not seen anything like a mirror described or anything of such "presumed value" listed in the inventory. I thought she meant this value as comparative, so I took a close look, just to be sure.

Six hundred seventy-eight objects were listed in the inventory. I was astonished to see "a looking glass" from the southeast parlor (the largest room) listed at $25. This particular mirror tied in listed value with a "bookcase" in the breakfast room, the two most expensive single items in the household after two Brussels carpets, $50 each. A dining table with a set of chairs was listed at only seven dollars for the group. The appraisal was so thorough as to list even trivial items such as towels, four tin pans, linens, tablecloths, feather mattresses, and "16 pair cotton Do [pajamas] all worse for the wear." Seven other mirrors of far less value were mentioned. Had Nicholas Brown once owned my mirror? Could Anne Brown Francis Woods, as his granddaughter—the only surviving female of that line and repeatedly mentioned in his will— have inherited it, thus placing the piece at Woods-Gerry?

It occurred to me while perusing the inventory that what I did not see was the industrialist's Newport desk, or secretary, or desk and bookcase, or any other item one might term an eighteenth-century mahogany workstation such as the one sold for $12.1 million in 1989, claimed by Christie's to have belonged to the first Nicholas Brown (1729–1791) and to have been passed to his son. During a second conversation with Denise Bastion, I brought up the omission of "the secretary" in Nicholas II's will.

"What are you trying to prove anyway?" She sounded annoyed. "All the Brown brothers had a secretary commissioned by Goddard. Anyway, it has always been spoken of by the family. It is word of mouth. Besides, we have photos of it placed in the house."

"Photos? From when?" I asked.

"The 1890s."

In an attempt to get us back on topic, I said I was not disputing the secretary the Brown family had sold at Christie's as a Goddard of Newport masterpiece of colonial design and craftsmanship. What I didn't say was how surprised I was to learn the historical record was based on hearsay, without any specific written documentation, unless as "bookcase" qualified. Regarding the critical issue of provenance, the public had been led to believe— on scant evidence—that the desk sold at Christie's was without a doubt the one belonging to Nicholas Brown I. That, and having spent the entirety of its existence in the house on Benefit Street, added to its romance and likely its price.

Instead, I asked Bastion if she knew anything about Anne Brown Francis Woods. No, she said. Then she offhandedly recalled, "Upon Nicholas Brown II's death, his son John Carter Brown was supposed to give Anne Brown Francis some cash, or something."

According to Nicholas Brown's will, I explained, Anne Brown Francis Woods was given a lot more than "some" cash. I was discovering that, unlike most women in the eighteenth and nineteenth centuries, the Brown women were not overlooked with rights to family-owned property. In addition to considerable cash, Anne had inherited not only her own portion but both her deceased mother's and sister's share of the family's banking and corporate stocks, dividends, and a staggering amount of real estate.

Nicholas Brown II had left his granddaughter acres of property in downtown Providence; his largest country estate, called Lippett Farm, in Warwick; and together with his son Carter, she was part owner of Turks Head estate, too, in Warwick. The will also indicated that Anne was entitled to some of the Benefit Street household inventory. What is more, when Anne Wood's uncle Carter Brown died in 1873, his wife, Sofia (born in the same year as Anne and decades younger than her husband), gave away the furniture in the Benefit Street mansion to his relatives. Years later his descendants made attempts to get those things back.

My foremost intention, I explained to Ms. Bastion, was to ascertain the provenance and track down the maker of a large, gilded Fox and Grapes mirror of the Rococo style. I thought it possible that Anne had inherited it from one of her grandfathers or her Brown uncle who was executor of Nicholas Brown's estate. When the Woodses constructed their own mansion and were trying to furnish it during the Civil War, good pieces were getting harder to come by and transport, leaving a chance that Anne had obtained the mirror along with some other things from the Nightingale-Brown House, and presumably she had installed her heirlooms at her residence at 62 Prospect Street.

Ms. Bastion clearly found my obsession with the Brown and Woods families odd and wanted to absolve herself from anything further to do with either subject. She proposed a match of like minds.

"I have an idea for you," she said. "Call Henry Brown. Here, let me give you his phone number. He seems to know everything there is to know about that family and has dedicated his life to researching his roots." In addition to depositing large quantities of family documents in the Rhode Island Historical Society, Henry Brown had donated some of John Brown's eighteenth-century furnishings he had inherited to the John Brown mansion, one being the trophy mirror that I believed had been mistaken for the one mentioned by the bridesmaid. At Bastion's suggestion, I called Henry Brown at his home, Spring Green Farm, in Warwick, Rhode Island.

Bastion was right. It quickly became clear that Henry relished the opportunity to discuss events of centuries past. He was quite forthcoming on the topic of his ancestry, his specialty, with anyone who was interested. He gave me the lowdown on Anne Brown Francis Woods as if she were a relative he had known in his lifetime.

"You see," he said, "Anne Brown Francis Woods's mother, Anne Carter Brown, was the only daughter of Nicholas II. Anne Carter Brown was married to John Brown Francis, her cousin, who had been raised across the street by his grandfather John Brown. One month after Anne Brown Francis was born in 1828, her mother, Anne Carter, died at her father, Nicholas Brown II's, house on Benefit Street in Providence, presumably from complications due to childbirth."

For the next thirteen years, until Nicholas died in 1841, Anne and her sister, Abby, lived under the wing of their grandfather Nicholas Brown II, a distinguished merchant, philanthropist, and member of the American oligarchy. Raised in an atmosphere of privilege, they had every advantage except the experience of living with their real parents. Their father corresponded with his daughters. The girls visited him and his new family at Spring Green in Warwick often.

As Henry spoke, the story of the woman who eventually became the wife of Marshall Woods unfolded. He confirmed what I had seen in Nicholas Brown II's will, that Anne at age thirteen came into an enormous inheritance when he died at age seventy-three, one of the wealthiest men in the country. In the same will, I had noticed that Anne Brown Francis and her sister, Abby, had been left the same share as their uncle Carter and even more than their other uncle, also named Nicholas. The will stipulated that should one of the girls die before reaching twenty-one, her sister would inherit her share. Abby died at nineteen in 1841, the same year as her grandfather. With these passings, Anne became one of America's wealthiest teenage heiresses.

Although a mine of information, Henry said he did not have much to offer about my mirror. He did have stashed at his house in Warwick some pictures and letters from Anne Woods he thought might interest me. The family fondness for the decorative arts was evident in gifts, Henry said. He had a letter written by Anne Brown Francis at age eight, thanking her father for a writing desk sent from Philadelphia, where the family routinely shopped for their furniture. Henry said he had some of that early furniture at his house and invited me to drop by sometime for a look, but first I had to catch up with the story of the Woodses.

PART TWO

A Privileged Family

CHAPTER SEVEN

The Woodses: A Nineteenth-Century New England Family

Because the Woodses—Anne Brown Francis and her future husband, Marshall Woods—would eventually build the house on Prospect Street in Providence, I hoped one of them would make reference to their furnishings. Where had they, or one of their ancestors, shopped for a whimsical Rococo mirror now in my studio in New York City? At the Rhode Island Historical Society's archives, I combed through Anne and Marshall's letters and diaries, looking for clues to their decorative taste. But my curiosity about the maker of a mirror soon mixed with a desire to know the family who for generations had passed before its glass.

I began with Anne as a twenty-year-old woman in 1848. I imagined her in May of that year, in the house where she was born, sitting at a desk, fingers stained with ink from addressing invitations to her July wedding to Marshall Woods. The ceremony would be held at Spring Green, the country estate her great-grandfather John Brown of Providence had built on Gaspee Point in Narragansett Bay. Anne's father, John Francis, a former Rhode Island governor, would be hosting the reception for one hundred guests.

Anne and Marshall had known each other since childhood—their families were connected by Brown University, where Marshall's father, Reverend Alva Woods, a Baptist minister, had taught mathematics and philosophy and served as interim president early in his career. After a series of teaching and administrative positions in the South, Alva returned to Providence in 1839 to serve as a Brown trustee. At the time, Marshall was fifteen years old and Anne was eleven. The Woodses and the Browns shared interests in religion and politics, and promoted causes such as higher education, the establishment of a hospital for the insane (Butler Hospital), prison reform, the abolition of slavery, and women's rights. While president of the University of Alabama, Alva—with his wife, Almira's encouragement—helped organize the Alabama Female Athenaeum, a Baptist college for women.

For the Browns, the equality of women was never an issue. Time had proven that not all male Browns had an interest in or aptitude for business. John Brown described some of the men in the family as having "developed tastes that were emphatically uncommercial." The elders saw no point in pushing sons into careers they were not suited for when there happened to be so many Brown women blessed with the talent for making money.

Anne had grown up with strong female role models on her grandfather Nicholas's side. Alongside the men in the family, the Brown-Ives women contributed ideas and invested capital from their own separate accounts. Dressed in hooded bonnets and long skirts, they inspected jointly owned Brown and Ives ships returning from Europe, Russia, China, and Southeast Asia. Anne's aunts and female cousins became principal partners in several of America's earliest corporations. They were part of a concentrated group of Rhode Island merchants who collectively owned and operated several privately held spinning mills and were involved in the building of canals to transport the goods from their factories. With profits from the textile mills, they purchased vast tracts of land that stretched from Pennsylvania to Ohio and Kansas. The aunts' continuous presence had a profound impact on Anne Francis. By example, she knew how important it was to manage her own finances and to seek out legal advice to protect her interests. Keeping everything—such as real estate, stocks, and heirlooms—in the family was a lesson Anne learned from the tradition of her women relatives.

With access to Anne's immense inheritance, Marshall knew he would never have to work for a living. After graduating from New York University with a degree in medicine, he realized he had no gift for the art of healing. Since childhood he had felt cursed with a weak constitution, and exposure to the contagious diseases of patients was a risk he and Anne agreed was not worth taking. Instead, they fantasized about traveling for extended periods in Europe. Marshall pictured himself stationed at the best hotels, mingling with artists and becoming part of the salon crowd. Instead of medical journals, he would devote his time to studying art history. He would join clubs and societies where international intellectuals gathered, attend lectures, and bask in the pleasure of living in historic cities.

Keenly aware of his public image, Marshall did not want to be thought of as a dilettante. Volunteering his time in an administrative capacity at Brown University, his alma mater, would provide him with prestige and was feasible. His father had clout as a trustee, and Anne's grandfather Nicholas II had donated so much of his time and money to the college that the name of the institution was changed from Rhode Island College to Brown. It didn't take long after the couple was married for Marshall to be named college treasurer. His high-profile marriage promised a charmed life.

In July 1848, Marshall and Anne Woods were married and made their way by train to Niagara Falls, their honeymoon destination, with no rush to be anywhere at any particular time. In Utica, New York, they were detained because their "clothes were not ironed." Such setbacks were of no consequence; they were in love.

When Marshall went out alone for the first time since the day of their wedding, Anne had a chance to compose letters and record her first impressions of married life in her diary. "Both of us are perfectly happy and supremely blessed in each other's love. I am almost too happy for this world. May God preserve him for as long as I live!"

The first two weeks of sightseeing and intimacy were splendid, but the couple's prime days of marital bliss were soon

suspended. Their plans to arrive (someday) at the falls were interrupted when Marshall stepped on a needle. He could not walk
without Anne's assistance and complained "that his whole frame
ached."

Anne, frightened, wrote to her father-in-law for help. "I am
almost frantic for what may ensue and am here alone! I pity his
poor mother but she can imagine what I suffer." On July 14,
1848, two weeks after exchanging vows with him, Anne confessed that her husband "wants his mother."

The infection worsened. This time, Anne sent an urgent
telegram from Auburn, New York, to Marshall's parents, stress-
ing the seriousness of their son's condition. "Dear ones," she
pleaded, "Lose no time in getting here. M is very ill. I am almost
insane! We long to go home but he can't move! He is threatened
with the most awful disease—the lockjaw! Need I write more. I
am almost deranged . . . Come mother and father. I will be a
child to you if yours is taken from you. Your child, Anne."

Alva Woods immediately wrote to his friend Dixie Crosby at
the Hanover Medical School in New Hampshire. Dr. Crosby sent
off a prescription for Marshall. "I advise friction to the whole side
of his foot that is insensible, with the following. For his pain
Asafetida, 1 gram of opium, ½ gram Belladonna, ½ gram Cam-
phor . . . mix makes 1 pint." Crosby went on to advise the
"endermatic use of morphine applying ¼ gram 3 times a day."

By the time Crosby's letter and prescription reached Providence in August, Marshall was fully recovered and the Woodses
were in New York City, shopping for wallpaper. Joined by his
mother, Almira, there to fulfill her obligation as family decorator,
the couple hunted things for the newlyweds' house on Waterman
Street. Anne, who at this point admitted to being without an eye
for home decor, happily deferred to her mother-in-law's "exquisite taste." When the house was purchased, two months before the
wedding, Anne had told Almira that she would "never even consider having a brush lifted to a wall" unless her mother-in-law
had selected the paint color.

When the Woodses returned to Providence, Almira was still
on the interior decorating crusade. She asked if Anne would like

to meet her in Boston to purchase more things for the house. Anne declined on grounds that must have pleased her mother-in-law: She could not tear herself away from Marshall. "When I got married I thought that I could come and go as I pleased," she wrote, but instead her sense of independence vanished. "I have my own precious husband to love me and be with me," Anne wrote rapturously. "It matters not if I see another living soul. I can't bear to go away from him, even for a few hours. It fairly makes me love spirited and sick."

Clearly, in the first few months of her marriage, Anne had no interest in carpeting, drapes, and trimming. Or mirrors. And it does not look as though Almira purchased any in Boston or donated one from her own collection to hang in the starter house. Although I uncovered plenty of peculiarities regarding mid-nineteenth-century marriage and in-law relationships, I kept hoping for some reference to my gilded mirror. Almira kept shopping, and I kept reading.

Spending the first Christmas with Marshall's parents in Providence provided Anne's opportunity to present to her mother-in-law a golden locket filled with her own hair. Almira's gift to the newlyweds was fine china plate to go with the immense collection of silver that Anne was beginning to amass. Anne was asserting herself as a young Providence hostess and was busy with a staff of servants decorating the house for the holidays. On January 2, 1849, the day after a New Year's party held in their own home, Marshall remarked proudly in his diary that "Anne was beautiful, beautiful, beautiful. I never saw her look better. All men in love with her as well as her husband. She was the beauty of the room."

She almost certainly was beautiful, but by January 1849, Anne was six months pregnant with her first child and exhausted from all the parties and recitals she had given over the holidays, to say nothing of the unrelenting task of attending to Marshall's every whim. Marshall, an only child used to being the center of attention, assumed it was Anne's job to indulge him as his mother had always done. Oblivious to the effects his hypochondria and selfish behavior might have on his "devoted" wife, he surmised Anne's busy holiday schedule was responsible for running her down. "Anne," Marshall wrote in his diary a few days later, "is fatigued from the party. It has made her sick. Dear child she is so precious. I can't bear the thought of her suffering at all."

The following weekend, Marshall was ill again. The house was brimming with servants. Nevertheless, Marshall kept a bell beside his bed to ring Anne whenever he wanted her attention. After recovering, he wrote in his diary, "Anne has been through another trial with me and come out of it more perfect in character than when she was first made my wife . . . Like a good wife she is willing to do as I ask her."

Such sentiment—or sentimentality—was fascinating to one looking back from a far more cynical century. The voyeur's reward in perusing private writing distracted me from my objective of finding a reference to a mirror hung in what was to be the Woodses' final home in Providence.

Could they have purchased it while abroad? I was practically certain they had not, but just in case Alan Miller, the carving expert, was on the mark, I decided to follow the Woodses to Europe. I turned to the couple's travel journals to see if England was on the itinerary of Anne's first overseas trip with Marshall. From the diary entries for 1852, it appeared the Woodses were not found anywhere near the British coast in that year. I vicariously joined them in France.

The mid–nineteenth century marked the beginning of the age of travel. More people than ever were scouring the globe with a thirst for culture. Wealthy Americans like the Woodses made up an Anglo-American colony in Europe with the goal of getting in touch with history, which many felt was not possible in the United States. With the introduction of ships powered by steam, and railcars moving at speeds up to fifteen miles an hour, travel gained more appeal than ever. Despite such improvements, it took the Woodses almost a month to sail from New York Harbor to the thickly settled port of Marseilles. It was Anne's first trip to Europe. She was twenty-four and had two small children in tow, Carter, who was seven months old, and Abby, who was three.

Anne's doting uncle John Carter Brown greeted the Woodses

Me and my mirror, back in Rhode Island in 2009.

Plate number 22 from Thomas Johnson's *One Hundred and Fifty New Designs*, published in London in 1761. This plate served as the inspiration for the carver of my mirror. Johnson's incongruous designs often included references to Aesop's fables and were wildly popular in the eighteenth century. Designs similar to his experienced a revival in the 1830s. (Courtesy of Redwood Library and Athenaeum)

It's easy to spot the differences between the Johnson plate and my mirror. Johnson's human figures were highly refined and meant for master carvers; the work on my model is primitive by comparison. The creator of my Fox and Grapes frame was clearly stretched beyond his range. To me, though, this naïve interpretation is seductive. In my long career as a restorer and gilder of mirrors, I have never come across a frame like it.
(Christie's Images Ltd., 2009)

If you examine the details of the figurative carvings on my frame, you'll see how much they have in common with the carvings on the fireman's trophy frame, which we know was manufactured by James S. Earle's firm in Philadelphia. The folk-art spirit of the carvings on both models are highly unusual and strikingly similar. (Friendship Firehouse Collection, Historic Alexandria, Virginia)

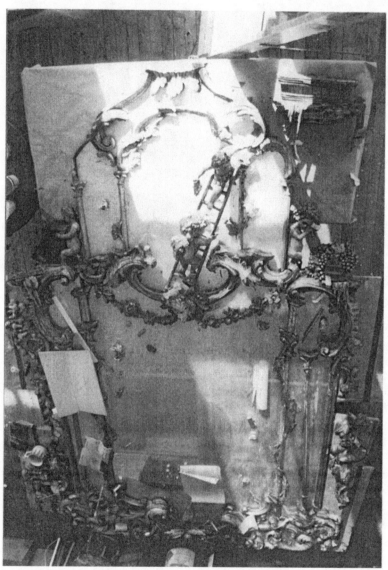

The frame, laid out on a worktable in my studio. This mirror, which was stored in a crate in an unheated barn for decades, was in poor condition when I discovered it, and needed months of restoration.

Working on the American dolphin sofa in my New York City workshop in 1995.

The dolphin sofa, displayed at the Detroit Institute of Arts. (Founders Society Purchase, R. H. Tannahill Foundation fund / The Bridgeman Art Library)

An 1858 portrait of Anne Brown Francis Woods, painted by George Peter Alexander Healy in Philadelphia. She was raised by her grandfather, Nicholas Brown II, the successful merchant and philanthropist for whom Brown University is named. When he died in 1841, Anne became one of America's wealthiest teenage heiresses. (Courtesy of Howard R. Merriman, Jr.)

Dr. Marshall Woods in the 1870s. Although he received a medical degree from New York University, he never practiced. In 1855, Marshall Woods served as a U.S. commissioner to the Paris Exposition, France's first world fair. Louis-Napoleón awarded him the cross of the French Legion of Honor for serving as a member of the jury of fine arts. (Courtesy of John F. Gifford)

The Woods-Gerry Mansion in Providence, Rhode Island, designed by the architect Richard Upjohn in 1860. Construction dragged for several years due to Marshall Woods's obsessive involvement with the project. (Courtesy of David Woods Merriman)

Abby Francis Woods at about the age of twenty-one. Tall, elegant, blond, and always impeccably dressed, she attracted suitors wherever she traveled. Her parents were relieved by her decision to call off her engagement to Charles Stewart Parnell. (Courtesy of Bay McClure)

Charles Stewart Parnell, nineteenth-century Protestant landlord and Irish nationalist leader, often claimed that it was Abby's "jilting" of him that drove him into a career in politics. (Library of Congress Prints and Photographs Division, Brady-Handy Photograph Collection)

Samuel Appleton Browne Abbott, a Boston Brahmin, lawyer, and businessman, married Abby Woods in 1873. He eventually moved to Italy with his mistress and, in 1897, became the first director of the American Academy in Rome. (From the estate of Priscilla M. K. Gifford)

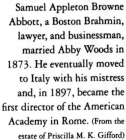

The Mott homestead on Block Island, built in 1750, is where our family spent summers.

The Gray Craig gatehouse in Middletown, Rhode Island, where my mirror presently hangs.

at the dock. On the way to their hotel, they made a stop at a jewelry store, where Anne's uncle bought his favorite niece a wristwatch encrusted with pink diamonds as a gesture to lift her ocean-lagged spirits.

To Anne, "the surroundings seemed wonderfully strange." She remarked on the beauty of the sunset and the colorful boats she saw from the small skiff her uncle rowed. This leisurely activity was in dramatic contrast to the lives of the galley slaves with sad and "horrid faces" whom she observed bound in chains on the decks of rotting ships.

Raising children was the most fulfilling aspect of Anne's life. "Mothering makes me extremely happy," she wrote in her journal in Rome in 1852. Describing herself as a "motherless child" on the anniversary of her mother's death, she prayed to God to spare her fledglings the same fate. Anne developed the habit of writing her children letters meant for them to read in the future and have as keepsakes should she die before they had any memory of her. This way, she thought, they would always know how much she had loved them. With her children present, Anne knew she was "cared for and loved in this frigid world." On the other hand, the burden of taking care of Marshall was beginning to wear.

Through the filthy cities of Genoa and Nice, and beautiful places such as Venice and Lake Como, the couple's plans were constantly altered and suspended because of her husband's incessant demands and complaints. Many times Anne confessed that "Marshall was not nice at all." "I have much fatigue and anxiety in both body and mind," she recorded in Florence. "Marshall continues quite ill with a severe attack of gout. At any rate what ever is the malady, he certainly suffered a great deal. I will not attempt to describe what I suffer on the occasions of his illnesses," she added. "Oh how very different I expected my life to be," she confessed to her journal. Continuing to grouse about her disappointing marriage, she wrote, "Four years since I looked forward to so much bliss and yet alas, never! I may truly say that had one month scarcely elapsed but what I have been nursing a sick husband. My only hope is that I can bear it with patience."

When Marshall was feeling up to it, he and Anne, escorted by an essential *valet de place*, made side trips to tourist attractions. Anne's general descriptions of the "dark, dismal and filthy" cities in France and Italy are similar to those of other nineteenth-century travelers, including fellow New Englanders like Hawthorne. Along rutted streets wide enough only for "foot passengers," she was astonished to find elegant palazzos decorated with trompe l'oeil exteriors squeezed among squalid, crumbling buildings that housed the majority of the impoverished population. Paying admittance fees to view the palaces' interiors, Anne made a note of the "superb marble floors of every color of inlaid marble" as well as of "all the costly gilding." On the walls of the Red Palace, gilded vines of grapes and leaves were carved in bas-relief. "The mirrors and the frescos and the splendid pictures surpass anything an American can have any idea of."

Needless to say, Anne's image of the gilded grapes and leaves perked me up, and her taste for ornately carved mirrors held promise, if without reference to one she may have already owned.

The Woodses had come to Italy to see the art, and it shocked them to discover so many masterpieces disintegrating from damp and neglect. Michelangelo's Sistine Chapel ceiling was peeling; Leonardo's *Last Supper* was hardly recognizable after a series of inept restorers had repainted large sections and tweaked the facial expressions of the apostles. It was reported that the Dominican friars at the Convent of Santa Maria delle Grazie had sliced through the painting to create a door to the dining refectory.

Anne blamed the Roman Catholic clergy for the destitute state of the Italian citizens. To her mind, priests were hucksters who invented superstitious rituals to manipulate the poor for the sole purpose of filling the purses of thieving popes and cardinals, who lived in splendor. She grew up in a country that espoused individual freedom and the republican ideal. Raised in a liberal family of philanthropists who believed in elevating mankind through education, she chafed at how the Roman church squelched any form of progressive political and scientific thinking among its followers. A pragmatist who was intolerant of most forms of faith not her own, Anne was blind to the mysteries of the Catholic religion and the glories of its churches and cathedrals. "If only a greater part of the money could be spent in sending the bible to these ignorant creatures, what a blessing it would be!" One of the basic flaws in Anne's reform theory was that the majority of the population was illiterate. She raged on repeatedly in her diary against the corrupt clergy. "The more I see of these disgusting Catholics the more I detest the whole sect. I can smell a catholic a half mile off, the horrid incense which is so stifling to me." With church bells ringing in almost every neighborhood and saints' statues in building alcoves on every corner, Italy must have been a trial for Anne Woods.

Anne's railings at the Catholic clergy echoed sentiments common among educated Anglo-Christians. For those who believed that the way to change corrupt societies and institutions was by questioning authority, the political structure of the papist church was the perfect target for recrimination. Charles Dickens, a member of the Anglican Church of England and a champion of individual rights, wrote unabashedly about his contempt for the monks. In *Pictures from Italy*, a serialized account of his experiences of living there in 1844, he wrote, "I have no knowledge, elsewhere, of more repulsive countenances than are to be found among these gentry. If natures be at all legible, greater varieties of sloth, deceit, and intellectual torpor could hardly be observed among any class of men in the world." These remonstrations contrasted with his feelings toward the Italian people, whom he regarded as charming and endlessly entertaining. He satirized their religious beliefs with more humor than scorn.

Marshall shared Anne's outlook on the Roman Church but didn't grumble the way she did. They had come to Italy to see the art, Marshall reminded his wife. If she could try to put aside her entrenched opinions about the way everyone should be, she might enjoy herself more, he added. The point of traveling was that it gave one an experience different from the way things were at home, and now that they were there, it was better to make the best of it.

Shortly after his lecture about tolerance, Anne agreed to accompany her husband on an excursion to a Franciscan chapel in the hills of Tuscany. Marshall wanted to see the precious hand-painted manuscripts and Old Master paintings kept there. If he did have to suffer fools, art was worth it.

Once they arrived, Marshall, poring over the pages of a rare medieval manuscript, was enthralled by the brightly painted figures and exquisitely formed lettering embossed with gold leaf. He was so immersed that he ignored Anne, who stood impatiently behind him, glaring haughtily at the monk. "Oh what a filthy dark dismal place," she later wrote. "I was never as glad when they said that ladies were not admitted behind the altar or into their garden. For I had had quite enough."

The Woodses preferred to commission American artists rather than Europeans to paint their portraits and sculpt family likenesses. Many of these artists could be found working and living part-time in Europe. In 1848, Hiram Powers, a Vermont-born Neoclassical sculptor, became internationally famous for his work titled *Greek Slave*. The marble statue of a naked female bound in chains was the subject of controversy when it toured the United States. Powers's roster of American clients included Andrew Jackson, John Quincy Adams, and Daniel Webster. Powers had been working in Florence since 1837. To support his family, the sculptor took on high-paying commissions from wealthy Americans who flocked to his studio.

One such client to call on him in 1852 was Anne Brown Francis Woods. In July she recorded frequent visits to the sculptor's studio to "supervise" the marble bust of the eight-month-old Carter, a hand of their three-year-old daughter, Abby, and her own hands in a praying gesture. Anne was homesick in Florence, so the hours she spent conversing with a fellow New Englander, especially one of such notoriety, made her feel less estranged.

With the vast quantities of fine art available in Italy, Anne remarked how astonished she was by "the amount of trash that Americans buy to carry home." Her policy was, regardless of cost, she would rather have a well-executed copy made of a truly great painting than own and overpay for something mediocre. This mind-set made me think Anne would not object to having a revival example of a Thomas Johnson mirror frame.

After living abroad for two years, the Woodses headed home.

Their travels in Europe clearly had an impact on their plan for a house in Providence. They wanted something based on a historical concept. In the land records held at city hall, they are recorded as having purchased a large plot on September 2, 1851, on Prospect Street across the road from Marshall's parents in a neighborhood packed with Anne's relatives. In 1858, seduced by Italian architecture and unscathed by the stock market crash the year before, Marshall and Anne seriously began to discuss building a new home. It would have to be large enough to accommodate the family and a sizable staff of live-in servants. They wanted high windows for light but also wall space to display their art collection, a garden planted with evergreens, and tall mirrors placed at advantage to bring the outside in.

When the Woodses interviewed Richard Upjohn, he was the president of the American Institute of Architects, the guild he had founded. Born in 1802 in Shaftesbury, England, Upjohn was trained as a cabinetmaker, engineer, and draftsman, and had apprenticed with a builder. Immigrating to Boston in 1829, he moved five years later to New York City to open an architecture firm. His early training in mechanics and the art of furniture making served him well in designing the glorious wood-worked interiors of his inspired and perfectly proportioned buildings.

He had gained national recognition for his ecclesiastical commissions. Upjohn's career took off when, at the age of thirty-two, he was hired to design a new edifice for Trinity Church in New York City. Many of his churches erected there still stand. I was surprised at how familiar I was with the architect's work before being introduced to him by the Woodses. Almost every day on my way to work I would walk past and admire the Church of the Holy Apostles on Twenty-eighth Street and Ninth Avenue. In the 1980s, I was hired to gild a chalice for the Church of the Ascension on West Eleventh Street. During the same period I frequented a nightclub on West Twentieth Street called the Limelight, disco dancing in the shell of what once had been the Church of the Holy Communion. All of these buildings were designed by Upjohn.

In the nineteenth century, blue-blooded families hired

Richard Upjohn for his flair for commodious designs based on the Renaissance style. In the spring of 1858, he went to Providence to meet the Woodses, inspect the site, and discuss costs. After finalizing an agreement, Upjohn went to work.

While the key events leading to the American Civil War were coming to a head in 1860, the Woods mansion was in early construction. As months passed and the official declaration of war was made, in 1861, work on the house understandably did not progress smoothly. The challenges of finding skilled men willing to stay on the job and obtaining materials threatened completion. Delays mounted. The project became an exercise in frustration for everyone involved. Rich, neurotic, and demanding, Marshall wrote the architect regularly with tedious lists of complaints, questions, and requests for work order changes. He made it clear that if Upjohn was to be paid his 5 percent commission, the house had to be completed on schedule.

The Woodses stayed in and close to Providence for the next four years, with Marshall showing up almost daily to keep a log and an eye on the construction process. By insisting on the best imported materials instead of those locally obtainable, Marshall the perfectionist subjected himself to extra aggravation. Challenging the architect on beam construction, he wrote, "I fear the wooden connection and substituted iron . . . These anchors are so important as regards springing of the floor that I request your close attention to it. Telegraph whether the anchors are to go on each beam where it meets together." Marshall wanted to use only Philadelphia brick. When the brick did not arrive on schedule, he demanded an explanation from Upjohn at his New York office. "You do not mention one word about the Philadelphia bricks. Where are they? When did they leave? On what vessel? Name the Captain!" In September, Marshall was discouraged to receive the news that a schooner had left for Providence with 71,000 bricks intended for Prospect Street. On the way there, the vessel encountered bad weather and the captain ordered that 4,000 bricks be thrown overboard. Of the thousands left, many had been damaged by improper packing.

Problems with labor also seemed never-ending. In one

instance, Marshall relayed his dissatisfaction with the bricklayers in a letter to Upjohn. "Mr. O'Connor's work goes on as well as it can with a few workmen, But I wish you would see that he sends on men of whom he knows the work." The brick was not leveled properly and had to be dismantled. "He must have men who are good masons and whom he knows. These are the men I insist upon having and if he does not give them, I shall give such a protest as will interfere with the payments, even though it may be, as would be the case, much against my desire. He cannot give good work with poor men. You understand this." Marshall pleaded with Upjohn to keep his complaints about the Irish bricklayers confidential. He did not want to "discourage" O'Connor, the contractor, from continuing with the work, since there was no one else around capable of taking over the job.

During the war, Upjohn traveled to Providence to check on his building and appease the Woodses, but as soon as the architect boarded the train back to New York, progress stalled again. "Since you were here last night, I have been called upon by a gang of Philadelphia brick layers," Marshall wrote. They charged that O'Connor had deceived them about the nature of the work and was not willing to pay them the same wages for rough brick as for the face brick. They threatened to go home. Marshall offered to pay an extra half dollar a day to each of the four bricklayers if they stayed on the job, but this strategy did not work. Money could not make up for what the laborers felt was O'Connor's betrayal. The disgruntled group walked off the job and returned to Philadelphia. "It is these detestable small savings of a 25 cent piece here and there.which seem to threaten the success of the job," Marshall complained to Upjohn. "I depend on you therefore to arrange for their immediate replacement." Marshall criticized the architect for putting him "at the mercy of any drunken workmen among the gang who refuse to obey orders and makes his fellows follow suit by sympathy. O'Connor did not impress me favorably and the next man YOU BETTER SEE YOURSELF."

After the outside of the mansion was completed, another year dragged on as the carpenter, the New York architect, and the overly involved and fussy clients tried to resolve the interior details. Were the doors still to be arched? What height should the dadoes on the stairway have, and the railing? "Was it too late to put in window seats now that the walls were up?" Marshall hoped not. What about blinds? What should those look like? Drawings were revised over and over again, making sure the design of the hallway paneling and the moldings and every other interior feature would satisfy the Woodses' meticulous standards. In 1864, to the great relief of everyone involved, the house was completed—on schedule—and the last payment made to Richard Upjohn.

With the Prospect Street mansion in Providence completed, the Woodses found themselves unwilling to build another house. Though they owned a house on Ochre Point in Newport, they sold it, along with the land on Bellevue Avenue they had purchased with the intention of building something more up-to-date. This did not mean they abandoned Newport. Anyone who was anyone spent at least part of the summer there, and the Woodses kept a toe in by renting villas from friends and relatives. They also continued to sojourn, and shop, in Europe with the same tribe from Philadelphia, Providence, and Boston they had always known.

I continued to look further through Woods papers for mirrors and other furnishings mentioned in wills. Marshall, pompous and materialistic, seemed to grasp the concept that, once you died, it didn't make sense to fret over things that weren't yours anymore. He left his wife in charge, obligingly signing his name next to hers in every legal transaction. Anne Woods, ever mindful of her short time on earth, frequently updated and revised her wills according to the circumstances of her life. In the dozens of wills I slogged through, two requests never changed. It was her "desire" that no real estate be sold and that "property remain undivided for as long as possible." This I assumed meant personal property. The same rule applied to inherited bank stocks, of which she had not once tapped the principal.

It was Anne's wish that, after her demise, all of her "old fashioned furniture" and silver inherited from her great-grandfathers John and Nicholas Brown would go to her children. A stickler for household maintenance, she had money put aside for restoring gilded frames. "Gilded frames" I assumed meant not only picture frames but gold-leafed mirrors as well. This perhaps explained why the Fox and Grapes mirror frame had been touched up on several occasions.

Carter Brown Woods, Abby's brother, died in the mansion on Prospect Street in 1930 at the age of seventy-eight. The house and most of the articles inside were divided up among his four married nieces. The mansion was left vacant until a couple with first-rate credentials appeared.

The Rhode Island senator Peter Goelet Gerry and his wife, Edith Stuyvesant Dresser Gerry, needed a new house in Providence. The Gerrys were gifted the house in 1930 by the Woods descendants for the token sum of ten dollars. My theory as to why the mirrors had not been removed before the Gerrys moved in was that they were large enough to be considered part of the interior architecture or else that none of the Woodses' granddaughters wanted them. On the walls at 62 Prospect Street the mirrors remained, until they were finally taken away and, for decades, shrouded from view in a barn in Clayville, Rhode Island.

CHAPTER EIGHT

A Scientific Matter
and Opinions from Experts

I enjoyed poring through diaries and letters and getting to know the Browns and the Woodses but so far had found no direct reference to the mirror. Both families were good candidates for my Fox and Grapes, but proof of purchase was eluding me. I decided to return to the facts for a while, to find out more about the mirror itself. I would start with validating the date of production. Such steps begin with an analysis of the wood, the hardware, even textiles. I would have to send samples to labs.

Along with a mirror's stylistic features, the type of wood used most often helps identify the country of origin. Its importance is "almost always" definitive, according to American decorative art authorities. In the process of authenticating an object, the trained or artistic eye is now supplemented—some might argue supplanted—by science. Antique furniture preservationists are beginning to use some of the same methods that were formerly restricted to painting conservators and archaeologists. I understand the advantages science can offer people who work in the fine arts. Using penetrating lights, conservators reveal the intentions of artists and the decisions they made as work was in progress. In addition, conservators can determine how to recover artists' original work when it has been overpainted by restorers. But to my mind, furniture is very different. I know many people would not agree with me, but I suspect the scientific methodology used on paintings, when applied to furniture, just serves American dealers as a way to instill buyer confidence. Technology works wonders as a sales tool.

Wood spores are now microscopically scrutinized. Large checks may confidently be inscribed after white-jacketed biologists and chemists toiling in laboratories can attest to region, bark, and soil. Papers must be written and spore slides produced and validated for the community of experts working together before anything of excessively high value can be deemed worthy. Using X-ray fluorescence spectrometers, paint on the outer casings of chests is analyzed. That I can understand. But I am amused when I see pictures of X-rays of early furniture construction in books. The methods of fine furniture construction are straightforward. The same techniques have been used for centuries. Even today, makers of traditional furniture build pieces in the same way. Joints are tenoned and pinned with small dowels, the sides of drawers are dovetailed, backboards, case sides, and tops are usually tongue-and-groove.

Nevertheless, these factors, in addition to proportion and materials, are no longer enough. All are benchmarks for determining value, but I suppose, with escalating prices, especially for Americana, more can always be done to keep the market viable.

Determining the wood is pretty basic, and quickly done by anyone who has spent time looking. But I am delighted that underpaid scientists in the United States are able to pocket money on the side via validation. I could plainly see the frame of my mirror was made from white pine but still had to wade through the lab process to settle the matter if I ever wanted to enlist the help of others to determine where the frame could have been made.

Whether evaluating drawer bottoms or pedestal bases, everyone involved with the American furniture club in 1995 used Donna Christensen for wood identification. She had worked for the U.S. Forest Service and gone on to start her own company, called CWIII, an initialism for Christensen Wood Identification, Information and Instruction. Tiny wood slivers from different sections of the frame were slid into marked envelopes and sent off to Christensen's lab in Arena, Wisconsin. Two months passed before she finished her analysis. She verified that the body of the Fox and Grapes mirror was American eastern white pine, also known as white pine, northern white pine, Weymouth pine, soft pine, and spruce pine. *White pine* is most commonly used for a species primarily grown in the eastern United States. The baskets of grapes were cherrywood, which I must say was an odd choice for carving since it is so hard and splinters easily with a chisel. Cherry trees, Christensen said, are indigenous to both America and Europe.

She sounded upbeat and pleased for me on the phone. "Aren't you excited?" she asked. "Usually American antique dealers and museum folks love to hear something is made out of white pine. It establishes that it is American."

I told her that I was not so sure the wood evidence would be all I needed for resolution, and that my case was far from closed. Christensen was perplexed. Wedded to the logic of science and a person who genuinely loved the natural world, and valued honesty, she did not grasp the "nature" of the art business.

I paid the wood spore lady's bill, the remarkably modest fee of $25 for her time, her opinions, and the folders and maps she had sent me, with all the regions where *Pinus strobus* grew in North America shaded in for easy detection. Included in that fat package were my original wood slivers, now returned as if they were as valuable as emeralds. Her supportive letter on CWIII stationery stated, "Antique pieces containing white pine wood are usually thought to be of North American origin utilizing eastern white pine."

Next I turned to a decorative arts conservator named Michael Podmaniczky, who works at Winterthur, the former country estate of Henry Francis du Pont. The museum in Delaware houses a vast collection of American furniture and offers programs to students of American decorative arts. Mike works as a furniture conservator and is in charge of gilded objects. I sent him screws, nails, brackets, and a few loose leaf carvings, all separated into sealed and marked envelopes for his analysis. What I got back for a small fee was a letter of encyclopedic discourse on the early manufacturing of hardware, namely, nails and screws. He wrote:

1. The small nail/sprigs are "L"-head, cut nails. Although the machine to make these was invented around 1760, broad availability of cut nails was not seen until the last decade of the 18th century.
2. The screw appears to be transitional, i.e., machine-cut thread and hand-filled slot. The machine for making cut screws was invented early in the 19th century.
3. The bracket . . . is a bracket. It appears to be cast and early; certainly in accord with the period of the nails and screws.
4. The gilded foliate element you sent me has had a long hard life. Under low power magnification, it appears that there are 2 campaigns of gesso (implying but not confirming) an earlier gilding, a thin wash of yellow bole and finally gold. The surface has been worn, with most of the gold gone, and much of the yellow bole worn away as well. This is an expected appearance for an object of this period.

I called Mike to try to clarify what his letter was stating, if anything, regarding the age of the frame. I wondered why it was necessary to use "low power magnification" when with just the naked eye I could tell that the leaf had been gilded at least twice. We had a short conversation about the age of the mirror. What "period" was he referring to? He was honest. He said he didn't know. He just repeated what he had stated in his letter about fasteners, which wasn't all that helpful.

Another specialist I consulted was Martin Bide, a textile expert and chemist to whom I was referred by a woman in the textile center of the Metropolitan Museum of Art. According to this woman, Bide, a professor at the University of Rhode Island, could determine the date of production of fabrics. When the glass had been replaced on my mirror, some of the original baize (a heavy green felt most often seen on card tables) had remained in the upper sections of the frame. When I approached Bide, he asked me to send him a piece of a substantial size. In his Scottish burr, he deemed it too frustrating to work with the "small bits" of cloth sometimes sent him.

This sounded promising. I sent Bide a fragment of the green baize used as a buffer between the glass and the backboards of the frame. I never got anything back in writing about the piece of material I had reluctantly hacked off. Bide delivered his conclusion by telephone. The green baize, he determined, was pre–industrial revolution. No synthetics had been used, only natural, organic vegetable and plant dyes, such as indigo. "Pre–industrial revolution" sounded good to me. This could set the date of manufacture to somewhere between the end of the eighteenth century and the middle of the nineteenth century. The first synthetic dyes were discovered by the British chemist William Perkin in 1856 while he was searching for a cure for malaria.

Having received little direction from Alan Miller, and still believing that the figures on the frame offered some clues to its maker, I turned to another expert, Luke Beckerdite. He was the man Leigh Keno had sent the mirror hardware to originally, but I had never spoken to him. Luke is the author and editor of books and articles on eighteenth-century American furniture and carving. He was once the curator and executive director of the Chipstone Foundation in Wisconsin, and later worked as a decorative arts consultant to Colonial Williamsburg in Virginia. He had written about immigrant carvers, like Henry Hardcastle, otherwise known as the Garvan carver, famous for his carved animals on eighteenth-century furniture, "chimneypieces, looking glasses, and pier tables," so I was extremely interested in Luke's opinion. In 2007, a Philadelphia tea table made by this carver sold at Christie's for $6,000,761.

Luke Beckerdite had seen everything American, so I wanted to speak to him to find out if, based on the pictures I mailed him, he had ever seen a mirror like mine. When I called to follow up, he told me that several years before someone had sent him a picture of a mirror he thought was almost identical to mine. He wished he could recall who the person was, he said, but at this point he had lost the information. What a letdown. Another frame to compare mine with was something I was dying to find. Luke Beckerdite, like so many other academics, tossed my mirror into the blanket category of nineteenth century. It seemed he could not imagine that a frame the size of mine, so full of figurative imagery, could have been made in America before the robber barons arrived on the scene, and therefore dismissed the subject as not in his realm of study.

Morrison H. Heckscher, chairman of the American Wing at the Metropolitan Museum of Art, is a pleasant man, a tweedy academic and the author of books on American furniture, including *American Rococo, 1750–1775*. Even though his area of expertise was the eighteenth century, earlier than it appeared the Fox and Grapes was made, I sent him pictures. He knows everything about Philadelphia carved pieces, and I wanted his thoughts. Our phone conversation went something like this:

"Very interesting, Maryalice. Where do you think it's from?"

"It came from a house in Providence, Rhode Island, which was owned by a Brown descendant in the nineteenth century. I don't know where it was made, but I believe the frame is American. I understand you wrote a book on frames, so naturally I'd like to know what you think."

"Who owns it?" he asked. When I claimed ownership, I could sense his loss of interest. The name Maryalice Huggins was not going to add a distinguished provenance. "Have you shown it to Luke Beckerdite? What does he think, and what do you plan to do with it?"

"Alan Miller has seen it, and I sent Luke Beckerdite photographs," I said. "Both feel it is late-nineteenth century, English, but I don't agree with them. To answer your last question, I'm not trying to sell the mirror. I am trying to find out where it was made."

"What Luke Beckerdite and Alan Miller say is very important in dating carving and making attributions, and we rely on them. What I'll do, if you like, is show the pictures to Bill Rieder, our European furniture guru here at the Met, and see what he has to say."

Despite Heckscher's demanding schedule, he made an effort to assist me. He left a message on my answering machine that he had spoken to Rieder, who agreed with me that my mirror was not English. This was exciting news. If it was not English, then it seemed likely it was American. If that were the case, being a Thomas Johnson design, the mirror was rare in a good way.

Heckscher then suggested I get in touch with Wendy Cooper at Winterthur. She is an expert on John Brown's furniture and wrote her thesis on the subject, he reminded me. Yes, I know she is the recognized expert on the John Brown collection, the topic of her 1970 thesis, I answered. But I did not agree with some of her attributions. I told him there was a mirror in the house she infers was the one mentioned in a bridesmaid's letter in 1788. For a variety of reasons, I said, I found her theory shaky.

Defending his colleague, he fired back. "Maryalice, Wendy Cooper is a scholar." Heckscher was only trying to be helpful. It was true that I lacked scholarly credentials in American decorative arts. And Cooper was a big deal, a woman who broke through gender barriers in the field. Maybe it was a good suggestion. In the meantime, I contacted Bill Rieder, whose formal title at the Met was curator and Administrator of the Department of European Sculpture and Decorative Arts.

Rieder did not recall receiving the pictures of the mirror from Heckscher's office, which is understandable when you think of all the things that appear on a curator's desk and then pile up in a corner of the floor. "If you would send me another set of photographs, I'd be happy to take a look and get back to you," he said. I confided how hard it was for me to get any American decorative arts experts interested in making new discoveries; anything unusual is treated as though it is not worth investigating if the time line is not in their area of expertise. Rieder seemed sympathetic. "That doesn't surprise me," he said.

Encouraged by his camaraderie, I began to describe the quagmire. I explained the confusion concerning the date of production and country of origin. "Some in the American camp say my mirror is English," I said. "The English believe it is American." Maybe because of the diversity of things made in Europe, those specialists seemed more expansive, I added. A mistake would not jeopardize their careers; nor were the stakes usually as high financially. I told Rieder I believed a descendant of the Browns of Providence, Rhode Island, had owned the mirror and there was a likelihood she had inherited it. As requested, I mailed pictures to the Met along with a letter with the wood description.

I was encouraged by the answer I received from Rieder seconding my opinion that the mirror was not English but American. He placed it in the second quarter of the nineteenth century—in keeping with carvings made after the 1825 reissue of Thomas Johnson's designs—and pointed out that English mirrors of that time were not made of American white pine. He also agreed with me that the carvings' "stiff quality" offered further proof of the mirror's American origins.

Rieder's opinion was an interesting follow-up to inquiries I had made the previous spring. In April 2000, I attended one of a series of lectures held at Sotheby's. The topic was furniture and objects that do not seem to fit a specific time. The speaker was Carolyn Sargentson, an English furniture curator from the Victoria and Albert Museum in London, my favorite repository for antique furniture. For me, an opinion from one who worked there would come near the last word. I carried a picture of the mirror along with me, hoping to show it to Sargentson after she spoke. This was pushy, and I had to muster up the courage to pull it off, but the opportunity was something not to miss.

After the lecture she was surrounded by a covey of admiring colleagues. I brazenly interrupted to introduce myself and show her the picture. "It's quite beautiful, isn't it," she said. "Do you own it? Are you going to sell it?"

Before I answered her, I had a more important question: Did she think it was English? I told her that her opinion would mean a lot to me. Sargentson gave me her address at the V&A and requested that I send her more photos. She promised to get back to me, a gesture she must have lived to regret. I sent her faxes and letters—relentlessly—throughout the following months.

Although it took a while for Sargentson to get back to me, the letter that finally arrived from the V&A contained more promising news. She had consulted with Michael Snodin, an ornament prints and drawings expert, and Frances Collard, a Regency furniture specialist, both of whom thought the mirror was likely American, although they weren't as certain as Rieder about its date. Snodin placed it somewhere in the 1820s or 1830s, while Collard was more dubious about my mirror being from the 1820s and placed it in the 1830s or later (although she admitted that she was "prepared to be proved wrong!"). The letter closed with an invitation to visit the gilding studios at the V&A the next time I made a trip to London.

The opinions from Rieder and Sargentson convinced me once and for all that the mirror was American and made sometime in the 1830s. But where? One of the advantages of living and working in Manhattan was that many of the people I needed to contact were there. Dean Failey was head of the American Furniture and Decorative Arts Department at Christie's. He relishes making discoveries in his field. He has a cheerful disposition, and it is always fun to speak with him about the latest things to hit the market. I knew he felt bad about missing out on the sale of the dolphin sofa for Christie's and my having missed an opportunity to make some money. About the sofa, he said, "You should have shown it to me. We would have loved to have had it. It's really a shame. I'm sorry about the way it turned out for you."

Dean arrived at my studio on an excruciatingly hot day. The man looks like a lampoon caricature of a British nineteenth-century politician. He is of medium height and wears his Irish red hair pushed back. His apple red cheeks seem even more pronounced from his way of perpetually smiling.

We both remarked about the scorching August heat, and I thanked him for coming in spite of it. Pulling on lapels to readjust a body uncomfortably stuck in a tight suit and tie, he perked up and reentered the moment. "So this is the mirror." Like others before him, he stood in front of it looking confused. After a minute or two, his posture began to soften. Then, in his tassel-toed loafers, he took two or three wide strides to view the colossal frame from both sides. He stepped backward and put his hand in front of his mouth as if suppressing something he was about to say. "It looks much different in person than it does in the photograph. Are there any marks of any kind on the back? We once had a frame, and there was simply a number on the back that turned out to be the address of the maker in the eighteenth century."

This was just the kind of story we both loved. Since the mirror was too heavy to safely turn, I showed him a picture of the back: nothing as exciting as an address, only pencil marks indicating assembly.

"You know," Dean said, "it looks a lot like Philadelphia to me. See this diapering on the swag? They used this design element quite a bit. You know," he continued, "it looks an awful lot like Reynolds." Then, taking back the compliment, Dean said, "But it just can't be. The glass is so big. I think it must have been a commission. I must say, I find something compelling about it. I really like it," he said finally. "It's very interesting."

Yet the word *interesting* was a polite way of being noncommittal.

"I agree about the proportions," I said. "It has to be nineteenth century, perhaps made by someone who worked in a shop at the end of the eighteenth century and the first quarter of the nineteenth whose style never changed much over time." I then asked Dean, "If a few people, experts, say it is early, say even the second quarter of the nineteenth century, will the strays follow?"

"Yes. Exactly," he replied. "No one wants to make a mistake. Keep looking. My feeling is that eventually you may come up with something." His face changed. He looked discouraged. "You know," he said, "it's sad what has happened to the business. It was so much fun. Now prices are so high, people are fiercely competitive, greedy. Every antique dealer is taking acting lessons to get on TV. *Antiques Roadshow!* Oh boy! It is getting harder and harder to get things, and it has taken some of the joy out of the field. I am not saying you are wrong about the mirror. It is charming and could be early, too, just out of the ordinary. If we could only find . . ." He didn't complete the sentence, because what needed to be found was conclusive evidence, which does not occur much in the world we play in. "You may eventually convince people," Dean said. "Maybe the frame Beckerdite spoke of will eventually show up. Another one to go by would naturally help a lot. But there is something about it, for sure. It has the character and elements of the Philadelphia school. Thank you for showing it to me, and good luck. Don't give up," he urged, giving me double thumbs up, then arching backward with one foot out the door.

Sometimes sending photographs of the mirror was enough to inspire a visit from a more curious specialist. When I sent pictures to Ron De Silva, the dealer I had worked with on the sale of the sofa, he called to discuss it. I said I had a mirror that appeared to have belonged to the granddaughter of the Brown brothers John and Nicholas. I knew it sounded far-fetched, but, confidentially, I was beginning to be persuaded there might be a chance Nicholas Brown II had purchased it for his Benefit Street mansion in Providence. I had seen an expensive mirror listed in the household inventory from 1841 for a room that could have accommodated it. But, unsurprisingly, there was no description except that it was one of the four most valuable items in his house. Anne was raised by her grandfather Nicholas Brown, I told Ron, and it was a fact that she had inherited some things from the house on Benefit Street.

Ron asked me if he could call Alby, as he nicknamed Albert Sack, my former boss. He knew his colleague had a passion for mirrors.

"Sure, call him," I said.

Ten minutes later, at the end of a winter's day, Albert Sack called me. "I hear you have a mirror over there," he said in his thick Boston accent. "I want to see it. Can we come now? Will you wait for us?" Albert arrived with a woman who worked in his Madison Avenue gallery. He walked over to the mirror, his voice tinged with sarcasm. "*This* is the mirror. You're kidding? What the hell was Ron thinking?" Then he began to look at it closely, front and sides. Stepping back, he stared at it in silence while he ruminated. Then he said, perplexed, "You know, when I first saw this, I thought it was preposterous. The size and all. But now I like it. I really, really like it. It looks . . . it looks"—he laughed softly—"like . . . Philadelphia. What wood is it made from?"

I told him it was American white pine. When Albert asked who had done the wood analysis, I told him Donna Christensen, which I thought would be the right answer.

"This white pine thing. White pine! White pine," he whined, flicking his wrist. "People overstate its importance. I don't always buy that." I mentioned the hardware and my letter from Mike Podmaniczky at Winterthur. I thought Albert might be able to interpret what Mike said since I was still confused. "If you have it here, let me see it," said Albert. I produced the letter, and he quickly read it.

"Mike says nothing," he scoffed. "Why do you think it may have belonged to the Browns?"

I told him my story about Anne Brown Francis Woods.

"Listen," he said, "there's a possibility I think I might be interested in buying this from you."

His associate looked shocked and dumbfounded, ready to throw a net over him and drag him out of there, but Albert continued to think out loud. "There is something interesting about this mirror. Some of the carvings really look an awful lot like Philadelphia and that school. Did Luke Beckerdite see it?"

"Yes," I answered. "I sent him pictures, but he was not intrigued." I explained that Luke said he'd seen one like it at one point but could not remember where.

"These people aren't always right, you know," he said scornfully. That was refreshing to hear from someone who had been in the business for at least forty years. Albert's assistant looked more and more concerned that the boss had lost his mind. She tugged his overcoat. "Let me get back to you," Albert continued. "I want to show pictures of it to Jack Lindsey, the curator of American decorative arts at the Philadelphia Museum of Art. He is an expert on Philadelphia carving. If anyone can identify a Philadelphia piece, he can. He is coming this week to examine a wonderful table we have in the shop.

"Now"—his voice went low and confidential—"I know that you have gone to our competitors with some good American furniture in the past, things we would have liked to have had. We would rather you did business with us in the future. We have the same clients, and we can pay you fairly for bringing them to us. Now," he continued, "if I bought it from you, we would buy it outright. We would give you a commission on a percentage of the sale in addition to the original purchase price. We like to do business this way now. It is more fair to the seller, and people end up happier in the end."

I had not thought seriously of selling the mirror before Albert showed up. I had believed it wasn't worth thinking about because I doubted I could ever come up with the kind of documentation required to sell it through such a dealer.

A week later, I called Albert Sack. He said he could not make an offer on the mirror without the backing of Mr. Lindsey. He never told me what Lindsey's reaction was to the photograph or the conversation the two had about it. "Maryalice, you may end up being right, but we just can't make an offer on something so unusual. We still go by the advice my father gave us, which was 'If it looks like a duck and walks like a duck, it's a duck.' The uniqueness of the frame is something we can't get around."

CHAPTER NINE

The Irish Question

Certain ties in the lives I researched seemed to coincide with the design of the fable mirror. A book about Irish looking glasses would soon raise interesting questions. One day when I was in Providence on one of my Browns and Woodses missions, my friend Susan showed me something she had found in the RISD library.

"Look!" she said excitedly. "Here is a picture of your mirror!" She handed me *Queen Anne & Georgian Looking Glasses* by Lewis Hinckley. A black-and-white photo showed Thomas Johnson's Fox and Grapes mirror described as a "Chippendale Carved and Gilded Wall Mirror." At the time the book was published, the mirror hung at Powerscourt, in County Wicklow, Ireland.

Susan was so happy for me, I hated to let her down by pointing out the difference between this mirror and my own. Although the mirror was indeed the same design, the scale was not the same. Lord Powerscourt's mirror fit over the fireplace mantel in his dining room, whereas mine was probably twice its size. The carving on mine was primitive in comparison with the other, feistier version. Pointing to the photograph, I said, "It's just earlier, and that makes a big difference. The two are related in the same way a tomcat is to a lion." But Susan was skeptical. She said I was beginning to sound like a snobby, nit-picking scholar. She fiercely upheld the author's argument that the

British had taken credit for the work of Irish artisans. The British had always exploited the Irish, argued Susan; they never gave the Irish credit for anything. I suddenly recalled a time I had shown my mirror to an English expert at Christie's named Orlando Rock after discussing another project. He'd shyly suggested the possibility of Irish manufacture. I had no firsthand reference to what he was talking about, thinking I had never seen Irish mirrors. I didn't ask him why he'd raised the possibility, and put the idea out of my mind. But as my recent research revealed, Irishmen worked in shops in England and America and, as Susan pointed out, were never given credit for their lineage. The mirrors they carved here were called American. Perhaps Hinckley was right. And maybe some of the English mirrors I had restored were misattributed, too.

In Hinckley's *The More Significant Georgian Furniture*, he stresses the importance of Dublin. "As one of the greatest capital cities of the eighteenth century, Dublin nevertheless stands alone in not being routinely acknowledged for the superb creativity and supreme excellence of the furniture produced there by its highly talented native and émigré craftsmen. Instead, with their great indifference to reality, English furniture historians have habitually claimed Dublin's fine and superfine Queen Anne and Georgian furniture as having originated in their own country, or even its far removed capital city."

The reasons Hinckley gives for such false attributions have everything to do with the marketplace value of English and American—as opposed to Irish—furniture. In his books, he argues that Dublin, a tax-free port, was more suitable than London for exporting Queen Anne and Georgian looking glasses. Why would the Scots, Welsh, or well-to-do English willingly pay excessive amounts for such highly taxed items when they could be bought more advantageously in Dublin? While shopping for furniture there, clients could also pick up Waterford crystal chandeliers. Irish glass was exported in vast quantities to America up to 1820. Waterford chandeliers are installed in Trinity Church, New York, and Independence Hall, Philadelphia. Glass windows and lanterns for coaches advertised by John Elliot and Sons of Philadelphia in the eighteenth century were also obtained from the Irish capital. Why not mirrors? Hinckley views Ireland as overlooked, and he details a history of mistaken attributions.

At the beginning of the nineteenth century, outside of Philadelphia, Dublin was the only place where North American white pine was shipped, the author states. Looking glasses sold by the Elliots in Philadelphia were advertised as sent from London. Imports from England were highly desirable in the American market of the eighteenth and nineteenth centuries, but the advertising misled. The *ships* were from London, but the furniture and frames sold by Elliott and Sons had in fact been manufactured in Dublin, the author believed. Pieces described as "Chippendale" and "thus presented as a London example" often, according to Hinckley, are Dublin masterpieces. He cites mirrors exhibited at the Metropolitan Museum of Art that have Irish design features and the John Elliot label. He notes, for example, that Prince of Wales plumes were never popular with American colonists working in shops in the eighteenth century and that eagles and eagle heads are repertoire features of Dublin furnishings. Hinckley explains that later, in the Hepplewhite, Sheraton, and Regency periods, looking glasses with eglomise (reverse painting on glass) also refer to Ireland. Scenes claimed as American Hudson views often are native Irish waterways. "In reality they depict rural effects with rustic fences and bridges, windmills, castles, and plaster-walled cottages with palm-thatched roofs, all crying for recognition as typical of Irish country landscapes."

Why such misrepresentation? Hinckley, a former Parke Bernet expert, writes, "Irish furniture was not popular so we called everything English. It is obvious that no such truly scientific research has ever been carried out in Great Britain, where attributions have always been based on extended deliberative judgments, opinions, beliefs or other forms of theoretical guesswork, as indulged in by even the most highly regarded English literary and museum authorities."

When I mentioned Hinckley's name to Simon Redburn, of

Sotheby's, New York, English Furniture Department, he was adamant. "Rubbish!" he said. "There is absolutely nothing to it."

"Four of his books presently circulate on the subject of Irish furniture," I said.

To this he replied, "The family must be reissuing them." But then he equivocated. "Hinckley does make *some* good points."

I asked him what those points might be.

"The books have some nice pictures of good English furniture," he answered.

"That's exactly the response Hinckley was up against forty years ago," I countered. "Has nothing changed since then?"

"No! No! No! It's absolutely preposterous," Redburn insisted in his crisp British accent. "Hinckley worked for Parke Bernet in the forties and was head of the English furniture division when he got this notion into his head that a lot of eighteenth-century English furniture was Irish. Let me tell you, there were no noteworthy cabinetmakers living in Dublin in the eighteenth century."

"None at all?"

"Well, yes, with just a few exceptions. Even Irish experts will back this up," he argued.

This seemed utterly illogical, considering all the beautiful Irish castles I had seen in books. "Didn't they ever purchase anything wonderful locally? Was there nothing of the national spirit in an Irish landlord's blood? Mr. Redburn, there must have been some high quality produced there. What do you think, for instance, of Hinckley's assertion that the Irish were known to extend the Rococo period from mid-eighteenth century through the mid-nineteenth?"

"Well," Redburn asserted, "the same is true in England in the same period. Irish furniture has very distinguishable characteristics."

"And they are?"

He briefly described the design flaws and second-rate carving characteristics of the Dublin school compared with the refinement of London craftsmanship. I took what he said to imply that Irish decorative arts were in essence rough, naïve, and provincial, whereas the English capital's furniture was just the opposite. No doubt about it. England consistently turned out some of the most extraordinarily gifted designers and carvers in the world. On the other hand, one of America's most celebrated eighteenth-century carvers, Hercules Courtney, was Irish-born, as were other fine craftsmen working in Philadelphia at the same time. This fact also might explain why English and Continental specialists were not enthused with American furniture. It lacked their high standards of excellence.

I brought up the American white pine debate. Redburn was also prepared to blow that theory out of the water. "Look, we have a chest right now," he said. "It's English. The wood is American birch. This fact is going to cause quite a stir with the American people! The wood, the wood! Americans are carried away with this. They make too much of it, qualifying that characteristic and source as near proof of having been made in America. American wood," he continued, "was shipped to England, especially at the beginning of the nineteenth century."

Again I felt the subtle rift between the American and English camps. Irish furniture was not even considered to be in the playing field.

"I have a mirror no one seems able to identify in terms of when or where it was made," I began, "from a design by Thomas Johnson."

"Oh yes," Redburn replied. "I know the exact model you describe. Grapes and Ladders. We've sold several of those over the years. They are English, made in the 1830s, sometimes a bit later. Definitely English. We have pictures of them in our archival catalogs. Just a minute, let me see if I can find one." He put the receiver down, and I could hear him rustling through papers on his desk as if to settle the pesky subject once and for all. "No, can't find it just now. But I'll look and get back to you."

"Any idea where they could have been made?" I asked.

"Outside of London somewhere."

"Where do you think 'somewhere' was likely to be?"

"Oh, I don't know."

"Then how do you know they were made outside London if you don't know where?"

I registered an annoyed silence on the other end of the line, and then, with solemn deliberation, Redburn spoke. "I have been in this business for a very long time. These mirrors are just decorative, of no great value."

" 'Just decorative'?" I asked, confused. "We are both in the field called 'the decorative arts.' What is the meaning of that anyway?"

Of course I knew what he meant: something a decorator, not a serious collector, would spring for. In either circle, the style and period he attributed to my mirror were neither popular nor exemplary, yet plenty of people had so far seemed impressed and even moved seeing mine. Had we arrived at the cliché that tastes change, that the value of an object moves from popular to unpopular and then back to a rediscovery of its merits?

I brought up the naïve carvings on my mirror, so different from the carvings on the frame from Powerscourt. Were the mirrors in his old catalogs primitive in feeling? "Yes, very flat," Redburn offered. "The earlier ones [meaning mid-eighteenth-century] were much better than the later ones."

My mirror, I ventured, had a cluster of ivy leaves set in the center. Was ivy a common element to the English execution of a Johnson design, or could it likelier have been an Irish embellishment? Redburn knew at this point nothing could shift my mind's persistent drift across the Irish Sea. I was hopelessly under the influence of the misguided phony Lewis Hinckley.

"Mr. Redburn," I said, "at least you're decisive. I look forward to seeing another example for comparison's sake. If so many mirrors like mine do exist, made by the same carver, it might be something interesting to look into. Do you have any idea who this person may have been, even if you aren't sure of the exact location?"

"I don't think we will ever know, unless that is, a label shows up at some point," Redburn replied.

"A likelihood against all odds." I sighed. "In America an Elliot label would be outstanding," I said, kidding.

"Or better still, Thomas Chippendale," Redburn volleyed.
"That would be perfect," I said.

Several months passed. I had been sending e-mails, letters, photographs, and voice-mail messages to Sotheby's with no reply. Early one morning, I called and caught Redburn at his desk. "I haven't called you back because I've been horribly busy these past few months," he said, his voice none too chipper at the sound of mine. I asked if he had received the pictures of my mirror and whether he thought it the same as those he'd had in mind when we last spoke. "Yes, it's similar enough," he grumbled. "Some firm was turning them out in England, unquestionably, around 1830 to 1840, after the reissue of Johnson's book; though I don't know precisely who 'they' were, or specifically where. There have been perhaps six of them that I have seen in my career, in the last twenty years, sold at Christie's in Kensington. In fact, I had one myself at one time."

This took me by surprise. "Then you must have liked it enough to own it," I said.

"No," Redburn snapped. "I did not like it at all. I thought it was ugly! I bought it in a lot, owned it for several years, and was glad to get rid of it! They are so big, seven, eight feet tall. No one can use them. The size is one of the things that make them worthless."

I was not getting the kid glove treatment now. There were no attempts to spare my tender feelings toward the mirror I loved. I could feel his exasperation and impatience. I pressed for one more answer. Had he seen any of these mirrors in America?

"No. In Kensington," he answered.

At this point I thought it tactful not to mention that height was not an issue in many English manor houses, or in many American homes. Size was certainly a factor but not categorically a flaw. The crudeness of the carvings was what turned people either on or off. America was in the midst of a second gilded age, and, as ever, architecture displayed one's success in the world. Modern castles and Sheetrock soufflés were presently being built coast to coast, all with cathedral ceilings and thousands of feet in floor—and wall—space. Almost any of that description could easily accommodate a large-scale mirror.

"There aren't any Johnson-style pieces in early America anyway," Redburn claimed, falling victim to his own circumscribed erudition.

"There certainly were," I responded. "Perhaps not mirrors, but other things."

"Well, I don't know of any examples," he admitted.

There was no doubt about the fact that Simon Redburn knew way more than I did. Extensive research had to be done to make text sparkle in auction catalogs when the great pieces came up. I had only recently brushed up on Johnson's designs in America. Yet I knew of seven examples of Aesop motifs used on Philadelphia case furniture and said so. Redburn was in no mood for further challenge at seven-thirty in the morning, and who could blame him? I had pushed the envelope unmercifully. I thanked him for his time, and he accepted politely. His judgment on the date of the mirror's production matched the consensus of others of his field and rank: English, second quarter of the nineteenth century.

I knew an American folk art specialist who once worked at Winterthur and later at one of the major auction galleries in New York, whose name she asked me not to mention. When she saw the Fox and Grapes in person at my studio, she said the carving reminded her of Pennsylvania Dutch carving. I asked her why experts seemed to be deaf when it came to anything new. This was just the way it was, she said sympathetically. My experience was no different from what she had put up with over the years. "Experts," she explained, "discourage challenges, and it is nearly impossible to revise their thinking. They only want to hear that which reinforces their entrenched beliefs."

Forging into a new direction, I asked what she thought of the notion that some wonderful American and English pieces might have been made in Ireland. "That idea is not something the galleries are promoting presently," she said without hesitation.

It turned out that it was only a matter of time before galleries would promote British and Irish sales together. When the Irish economy began to boom, the market suddenly responded by discovering fabulous new-to-the-market Celtic inventory for clients who wanted antiques made in Ireland, a badge of national pride.

And I still didn't know who had made my mirror or where it was manufactured.

CHAPTER TEN

The Scryer

Through the ages, there has been something about a mirror and its capacity to reflect life that has summoned interpretation, urging those reflected to reflect in turn.

Most civilizations have claimed truth seekers practiced in the art of scrying. A scryer is one possessed of mystic powers to receive information from "beyond" by peering into shiny surfaces, such as mirrors, crystals, and bowls of oiled water. Not everyone had the ability to scry. Virgins, children under the age of ten, and certain "chosen" adults were believed to have the gift to "see what ordinary mortals could not." The ancient Chinese, Sumerians, Hebrews, Persians, Romans, and Egyptians were all adherents. Even after the Catholic Church forbade scrying, replacing it with superstitions they devised, scryers maintained special followings well into the nineteenth century.

The vengeful queen in the Grimm tale asks her mirror who is the most beautiful in the realm, and the truthful reply—Snow White—predictably twists the royal tiara. Children's stories about mirrors left a subliminal impression on me. My earliest exposure to mirror scrying occurred when our family was living in Manchester, New Hampshire.

My mother had the distinction of hosting one of the first children's shows on television. Known as *Romper Room*, it was broadcast live out of Manchester and attracted an audience throughout

New England. On the air, Miss Alice, as she was called profes-
sionally, was beautiful. Like Snow White in the Disney classic,
she was a dark brunette with large, sparkling eyes. Her wide
smile revealed a set of perfect teeth; her bright red lipstick was
the only makeup she ever wore.

At the conclusion of every *Romper Room* show, the camera
would zoom in on Miss Alice as she peered into a round handheld
mirror. Props in place, she would begin her incantation:

> *Romper, bomper, stomper, boo.*
> *Tell me, tell me, tell me, do.*
> *Magic mirror, tell me today*
> *Did all my friends have fun at play?*

Then my mother would call out the names of children she
claimed to be able to see through her mirror.

To her gullible viewers she was a scryer, a clairvoyant capable
of seeing their every move through her magic mirror. I knew my
mother was just an actress who needed her TV job to help support our family. But hearing this week after week during impres-
sionable years may have prompted my own early attempts to scry
the polished gravestones on Block Island, and as an adult driven
me to scry into the Fox and Grapes mirror.

Thoughts of where the mirror was made receded for a while as
I escaped to another time with my adopted historic family.

I had followed Marshall Woods and Anne Brown Francis on
their honeymoon and their first trip to Europe with their young
children. I was fascinated to get to know their daughter, Abby.
She had spent much of her life abroad and witnessed one of the
biggest urban renewal projects in history: the reconstruction of
Paris. The visionaries Louis-Napoléon (Napoléon III) and Baron
Georges Haussmann transformed what had been a medieval city
festering with slums, crime, and the homeless into a light-filled,
modern metropolis. Wide boulevards replaced narrow, dangerous
streets, and along them acres of new limestone buildings were
erected. New housing, theaters, parks, train stations, a horse racing track, and glamorous hotels changed the city from a place

everyone could not wait to leave into the epicenter of commerce and intellectual and artistic life—the place, from then on, everyone dreamed of visiting.

Through letters addressed to her mother, I trailed along with Abby and her father on a trip they took together, a Grand Tour to celebrate her twenty-first birthday. Now, when I looked into the glass of the Fox and Grapes mirror, I thought of Abby Woods. But something was in store for me I had not expected. Abby Woods, a quintessential American girl, inadvertently had a greater influence on the Irish and Ireland than she would ever know.

In January 1870, Marshall and Abby sailed out of New York Harbor aboard the *Java*. As the ship's propellers churned the thick water of the East River, a loud horn signaled departure. From the top deck near the pilot, father and daughter waved to mother and son, who were seeing them off from the wharf. The passage home had not been booked. The itinerary would involve no definite timetables. It was vaguely assumed that they would be back in Providence within a year.

Once outside the harbor, the ship began to pitch and roll. Abby had never experienced a journey to Europe without seasickness. Her luggage contained a small pharmacy and standard remedies such as hot water bottles and tins of soda crackers. After dinner at four o'clock in the main dining room, Abby returned to her stateroom. A stewardess helped her out of her traveling clothes, into a nightgown and wrapper, and she slipped into bed, where she was resigned to stay for most of the cruise. A string dangled from the corner of her bed and ran along a wall to a bell in her father's bedroom to signal him should she need anything.

The purpose of this trip was different from that of any other trip Marshall had taken with his family. Abby was the marrying age, and her father hoped she would soon find a husband with a surname people on the international circuit would instantly recognize. Marshall had letters of introduction with him to ensure entry into the strata of society and cultural institutions that matched his station in life. Father and daughter anticipated going to places they were accustomed to visiting, and those where they had never been.

When she was a child, Abby's favorite book had been *The Thousand and One Nights*, and her dream was to visit the exotic territory of the tales. With her birthday approaching in May, Marshall had agreed to take his daughter to Egypt. From there they would move on to Jerusalem, which Abby, a devout Baptist, yearned to visit. They would explore the ancient ruins of Greece, and they both wanted to see Russia, especially St. Petersburg, known for its lavish Neoclassical palaces set along the Baltic Sea.

Marshall, an art historian, was responsible for promoting programs that broadened public awareness of the arts in America and abroad. He had served as a commissioner to the Paris Exposition of 1855 and as a member of the jury of fine arts. It was France's first world fair, instigated by Louis-Napoléon as a way to glorify painters, sculptors, and photographers, thus giving universal exposure to new French work. It was there that Marshall had become acquainted with the leading artists of his time. Painters such as Delacroix, Courbet, Corot, and Rousseau were exhibiting at the fair and became part of Marshall's circle of acquaintances. When the exhibition closed, the emperor awarded Marshall Woods the cross of the French Legion of Honor.

Marshall had a thirst for culture and thought of his daughter as his protégée. On the Continent, the Woodses usually filled their time visiting architectural sites and picture galleries, and attended as many musical events as they could fit in between society balls and salon fetes. It was their habit to spend the majority of their time among Americans living abroad, familiar friends and relatives from the Northeast.

Arriving in London via Liverpool, Marshall and Abby checked into Mauigy's Hotel, on the corner of Charles and Regent streets. A newly installed hydraulic lift took them to a high floor, where they found their large suite. The windows facing the street did not offer much of a view. "Outside the fog is so thick that it is impossible to see people walking in the street," Abby complained. Even by early afternoon it was so dark in her bedroom that Abby was obliged to dress and to write letters by candlelight. Gloomy weather persisted throughout their time there, making it difficult for her to navigate along the arcades and settle into a smooth shopping routine.

In the lobby of the hotel, Abby and Marshall dispassionately observed two women hobbling about with what had come to be known as the "Alexandra limp." Three years earlier, in 1867, the Princess of Wales had been struck with rheumatic fever. Because the disease left the princess slightly lame, her devotees attempted to imitate her crippled gait by wearing heels unequal in height. Small dogs held on jeweled leashes kept wary eyes fastened on their mistresses as they limped along. Abby, who loved animals and especially dogs, thought it unconscionably cruel that their fur was dyed to match their mistresses' hair in tints from pink to blue.

Marshall and Abby made the best of their short stay in England and ordered their affairs for the journey ahead. In a hired brougham, the two set out on errands, buying the things for which London was famous. The English excelled at riding apparel, their sporting outfits regarded as the best-made in the world. As far as Abby was concerned, it was the only thing the British did well when it came to clothes. Like every other woman who could afford to do so, she preferred to find her finer dresses and accessories in Paris, the capital of fashion and taste. Marshall, being slightly deaf, stocked up on ear trumpets and bought a new thermometer while Abby spent the day being fitted for riding apparel.

Since Abby anticipated riding a fine Arabian horse in Egypt, she needed an outfit for hot weather, too. She ordered a robin's-egg blue lightweight linen habit. The fitted jacket featured a shawl collar and overturned cuffs. The jacket, devoid of outer buttons, was fastened at the waist from the inside, which gave it a neat tailoring. A cream silk cravat was selected, its ends finished with fringe.

In the parlor of their London suite, the Woodses began to

interview prospective servants to accompany them east. Abby
hated doing everything herself and had no faith in her father's
ability to open trunks. "I must get a maid as soon as possible,"
she wrote to her mother, "for I do not want to be lifting trays all
the time." An Italian courier named Cataldi came highly recommended. He had once been hired to travel with the Iveses,
cousins from Providence. Cataldi would serve as valet for Marshall and was a superb French cook. Looking no further, the
Woodses hired Cataldi and Elizabeth, his English wife, who
spoke several languages, as Abby's personal maid. During the
Victorian period, it was nearly impossible for an upper-class
woman to dress without assistance, and moving anything in a
tight dress was a chore. Elizabeth knew the art of massage and
claimed she did not mind being awakened at two in the morning, when Abby would be returning from parties. Hiring a married couple seemed the perfect arrangement. Several days later,
the four sailed across the English Channel by Southampton
steamer toward France.

After Providence, Abby thought of Paris as her home. The
Woodses occupied a suite in the familiar Hôtel du Louvre on Rue
de Rivoli. Within minutes of settling in, while Elizabeth stayed
behind to unpack, Abby got down to business. In a hypertrance-
like state, she flung herself into a carriage and headed straight for
Vignon's, the dress designer whom her mother had so often
employed and who was known for concocting outfits for Empress
Eugénie.

Abby's obsession with couture was not restricted to stocking
her own closets. She was assigned to choose a wedding gown for
her cousin Hope Goddard, her best friend of the same age in
Providence. She also had her mother's measurements with her.
Born and raised to please, Abby flooded not only Vignon's but
also Coulbert's, another top dressmaker, with orders to supplement her mother's already overample wardrobe. "You may be
sure Darling that I shall endeavor never to get anything for you
that is ugly," she assured her mother. "My own experience teaches
me that it is best to go always to the best places for everything."
Shipments of trunks were facilitated by departure dates in news-

papers listing names of passengers headed for Providence. Abby bombarded these connections with requests to hitch her luggage to theirs, that it be safely delivered to her dressing room closets at 62 Prospect Street.

Abby bounded out of her Paris hotel apartment daily to shop. New attire was ordered for teas, boulevard walks, balls, operas, and theater outings. For women of her class, four complete dress changes were required during a given day and evening. Abby had to be organized in order to shop, as she struggled to create a look of her own through consultations with Parisian dressmakers. Even with assistance, getting in and out of the overornamented costumes consumed several hours.

She ordered bonnets elaborated with handmade lace veils, bows, and artificial flowers. She purchased custom-made gloves by the dozen. The only time permissible to remove one's gloves was while eating, with pairs needed for different hours of the day and evening as well as to sleep in. Shoes and stockings matched the color of every outfit, ornamented in a variety of agonizing choices: gold and silver buckles, enameled, jewel-studded, crusted with bows, flowers, and insects. Flounces and puffs were trimmed, pleated, and kilted, with wrenching decisions having to be made in that area as well.

Stiffly structured corsets trimmed in lace contorted the skeleton and compromised organs. As much as physicians railed against these contraptions, blaming the wearing of corsets during pregnancy for the high rate of infant mortality, women continued with clothing they could barely move, or breathe in.

Parasols or sunshades charged with frills accessorized each spring and summer dress and protected Abby's fair complexion. Chatelaine pockets of velvet or suede hung on thin chains, the initials AFW and the Woods family crest embroidered in silver thread. Selecting ribbons for hair and lockets was a chore in itself. Large decorative handkerchiefs were standard in a white-gloved hand, along with one's hand-painted fan.

In 1870, while Abby was in Paris, she rode upon the crest of a fashion revolution—the bustle—ending the crinoline's twelve-year term. The wide metal cages embedded with horsehair worn under skirts that made women look like tea cozies were being phased out. For hostesses the transition meant more room at parties, the crinoline's awkward circumference having taken up the space of five or six guests, the train alone, the space for ten standing men. One journalist wrote of the crinoline, "Every woman today is a tempest. She can not enter or leave a room without knocking over everything in her path; and, whenever she takes a step, it sounds like rain or hail, according to the stuff her dress is made of."

The new designs, with yards of material hanging in the back, struck some men as equally absurd. A minister in the English government joked that it was a waste of taxpayers' money to clean the streets when ladies were doing such a good job sweeping up with their trailing skirts.

If only for safety's sake, Abby welcomed the change. The bell contraptions she had grown up wearing presented fatal potential. Too many female pedestrians were killed or maimed when their skirts became entangled in the spokes of passing carriages. Ladies were blown down by the wind or, worse, swept off cliffs, some of the lucky ones saved when layers of hooped cloth served as parachutes. Standing next to a fireplace could be fatal. When she was encased in metal and inflexible wood rings, it was almost impossible to roll a woman in a rug or heavy drape when a flame licked her hem. Max von Boehn of Munich wrote of the craze for skirt width in the 1860s, "Take what precautions we may under fire, so long as the hoop is worn, life is never safe! All are living under a sentence of death which may occur unexpectedly in the most appalling form."

Abby endorsed the new silhouette. It was beautiful to behold from every vantage. The straight front was more flattering, especially on her tall and slim frame. The half hoops, called crinolettes, emphasized the arrangement of material in the back to create the bustle, which trailed over the floor. Placing the weight of the dress and hair toward the back gave women the appearance of leaning slightly forward; hence the style was christened the "Grecian bend."

Elizabeth, the traveling maid, did a fine job of arranging

Abby's hair for daytime. She could set simple plaits (or curls) with finesse. But Abby's evening agenda demanded something more sophisticated. A Parisian coiffeur was booked on a regular basis. Staying au courant required a hairdresser with the artistic hand of a professional florist. To form the large chignons then in vogue, Abby's fine hair had to be woven with hairpieces. The supply of additional hair came "from peasant girls in Germany, Italy, and France. Hair cut from prisoners, paupers in the workhouse, and even, it was rumored, from corpses and patients in fever hospitals. In Catholic countries large quantities of hair came from novices entering convents." The requisite delousing, processing, and dyeing did not add to the luster of the finished product. As Abby patiently sat on a stool before a dressing table mirror in her bedroom, the hairdresser's hands flew around her head, crimping, twisting, braiding, and pinning her hair, then, last, inserting "combs spangled with jeweled confections and artificial flowers," and perhaps, as a finishing touch, a faint sprinkling of gold dust.

Marshall wanted his daughter up-to-date and criticized Abby if he found anything about her otherwise. She was forbidden to wear a dress if it was a season too old. Women's clothes were badges of wealth. Marshall considered his daughter's appearance a reflection on him and his circumstances. He therefore refrained from scolding her when the bills began to pile up. In less than a month, Mlle Woods's purchases at Vignon's alone added up to the sum it would cost to send four young men to Brown University for a year of tuition, room, and board. (As treasurer of the university, Marshall made the calculation.) But if extravagance was part of what it took to attract the right man for his only daughter, the end would justify the means. He felt slightly relieved that at this point Abby had not been asked to a court function, an invitation that posed a serious threat even to a royal bank account. At Compiègne, one woman in attendance was overheard grousing that she "had to sell a flour mill to meet the expense."

Abby enjoyed the shopping and the clothes more than the parties where she wore them. High society bored her. "I dislike company and what is the use of going about seeing people," she complained to her mother just before leaving for a dinner party at the swishy address of her cousin John Meredith Read, who was consul. "I shall have a perfectly stupid evening." When the hour arrived, Abby, escorted by her maid, was dropped off at the gate in front of the Reads' house. As she ascended the stairs alone, she braced herself for a tedious evening. The next morning she recorded the following scene.

Passing through the front door, she was greeted by a liveried servant who announced, *"Voici l'entrée de Mademoiselle Woods."* This was just the kind of social etiquette Abby thought pretentious and ridiculous. She shuddered at the barrage of personal advice encountered at every dinner party. Mrs. Read (the former Delphine Pumpelly of Albany), whom Abby described "a thorough and entire woman of the world, and not very good either . . . fond of men and society," told Abby that she "should paint [her] eyes like she did hers" and that she was determined to get some of Abby's "Puritan ideas out of [her] head."

"Well, Abby," Mrs. Read said seriously, taking her aside, "you will want to marry. When you were in Albany, I picked out Bradley Martin for you and it was not his fault that you did not marry him. I advise you to think seriously of being married and why should you not marry a titled foreigner?"

Once set free from Mrs. Read on this particular evening, Abby ran into her great-uncle Carter Brown.

"Well, how are you?" he asked.

"Very well, sir, and quite gay," she answered.

"Well," her uncle said, "let me give you some advice that you will take or not as you think best. You should marry a Frenchman. Some of them are very fine fellows and you are just the girl to be the head of some fine establishment and to be called Mme la Princesse or Mme la Duchesse."

"Uncle," Abby replied in exasperation, "no title could tempt me to marry a Frenchman."

"Well, of course not, if you can not love him, but do not think you must settle down in a two-penny town like Providence or throw yourself away on a bag of wind, a piece of straw, or a mess of pottage." His last words as he drifted off were "This is my advice sincerely."

Abby knew girls who had married into European royalty. This seemed to be the goal of every young American her age. The daughter of Hockson Field of New York City had married an Italian prince. After seeing them together recently, Abby admitted to being a bit envious. She found him "very handsome, rich and fascinating from one of the oldest Roman families." Even she, who had few illusions about the significance of a title, was impressed. Without a word spoken on this specific topic, Abby sensed how her "father had wished she stood in her place."

As to a perfect match, Abby was able to describe to her mother precisely the type of a husband she dreamed of marrying.

> I always envy girls who can feel so intensely as cousins Lully and Hope do, after all it must be a great happiness to adore a man as they do. I wish it had been my nature. When I think of it, it almost frightens me for I care for no one in this way at all. I must have a man whose soul is not absorbed with his business and me but whose mind is inclined to literature and is fond of reading and who can educate and improve me and whose life is not limited to the mere humdrum of eating, sleeping and making money, one who can instruct me and whom I can say how intensely amusing he is and how superior he is. Such men I know are seldom seen and I probably shall never see him. I yearn for a strong intellectual mind to admire. I think it probable that if I don't marry soon I shall never marry at all. But I do not care. To be bound to such a man as I describe would be happiness.

American contacts in Europe were certainly doing all they could to arrange just the right introduction. A friend of Marshall and Anne Woods from Boston and Newport had retained a residence in Paris. Mr. Charles Stewart, an American railroad tycoon, lived his bachelor's existence in an opulent limestone mansion at 122, avenue des Champs-Elysées. The rooms were lit by enormous crystal chandeliers and filled with fine French antiques, articles of Roman antiquity, and Old Master paintings. In the back of the house, a pleasure garden adjoined the Elysée Palace. Weekly fetes were held there to introduce Stewart's Anglo-American friends to the nexus of cultured European society. The premier precincts of Paris were swarming with eligible young bachelors from the fiscally depleted European aristocracy, on the prowl for rich American brides. Abby Woods, a daughter of fortune, was prime prey.

The nephew of the host was staying at his uncle's for the weekend and was present at a winter soiree being held there. Separated from the other guests, the young man stood in the central hall and leaned against a highly ornamented bronze balustrade. Arms folded, he stared at a clock decorated with mythical figures, centered on the ledge of a marble fireplace mantel.

At twenty-four, he was tall and dashing. His auburn hair was worn slightly long and curled up at the nape of his neck, extending over a stiff, high-collared white shirt. His sculpted sideburns, thick mustache, and arched dark brows accentuated a pale complexion and chiseled features. His piercing, red-brown eyes followed Abby as she glided across the Persian-carpeted hallway and left her calling card with the attendant.

Abby, almost six feet tall, wore a blue silk dress with short, pleated, funneled sleeves that capped her shoulders and exposed her long, thin arms. Around her neck a gold locket hung by a simple black ribbon. Her strawberry blond hair was gathered at the crown of her head and fell in the back in a cascade of ringlets touching the triple-laced edge of the upper bodice of her dress. She wore long jet earrings in the shape of half-moons and stars that contrasted with her translucent blue eyes and creamy skin. As Abby stepped through the doors of the reception room, he trailed her in pursuit of an introduction. Abby was about to change his life and alter the course of Irish history.

Should Abby remain true to her ideal of a husband, this man—on this evening—did not qualify. He was not one who cared much for literature, and he could barely recite a poem without laughing. But he would become a muse for some of Ireland's most famous authors and poets. He was a young Protestant Irish landlord from County Wicklow who would one day be described as one of the most remarkable politicians of the nineteenth century. His name was Charles Stewart Parnell.

Beneath the coffered ceilings of the gaslit drawing room and beside a painting called *Two Cupids' View of Naples*, Charles and Abby struck up a lively conversation. They found they had a lot in common. Both shared an affection for animals, a passion for horses and riding. In his upper-class British accent, Charles described country life in Wicklow. Dogs were among Abby's favorite topics, and so he told her about the sporting setters and hounds he owned to hunt grouse. She in turn related tales of Gyp and Boxer, her canine companions at home in Providence. Charles amused Abby with his far-fetched ideas. When he spoke abstractly about the future of science, she listened, mesmerized. Someday, he said, man would embark on a voyage to the stars. A way would be found to support human life in a different atmosphere. He prophesied that a celestial world beyond our own planet would be discovered, just as Columbus and other early explorers had discovered new lands on earth.

Charles told Abby that America and its politics fascinated him, especially the Revolutionary and Civil wars. He confessed he had never been to the United States even though his American-born mother had inherited a house in Bordentown, New Jersey. Sometimes he thought about starting a business there, the sort, though, was left unclear. Charles wanted to plant the idea in Abby's mind that he was not tied to his life in Ireland and was open to emigrating if the right opportunities arose.

Abby was flattered by Charles's attention and happy to meet someone her own age who, like her, seemed not to care for society but yet to be part of it. No one she had ever met seemed to care less about the opinions of others. He was not a member of any club and had no interest in joining any. She was enchanted by the Irishman's reserved, masculine manner, his shy, boyish smile, dry sense of humor, and individual outlook on life. That evening Abby was swept up in the moment while Charles was thrust into thoughts of his long-term future.

Charles found Abby's good looks, American accent, polished manners, and positive outlook on life inescapably seductive. Her effusive personality, combined with her family's inherited wealth, presented a most compelling package. The money would help maintain Avondale, a property he had inherited from his father. Located in the lush mountains just south of Dublin in a district called "the Garden of Ireland," Avondale comprised 4,500 debt-ridden, wooded acres and a "shabby genteel" manor house. One hundred and fifty men and their families worked on the estate and lived in the housing built for them, many of them never paying rent to a lenient landlord. Charles was also part owner of an enormous game-hunting lodge in Aughavannagh, a former army barracks built in 1804 that could have used major improvements. The burden of supporting his mother and sisters was his responsibility as well.

Dreams of house restoration and of paid-off creditors could be realized quite efficiently if he could persuade Abby to marry him. As love has the power to expand, the utopian projected his desires and fantasies onto Abby. Propelled into thoughts of a new life, one that offered a secure and prosperous future ensured by the Woodses' holdings, Charles began to imagine his options as limitless.

In the following weeks, Charles and Abby both fell in love for the first time. His feelings for her quickly gained precedence over his initial material considerations. Locked arm in arm, the couple was seen walking in public gardens and on the fashionable boulevards of Paris and attending social functions. People began to assume their future together was sealed.

In February, the Woodses prepared to leave Paris for the journey ahead. "I shall enjoy myself and like the bustle of traveling," Abby wrote to her mother. "I think I have the spirit of adaptation since leaving home." While Abby saw to packing her trunk with the help of her maid, Cataldi coordinated the itinerary with Marshall in the adjoining parlor.

Charles saw no reason to stay in Paris without Abby there. Before leaving, he asked her to marry him. She seemed receptive to the idea, though without committing herself. Confident about his future with Abby, he returned to Avondale to oversee the various businesses he had initiated there. To help defray the expense of maintaining Avondale, Charles had set up a lumber mill on his heavily wooded property. The Avonmore River just outside his house continued to trigger his imagination as it had throughout his childhood. Convinced gold deposits lay beneath the waterway, he was superintending a chemical analysis of the riverbed.

Still, the former flirt of the Irish countryside returned home a changed man. To his household staff and tenants, Charley appeared withdrawn and more mature. He focused on sprucing up the interior of Avondale, anticipating the reception of his future American bride. In the following months, while he was playing cricket with friends and bird hunting in the hills and valleys of Wicklow, his mind and heart seemed elsewhere. Now he only reluctantly accepted invitations to functions held by the local gentry. It became clear that Charley, once considered a catch by the daughters of Protestant landlords, had been plucked away from the pool of eligible local bachelors.

There was one barrier in the way of the couple's future plans: Marshall Woods. Charles Parnell was not the brilliant match the doting parent had in mind for his daughter. He appeared an ordinary gentleman—courteous, well-spoken, and intelligent, but lacking direction. Marshall was careful not to say too much. He decided to intervene through his wife, who corresponded with Abby regularly and whose advice his daughter sought about everything. In the meantime, Marshall began to investigate the suitor's background. His closest friend and relative, John Read, a man of monstrous social stamina, who as the American consul to France made it his business to know the personal facts about everyone who wandered among their set, provided details. More information was gleaned in gossipy men's clubs. What Marshall discovered was worse than he could have imagined.

Dating back to colonial Philadelphia, the Browns, Francises, and Stewarts had been friends. Marshall and Anne knew Charles Stewart, who spent at least half the year in Paris and summers in Newport. Oddly, nothing much was ever said about his nephews. Charley's mother, Delia Tudor Stewart, had been born in Boston. Her crusty and debauched father, "the Commodore," also nicknamed "Old Ironsides," was a naval hero in the War of 1812. He left his family to live with his mistress when Delia was nine. She was raised by her mother and grandmother. In her teenage years, she had been a dark-haired, blue-eyed beauty with a manic personality; she was called the "Belle of Washington, D.C."

In 1835, John Henry Parnell and Lord Powerscourt, neighbors and cousins from County Wicklow, Ireland, visited the U.S. capital together. The Commodore's daughter smote both men. At twenty, Delia Stewart, lacking all common sense, selected as her husband the handsome John Parnell instead of Lord Powerscourt, a titled man of wealth. The couple was hastily married at Grace Church in New York City on May 31, 1835. Immediately after the wedding, Delia moved to John Parnell's ancestral home in Ireland.

Being a country squire's wife did not suit Delia. Raised in cities, where she could indulge in her preoccupation with social climbing, she hated provincial life. From the start, the marriage was disappointing—and stormy. She gave birth to twelve children, of whom only five survived to adulthood. As a mother, Delia was unnurturing and scattered, "offering little stability to the household." The Parnell children ran wild under minimal supervision. At Avondale, household staff came and went amid the chaos. To escape, Delia spent long periods in Paris, her daughters in tow. The three boys, all under the age of seven, were left behind with their father. How different, Marshall thought, Delia was from his solid Anne, who ran the family's affairs with a velvet fist and was obsessively entwined in the lives of her children and husband.

Marshall was stunned to learn of Abby's Irish suitor's patchy education, a far cry from his own and that of his son, Carter, then finishing his last year at Hopkins Academy in Massachusetts and preparing to enter Brown University in the fall. Charles's home schooling had proven ineffectual. Several tutors quit when unable to manage their defiant charge. By seven, Charles seemed cursed with an unmanageable temperament. His father thought the best solution was to send him off to a Somerset boarding school exclusively for girls as a way to soften him up.

John Parnell had taken Charles there himself. He explained to the kind Mrs. Muirley, who ran the school, that he thought his son was in need of some "mothering," which he hoped she could provide. Because he was the only male student, the headmistress doted on him, and Charles seemed relatively happy there. Within the first year, however, he contracted the typhoid fever that swept through Ireland as a result of the potato famine and had to return to Avondale to recover.

When Charles was eight, his mother put in one of her rare appearances at Avondale and finally decided to address her son's education. Charles was sent off to a school in Kirk Langley, Derbyshire, run by the Reverend John Barton and his wife. The young pupil "liked the games there," but again his residency was short-lived. After Charles was provoked, he threatened to clock the headmaster and was asked to leave. Nervous, irritable, withdrawn, and given to outbursts of anger, Charles was never popular with his classmates or teachers. Plagued by panic attacks and prone to sleepwalking, he was afraid to be left alone at night. Whenever possible, he was assigned to first-floor dormitory rooms to avoid the danger of falling down stairs.

Charles had no respect for authority. Breaking rules and defying orders without fear of the consequences was a key component of his personality. Greek and Latin had no appeal for him. He wanted to study only subjects that interested him. According to Marshall's sources, that meant horses, fishing, and cricket.

Charles was used to doing exactly as he pleased. At boarding school, he chafed at any kind of restriction. He was most content spending his days in the sylvan hills of Wicklow. When other children were away at school, Charles and his brothers kept themselves happily occupied constructing ponds, building rafts, fishing for trout in the Avonmore River, and launching rockets they had made out of gunpowder. He and his brother John liked "visiting the ruined fort, and haunted cottage on the estate." During extended periods spent with relatives, the Howards, Charles hunted grouse near the moors, organized donkey races, and defended his position as a first-rate batsman in cricket.

When Charles was thirteen and attending yet another school

in London, his father died suddenly. Marshall was horrified to hear that Charley was the only one in his family to attend the funeral. How pitiful, Marshall thought. The Parnell family dynamic was very different from that of the Woodses. "We are a peculiar family," Parnell once explained. "We are all very fond of one another, but somehow, we do not get on so well when we are too much together."

The books in the library at Avondale had not been replenished since the death of Charles's grandfather. Charles entertained himself there looking at illustrated and "outdated editions to do with mechanical devises, scientific inventions, astronomy and horse breeding." He may also have stumbled upon pamphlets his incorruptible politician grandfather had published on social justice, the liberal ideas between the stitched bindings insinuating themselves subliminally.

Never having shown any interest in a formal education, Charles, at eighteen and seemingly out of the blue, got the notion to attend Cambridge. He was not prepared to take the entrance exams. Reverend Wishaw, who operated a cramming institution, was hired to spruce up the young man's manners and see if it was possible to turn "his academic deficiencies around." It was not long, however, until Charles's belligerence reared itself again. Given an ultimatum, for "the first time in his academic history . . . he backed down from a confrontation." Despite his handicapped scores, he was admitted into Magdalene, the college with the most relaxed standards in Cambridge.

The unchallenging curriculum let him muddle through for three and a half years. The last semester ended in a suspension because of a drunken street brawl and resultant court appearance. Charles never returned to graduate, either because he did not have the money or, more likely and in character, because he simply did not see the point of wasting any more time there. A classmate was quoted as claiming Charles "one of the three or four genuine loafers in the college at the time . . . keen about nothing."

Charles Parnell was hatched from a family of eccentrics who had never trod the straight and narrow. He was nevertheless firmly of the upper class and thought himself so. A person who knew him well observed that "once [Parnell was] entrapped into what is odiously called a social function, his charm was irresistible." His "own social interests and tastes would have made him an ideal clubman—undemonstrative but in a quiet way affable and *facile à vivre*. He was a batsman of considerable repute in the cricket world, a straight rider with the Wicklow hounds, a devout seeker of the grouse who was to be found on the mountains earlier than the sun, an athlete of the toughest thews and sinews for all his seeming delicacy of build, the best man at handball and the best man at chess."

Throughout his life, Charles demonstrated "a complete impatience with religious instruction." He rarely stepped into a church and politely declined the invitation to attend services when called upon. Of a scientific mind, he did not believe answers to the mysteries of the universe could be found in creationist doctrine. "The only immortality a man can have is through his children," he said. Furthermore, to assume that the earth was created for the benefit of mankind made no sense to him at all. The beauty of a starry night sky, the sound of rushing rivers echoing through mountain ravines, was enough solace to put his troubles and the world in perspective.

Marshall Woods did not see how Charles's agnosticism would mesh with his daughter's religious beliefs. Abby, a devout Baptist, read her Bible every day. He lightly raised the question with his daughter, who revealed that Charles was unfazed that Ireland was predominantly Catholic. Marshall was relieved to know that Wicklow's population consisted mainly of Protestants.

Marshall wondered if Charles had mentioned to Abby, or if she had otherwise heard of, his coming of age party, held at Avondale in 1867. It had been a "Leveresque" event and turned into a scandalous three-day affair. Charles's original plan to host some cricket matches was undermined by his sister Emily. She and her military officer husband, Arthur Dickensen, a perpetual drunk, arrived at Avondale with a crowd of soldier friends and a large number of ladies. "In every shady nook and corner were to be seen an isolated couple engaged in the pleasant pastime of love-making," Emily had laughingly reported. In his defense, Charles had disapproved of the way things turned out and, in a sour mood, had separated himself from the scene going on at his expense, not so much because of the moral laxity of the guests as because after two days not a single cricket game had been played. Finally, in disgust, he declared the party over and packed the rowdy bunch off to the train station, albeit too late to redeem the reputation of Avondale.

It seemed obvious to Marshall that Charley was not on the path to a stable future. Once the facts of his background were gradually and selectively unfolded, Marshall was confident that Abby would conclude Charles Parnell should be tossed from the ring. An alarmed Marshall wrote Anne in Providence, outlining everything he had heard about the Irish suitor along with unfortunate portraits of the entire Parnell clan. A short infatuation might be fine, but in the long run Charley did not measure up.

The Irish connection prompted me to reexamine the cluster of ivy placed beneath my mirror frame's golden ladder. I wondered whose idea it was to place it there, the twig a national symbol representing the man who had once stood before the glass. The ivy appeared to be a later addition, because the carving did not synchronize with the rest of the frame. Was the person who made it Irish, and could he possibly have known about the Woods-Parnell connection?

As extraordinary as it sounds, Charles Parnell would almost certainly have encountered Fox and Grapes mirrors on both sides of the Atlantic. One hung in Lord Powerscourt's dining room in Wicklow, Ireland, shown in Lewis Hinckley's book on Irish mirrors, while another graced a wall in Abby Woods's house in Providence, Rhode Island. The fable's message with regards to Parnell's life had become more compelling to me than the matter of who had made it and where, or the manner in which it had inspired designers like Thomas Johnson. With an eye on Abby and her legendary Irishman, I continued to forge through the nineteenth century.

CHAPTER ELEVEN

Travels East

Abby, bundled in flannels and furs, and Marshall, clutching his silver thermometer, boarded the train to Venice to look at art. A week later, to Abby's delight, Charles appeared at their hotel on a surprise visit. He gave her a modest gold ring. This put Marshall in a foul humor. The young couple ignored him and walked along the icy canals, happily taking in the sights together, while Marshall stewed. Charles's visit, however, was cut short after he received a telegram from his uncle in Paris, warning him about the Roman fever epidemic rumored to be sweeping Italy. Abby begged Charles to stay. But Charles, a hypochondriac like her father, swiftly threw his clothes into a suitcase and was gone.

A few days later, the Woodses were on their way to Egypt. As the steamer pulled into the harbor in Alexandria, they were "at once surrounded by little boats which contained hundreds of screaming Arabs," Abby noted. When the gangplank was lowered, Cataldi "kept them at arms length by blows and threats." For Abby and Marshall, the strangeness of everything was captivating. They noted the Arab women, covered but for their eyes, the men in burnooses. Marshall, enthralled, could not help repeating, "What would Mama say if she were here."

By 1870, Egyptmania had captured the minds of the West. Books and travel journals were written about the subject, and the decorative arts followed suit, referencing the pyramids and the

artifacts discovered inside tombs. Even though Egypt had become a prime travel destination, Abby was surprised to find
Cairo packed with tourists. "It is so much like a continental
town," she wrote, "being so full of English it seems as though we
were in England. It is astonishing to see so many foreigners traveling here especially Americans and English." In her room, one
window looked out on a street where a steady stream of Western
ladies could be seen riding camels and donkeys. An opposite window opened onto a garden of palm and fig trees. With the scent
of jasmine and orange blossoms in the air, and the newness of
everything foreign, Abby was content, thoughts of her future for
the time put aside. She soon clicked with a group of British men
and women her own age. After dinners together they took turns
holding impromptu parties in their rooms that lasted through
the night.

Tourists prepared to make for the pyramids at a relatively cool
5:00 a.m. Wearing a light tibet dress, a straw hat covered with
white gauze, and with her hands sheathed in dogskin gloves,
Abby was ready for adventure atop a donkey. As Marshall had put
on some weight over the years, he was assigned a slightly larger
donkey. Dressed in his English sporting outfit, Marshall held the
reins in one hand and his engraved brass ear trumpet in the other.

Joining a group of tourists and several guides, they proceeded
toward the Sphinx. As the sun rose, it cast an orange glow on the
desert sand, illuminating the path. Dismounting at their destination, Marshall, already miserable, reached into his saddlebag to
retrieve his thermometer and check his watch. At six o'clock in
the morning, the temperature registered one hundred degrees
Fahrenheit.

Few ladies could climb to the top of the pyramids. Abby was
a proud exception. She believed the climbing to be a critical part
of the experience. It was impossible to get where she wanted to
be, though, without assistance. Led by what she described as
three "filthy Arabs she would never have dreamed of letting
touch her," she bravely hiked up her skirts and was hauled to
the top.

When their visit to Egypt had come to a close, father and daughter headed to the Holy Land. Marshall found fault with everything in Palestine—food, transportation, the very rhythm of the trip, with its constant moving and packing. The boat and hotel accommodations fell short of his standards, to say nothing of the heat, dust, and humidity. Abby, on the other hand, rarely complained. She found novelty in everything she saw. Like many Victorians, she had a fascination with the erotic and exotic the Mideast provided and was not about to skip visiting a harem. She could scarcely wait to observe how a multitude of consorts managed dwelling under the same roof, although she felt skeptical the arrangement was a happy one. Abby, so thoroughly American and so well traveled, wondered how a woman could spend her life sequestered behind a gated wall and never be free.

Even in the sweltering climate, Abby always tried "to look like a lady," which, she could not help noting primly, "was unusual in this part of the world." Keeping her fair skin from burning and freckling involved an endless duel with the blistering sun; many evenings were spent with Elizabeth fashioning hats of wire and muslin. Some blemishing was inevitable, but vanity could not keep Abby inside and on the ground. A practiced equestrian, she rode an Arabian stallion along the ancient roads. Resting spots atop steep hills offered bird's-eye views of the vast, shrubbed landscape.

The Woodses joined a large party of Quakers from Philadelphia to tour the holy sites. A caravan of donkeys, horses, and provisions headed for Jericho, Jordan, and the Dead Sea. Thirty armed guards led the way and served as protection against the Bedouins. "Ten consulate guards, five dragomen, four Sheikhs, twenty luggage muleteers, eight bodyguards, and seven other attendants made up a party of over a hundred." Base camp was set up at the foot of what Abby described as the Mountain of Temptation. Outside each three-room tent, a flag on a tall pole was set in sand. A neighborhood of white canvas tents was laid out in rows. At night, the oil lantern light within each filtered through the pinned-backed flaps serving as portals. Between the corridors of tents, fires burned through the night to keep wolves away. The guards and muleteers kept watch over belongings as the tourists slept on their cots. Just out of the campfire light, Bedouins stalked nearby hills, their bodies and horses a shade darker than the night. Abby was enchanted with the romantic atmosphere and loved camping. Marshall, however, was "in actual despair."

Abby seemed to attract admirers in every part of the world. In Egypt, a rich, handsome German baron proposed to her, an incident she seemed to shrug off without a serious second thought. Several Arabs were spellbound by her Anglo-American looks and natural athleticism. She was about to retire to her tent one evening when she was approached by one of the guides. A dragoman, Sheikh Abdel Hassan, gave Abby his evening Arabic salutation. "Taking his hands once to his heart and then to the head and again to his heart," and then grasping her hand and kissing it, he said, " 'May the white lady be blessed and a happy sleep tonight. Abdel Hassan will watch that no harm comes to her and may the god in the stars look at her until morning.' " Prayed through the night and admired during the day, Abby felt well protected by the land's native men.

After she rode for eight hours straight, cantering toward the Dead Sea, Abby made a lasting impression on the son of a sheikh. When she dismounted, he noticed how gently she spoke to her horse while stroking its sweaty neck. He rode up to where she and her horse stood. From his saddle, he admiringly looked down at her. "You went through the air as swiftly and as steadily as an arrow," he said, beaming.

"This horse deserves the credit," said Abby, as she squinted up at him in the sun. The sheikh's son then presented her with his photograph as a gift. The image, she told her mother, "was an excellent representation of how they all looked." She proceeded to her lodgings, where before sleep she mounted the photograph onto one of the black pages of her personal scrapbook entitled "The East 1870."

Every moment was not perfect. Each day brought its burdens. "I was disappointed in the church of the nativity where Jesus is said to have been born," Abby wrote. "It seems to be unreal and a terrible desecration to have Catholics all about and a disgusting priest running around such a holy spot." Gradually, she appears to have adapted to sharing the sacred territory with Papists. In her travel log, she marked places named in the Bible. She had to pinch herself once when she found herself at the foot of the mountain where "David wrote so many of his beautiful psalms," and the spot where shepherds first lay beneath the eastern star.

The only way to reach such landmarks was on horseback, and poor Cataldi and Elizabeth were not used to such active employers. Unable to keep pace with the others, they often fell behind and on occasion had to make their way back in the dark without the protection of bodyguards. When the exhausted servants finally reached Jerusalem on horseback at ten at night, they could barely move. Marshall excused Cataldi from preparing dinner, with Elizabeth reduced to light duty, merely asked to fix Abby's hair in simple braids before the Woodses left to dine at the table d'hôte.

They were seated at a table lit by lanterns dangling from a cord strung from the kitchen to a mud wall. Colorful carpets were strewn through the patio and placed underneath their feet. The Woodses took a detour from their regular French diet, adventurously ordering dishes from the traditional Middle Eastern menu, served on hammered metal plates. Experiencing spices new to them, father and daughter began to compare the dinner with meals served at home. As Marshall seemed to be in fairly good humor, Abby thought it an opportune time to broach their return to Providence. But her father, annoyed, lit into her. "You are spoiling all my pleasure by always bothering me with this question," he said. "I have traveled to the east explicitly for you and now I would like to enjoy myself for a bit longer before going back to America. I will need quiet in Paris for some time when we return to the continent. You seem to be enjoying yourself. Why do you always insist on rushing back home? We have only been away for three months. What about our plans to see Russia?"

Abby knew protest was useless and dropped the subject.

Using the nineteenth-century invention of photography, the Woodses, like everyone else, became obsessed with recording their images. In letters addressed to Prospect Street, Abby asked her mother to send along her most recent tintype—"Just as you are now in the street, dressed in black," she pleaded. Marshall requested portraits of the family dogs, on evidence the only things he missed about Providence.

While Abby and Marshall were in Jerusalem, a telegram arrived from Anne Woods saying that John Francis, her half brother, had died in Italy. Abby worried about what would happen to her mother's two half sisters, who, in their thirties, were regarded as past their prime, and who had made the mistake of turning down marriage proposals in their youth. "Oh what a lesson to old maids," Abby sighed. How would they manage in the big house in Warwick with no man to watch over them? Marshall's immediate question was who would inherit Spring Green, whether his wife might be mentioned in the will. Both saw the uncle's demise as a setback. "This destroys our traveling plans entirely," moaned Abby, who at that moment had no yen for Rhode Island.

While Marshall stood at the telegraph station all day communicating with his wife back in Providence, Abby was in a quandary about what to wear. "I scarcely know what to do about mourning," she conceded. "I must put on the appropriate clothes but must wait until I get to Paris. I shall choose dead black silk and perhaps light French crepe. There will be so many who know of the relationship I must be seen in it," she added. Abby, lost in such circumstances, plied her mother with questions on Victorian etiquette. "Do I wear mourning for six months or is it nine?"

Anne knew her husband would want to do the right thing by her with a death in the family. He assured her he would rush home if she needed him there, but with nothing more to be done, Abby and Marshall finally received the telegram they were waiting for:

CONTINUE YOUR JOURNEY—
LOVE MAMA

Permission granted by the matriarch, the Woodses boarded a steamer for Greece. "My clothes are getting shabby from traveling so constantly in boats," Abby complained. "I have a nice silk costume but when I put it on Papa always says it is too handsome and attracts attention, and he is right for in this part of the world it is better that a stranger should not know anything about you or your circumstances."

In Athens, political events kept them confined to the hotel, halting their plans to view the Acropolis. With few options left, the Woodses decided to return to France that summer. They took the train from Paris to Trouville, one of the oldest seaside resorts in France, and with a reputation for attracting not only international tourists but artists and writers. Marshall always wanted to be wherever the new impulse in art was occurring. Eugène Boudin had exhibited *Bathers on the Beach at Trouville* just the year before, in 1869, and was promoting the idea of painting outside.

The hotel in Trouville overlooked the English Channel and was filled to capacity in July. An enormous staff catered to the summer guests who streamed in from all of Europe and from America. After camels and donkeys, the superb accommodations were a relief to Marshall. Abby's only complaint was that the beaches were "not nearly as nice as the ones in Newport."

In the lobby of the French Hotel, its people checking in and out with their luggage, Abby felt the more homesick for Rhode Island. From the porch that faced the sea, she watched horse-drawn carts carry guests to the shoreline pavilion and decided to head that way herself. After changing into a frilly bathing costume with three-quarter sleeves and pantaloons poking out beneath a skirt, Abby was escorted to the water's edge by a Swedish *maître baigneur*, who took her hand and led her into the sea. For what seemed a long time she floated and bobbed atop the waves, listening to the surf and the muffled voices of other bathers nearby. When she emerged, buckets of fresh hot water were poured on her feet, an experience so "divine" she recommended the custom be adopted at Bailey's Beach.

By eleven o'clock it was time to meet her father for breakfast in the dining room. As ever punctual, she quickly spotted him in formal dress with his long beard trimmed, seated in a corner beside a fluted pillar. Behind his chair, rows of potted orange trees created a natural-looking barrier affording privacy. He seemed pleased to be back in Western civilization, where he understood the language and had a renewed appreciation for modern conveniences. With his folding reading glasses set on the tip of his small nose, he looked thoroughly content to be alone with the day's edition of the London *Times.* As he turned a page, he glanced at the watch pinned inside his coat pocket. He noticed his daughter coming toward him in mirrors fastened to the wall between the windows. Abby held a packet of letters in one hand and a hat in the other and weaved her way toward him through a maze of round tables covered with white tablecloths and surrounded by half-empty chairs. Marshall smiled at her as the waiter pulled out her seat beside him. In French, they both ordered breakfast.

While they waited to be served, Abby told her father how wonderfully healthy she felt after a morning swim on a bright, hot day. The Woodses had been in Trouville for a week, and mail from home had just arrived. Abby told her father of a friend who had recently made a great match. This news hit a raw nerve. "Well, she can get a man and you can't," Marshall snapped, lifting a teacup to his lips.

Stunned by the cruel remark, Abby looked blankly at her father. She now clearly understood that Charley did not figure in his mind as a "match." With Marshall in a sulk and herself less than enamored with him, it was not the best time to bring up the sore subject of heading back to Providence. But she couldn't help herself. "Papa," she said, "is there any possibility that we might go home in August?"

Marshall, having been nagged on their departure intermittently for months, stiffened his back and stared at Abby. "When will you stop," he snarled. "I oppose the idea of heading home so soon. Before leaving I will require to take the waters in Germany. Of course if you want to sacrifice my health, we can take passage for the 20th in the *Cuba.*" Letting that impact settle, he picked up his newspaper and finished the column where he had left off.

Abby tried to disguise her disappointment at not being a part of the Newport summer scene. She missed her mother, her friends, and cousins. Being on holiday so long, never knowing when it would be over, made time move slowly and her life seem without much purpose. She barely touched the food delivered to the table. Resigned to another day of finding pleasant things to occupy herself, she blankly stared out the window to the line on the horizon.

Marshall's discouragements concerning Charley were beginning to take hold. The last thing Abby wanted was to disappoint her parents. She started to think how she might put her thoughts in a letter to Charley without devastating him, unsure she had the courage or ability to express her doubts in person. Charley could be persuasive, and she did not like confrontation.

The reasons for her confusion were not precise, which she had trouble addressing rationally. Charley had been a surprise at a moment in her life when she was feeling more independent than usual. They'd had a good time together. She had to admit she enjoyed his company more than that of anyone else she had known. There was something about him that suited her, unconventional though he was. When it came right down to it, though, Charley was not the type of man she was hoping to marry, and she did not think she could follow through. She felt responsible and ashamed for words she now regretted and promises she thought she could not keep. She half blamed Charley for pressing ahead so quickly. On the other hand, she could see how her actions might have been read as reciprocal. A decision was due, but the confidence and self-reliance she had developed away from home seemed to dissolve at the thought. She wished for her mother to lend advice. "I am more troubled than ever and perplexed," she wrote wearily after the gold ring Charley gave her broke in half. "Were I at all superstitious I might think it was a bad omen." Night after night a ghostlike figure dressed in black appeared in her dreams with a warning. "Be careful what you do," he would say, pointing a finger at Abby, "for you do not know your own heart."

After two weeks at their shore resort in France, Abby was

hard put to concentrate on anything besides her entanglement with the Irishman. "Papa is very kind," she assured her mother, "but he does not understand how I feel as you would." Having tired her father on the matter and making do without her mother, Abby spent more hours than usual with the Bible in search of consoling passages.

Marshall spent a week at a German spa soaking his gout-afflicted body in mineral waters. Kneaded, wrapped, and set on a starch-free diet, he felt restored enough to continue by train from Berlin to Cologne. Their departure coincided with the official declaration of war between Germany and France on July 19, 1870. The feeling in the streets was palpable. "The excitement is as great in Berlin as I ever saw it in America during the time of our worst troubles," said Abby, alluding to the American Civil War.

As the Woodses pushed through throngs at the train station to buy tickets, they were informed that an estimated "8000 soldiers were already heading to the frontier." The front of their hotel was crowded with people cheering and singing the national hymn. Abby was not so concerned for their own safety, what with their American passports and letters of introduction. The biggest concern was "that all letters will be stopped." Her family and friends would panic at the thought of father and daughter stranded in the hinterland.

On July 24, 1870, when Marshall and Abby got off the train in Cologne, the station was full of militia heading for the Rhine. Unable to find a carriage, they walked toward the central part of the city. They were stopped several times by the police, who wanted to see their papers. The Woodses were stunned to hear that there were only two rooms left, but they took what was offered without Marshall's usual inspection.

The streets were filled with screaming women and children sending husbands and fathers off to the war. The king's palace was next to the hotel, and Abby and Marshall could see and hear the crowd gathered there in patriotic song. For Abby, that was the one bright spot in a trying day. "You can imagine how fine it was for the Germans are such fine musicians," she reported to her mother.

They were there when the French secretary put into the hands of Count Bismarck the declaration of war made by Napoléon III to the King of Prussia. All foreigners were advised to evacuate the city. In a matter of days the trains would refuse to accept anyone other than military. The Woodses' plan for St. Petersburg was not looking good. It was possible to get to St. Petersburg from Stockholm, but the Baltic Sea was no longer safe; the lighthouses had been extinguished along the entire Prussian coast. Heading back to France was the only alternative.

The Woodses followed the war by newspaper in Paris and through political insiders such as their diplomat cousin John Read. "All my interests are with France which I love like a second country," Abby sighed. "My whole heart and sympathies go out with France and I am as enthusiastic as any French woman."

Despite events on the larger scale, Abby continued to dwell on her own concerns. The outset of the Franco-Prussian War sorely affected her shopping, and Charley was still much on her mind. Her mother advised postponing any decisions about marriage until she returned to Providence, where they could discuss the matter in person.

As foreigners funneled out of France to safer places, Abby endured, living up to her commitments. She still figured into a shopping network with relatives at various points on the globe and felt obliged to hold up her end. Her cousin Hope's wedding attire, which she had agreed to acquire in Paris and had already picked out, had yet to be completed.

Marshall decided the most sensible solution was to drift back to the shores of Trouville until things cooled down in the capital. He and Abby resumed their routine of swimming, afternoon carriage rides through the boulevards, walks on the beach, reading, and mingling with other guests.

Abby bided her August at the resort in certainty that the situation would straighten itself out with France victorious. Her optimism went unrewarded. News filtered to them of France's defeat. Paris was in a state of siege. Thinking of all the unfinished dresswork at Madame Vignon's shop, Abby panicked. "Therefore we should get back to Paris and I shall immediately order all my things for perhaps we may have to leave," she wrote.

In Paris, the streets were quiet but filled with those trying either to escape or to protect the city. As the situation continued to decline, members of the American Paris colony began to strategize their exit. The Woodses postponed their own departure for as long as possible. Marshall wanted to observe further, and relished being in the thick of things.

Abby finished her shopping for her cousin's wedding. "Yesterday I ordered the rest of Hope's clothes: her corsets, gloves and thirty yards of light pink silk flounces. Her other dresses I ordered before," she wrote her mother. The gown's design was complete and the bill presented. "The wedding dress is to be made of white gauze, very thick and handsome, trimmed with tulle and orange flowers and it is to cost including wreath and everything, nine hundred francs, with an under petticoat. I do not think it is too much, when you know the immense amount of silk it takes for the train. The blue silk is to be seven hundred and fifty francs. I hope I have not paid too much but I determined that at all events it would be as handsome as possible." Even Hope's pennywise mother, Mrs. Thomas Goddard, Abby remarked, "could find no fault with it."

As conditions in Paris declined, the everyday things the Woodses had taken for granted became impossible; the mail became so unreliable that Marshall began to send his correspondence by balloon. Pressure mounted for Americans to leave. John Read went to the Woodses' hotel, recommending they make preparations to evacuate the city at a moment's warning. Read was frantic. He had not seen or heard from his wife in a week, nor did he know the whereabouts of his seven-year-old daughter, whom he had dropped off at a convent in Passy a year earlier.

Conflicting accounts of the war seeped into the headlines. A Paris paper reported the Germans defeated, the French having taken 40,000 prisoners. The news in the papers and on the street, though, was incorrect. It was France that had been defeated.

Marshall, ever peripatetic, was curious to see how the French were preparing for war. On August 15, 1870, he and Abby drove out to the Bois de Boulogne. They hardly recognized the entrance. The gates had been taken down, and in their place a drawbridge provided access through the fortifications now surrounding the park. "There are over ten thousand workmen on the fortifications around Paris," Abby reported. Others manufactured artillery around the clock. "People don't know what to think," she said. "It is very sad and everyone feels as though it will be very hard for France. Should they again be defeated we will have to leave at once as there will be nothing to prevent the Prussians from coming directly into Paris." Driving through the bois that evening, Abby described the scene of 400,000 men working under gas torches as "beautiful." "The moon was full and you can not imagine how picturesque the scene was. I never realized the patriotism of Paris."

An atmosphere of doom descended upon a city that swarmed with soldiers. The parks were transformed. "The beautiful trees were cut down to the lake itself and filled with strong earthworks," grieved Abby. "Droves of livestock were herded into the park for provisions. The garden of Luxembourg is a feeding place for cows, sheep and pigs."

The French press continued as an unreliable source. The only newspaper that seemed to get the story straight was the London *Times*, could a copy be obtained. The Woodses found themselves in Paris when the French army was defeated. The Napoléon dynasty had ceased to rule France. "I was in the crowd when the Republic was declared," Abby reported. "I would not have missed being there for anything." The Place de la Concorde was packed with people and armed soldiers. Citizens shouted, "*Vive la République!* Death to the English. Death to the Emperor." With the new membership of the Republic announced, the people cheered and tore apart the former flag. Every shop that displayed the eagle and obsolete initials was ripped down. People poured through the Tuileries' gates, discarding the emperor's arms as they rushed toward the palace and stormed the private apartments looking for the empress. But Eugénie had managed to slip out of the country days earlier, accompanied by her dentist.

The Woodses observed what was going on from their carriage

parked in the Champs-Elysées, then proceeded to the bois to see how events had unfolded in that part of the city. The overall spectacle was disheartening. "I am so disappointed in the French people, and feel so dreadfully for the Emperor," said Abby. Upon their return to the oasis of their hotel on the Rue de Rivoli, she could hear droves of men singing the "Marseillaise" outside. "I never heard anything so perfect," she noted. "They kept the best time."

When Abby got back to the hotel, she found a package from her mother. It contained her mother's recent tintype and a locket of her hair. There was also an envelope marked "Private." Abby eagerly tore off the seal to catch up on the latest Providence gossip.

She nervously stroked the side of her cheek with the hair as she read the shocking news. Her cousin Nettie was in love with William, a Negro servant of the Woodses. Not only that, a male friend of Abby's had switched his affections from daughter to mother. The couple, with their preposterous difference in age, were flaunting their love in public. Anne had had a talk with the young man urging him to end the undignified relationship, but he did not appreciate her unsolicited advice.

Abby and Marshall Woods were among the last Americans to leave Paris. Crossing the channel for England, Abby chastised herself. Why, she pouted, had she not bought more gloves in Paris!

In London, an old acquaintance of Abby's, George Bradley from Albany, came to visit. Their paths had not crossed for several years, and in May both had turned twenty-one. Since the last time, Abby thought he had "improved" and—pleasant surprise—grown to be "quite good looking" as well as "handsomely dressed." They spent the morning talking in her suite's living room and, finding the company so agreeable, continued to catch up over lunch.

As the day progressed, George felt he should let Abby know what people were saying about her. He had heard she was engaged to Charles Stewart Parnell. "George," Abby noted, "openly displayed his disapproval. He simply could not bear him." Like others who had encountered Charley, George found him enigmatic, aloof, and socially stiff. They called him "the Sphinx." Abby was not blind to Charley's foibles. Although he could be charming and sociable when he felt like it, the Irishman found the subjects of most people's conversation mind-numbing. So she well understood what George was talking about when he voiced his criticism. "I do not wonder why people dislike him," Abby said, "for he treats people so coldly and so contemptuously." The day with George left Abby once again with the jitters about a future with Charley. "What shall I do?" she frantically asked her absent mother. "What can I do to get out of this?"

The letter to Charley could be postponed no longer. Abby wrote her mother, "Today I am so blue and unhappy that I can scarcely write. Do you remember how often we talked about my ever having to write a letter as the one I sent yesterday and how difficult it would be and how we said we should have to think it over together? How strange that I should have to write it entirely alone and that I should not even ask you about it. I don't think in justice I could have done otherwise. . . . How much I blame myself."

Abby waited "with great anxiety" for Charley's answer acknowledging her decision not to marry him. She wondered if he would ever want to see her again. "It would, I think, be wiser if he did not see me. It will only be a trial for us both," she opined. Soon a letter arrived postmarked Wicklow. With trepidation Abby opened it and was baffled to find that Charley never once referred to the letter she had sent. What she did not realize was that this was typical for a man who never took no for an answer. He was perceptive about human nature and rightly sensed Abby's parents had influenced her to break off the engagement. He was not about to let her off the hook that easily. He rushed off to Paris to find her, but it was too late. She was on her way back to America.

CHAPTER TWELVE

Parnell Comes to America

May 6, 1871

THE WESTERN UNION TELEGRAPH COMPANY, NEW YORK, RECEIVED AT PROVIDENCE, MAY 6, 1871. TO MISS ABBY FRANCIS WOODS

I SHALL BE AT PROVIDENCE AT SEVEN THIRTY THIS EVENING TO SEE YOU.

CHARLES S. PARNELL

Charles Parnell came to America for the first time in 1871, his underlying goal to see Abby Woods again. Used to getting his way, he had not given up on marrying her. This time he wanted to impress the Woodses by presenting himself as a man of the world, with a good shot at success. With him were letters of introduction to those potentially able to aid him should he decide to resettle in the United States.

When Charley arrived at the Providence station, he was greeted by a Woods servant and delivered to the brick mansion at 62 Prospect Street. He was warmly welcomed, with an offer to stay with the family for several days if it fit into his schedule. Abby was friendly, which Charley mistook as a sign of rekindled feelings. Abby, like Charley, had a tendency to see things the way she wished them to be instead of the way they were. She wanted to believe that after one year since she wrote the letter turning down his marriage proposal, he was content to be marginalized to the role of her "friend." Charley, however, was bent on convincing her to change her mind about marrying him.

The front parlor was scented with cut flowers placed around the room on bookcases and marble fireplace mantels. Daylight streamed in through the large windows that faced the courtyard. Abby was sitting on a fringed velvet sofa reading when Charley entered the room. She could feel his tension and, after placing her book on the table beside her, rose to greet him. An awkward silence fell, and then Charley proposed they go outside, as there was something he wanted to speak to her about in private.

Mirrors on the wall reflected the pair as they exited through the French doors that led to the garden. On a brick path, they passed staggered rows of blossoming rhododendron and Roman statues surrounded with boxwood topiary. Between a pair of marble urns, they found a stone bench where both sat. When Abby finally asked him what he wanted to say, Charley responded by demanding to know why she had broken off their engagement. He told her he still loved her and still wanted to marry her. She felt cornered. Her guilt and confusion made her angry enough to deliver a cutting answer, one that would drastically change his life and affect an entire culture. She told him "he was only an Irish gentleman, without any particular name in public." Her mind, he now realized, was plainly set beyond persuasion. He had encountered a will to match his own. Defeated, Charley left Providence.

There was one thing Abby had failed to mention: by this time she had her eye on a man with better prospects. A female cousin of Abby's had recently died. The cousin's rich young husband, Sam Abbott, was now available.

From Rhode Island, Charley went directly to visit his brother John, who had become a peach farmer in Alabama. When Charley reached the plantation, his brother described him as "sullen and dejected." For days Charley made no reference to his broken love affair. Staying behind in the house while John attended to his orchards, Charley, who had had episodes of "melancholia" throughout his life, now slid into deep depression.

Mrs. Myrna, John's housekeeper, became concerned that throughout the day, Charley would sit before the fireplace, "holding his face in his hands sighing bitterly." Finally, Mrs. Myrna felt she had to say something. "John," she insisted, "you must speak to your brother about what is troubling him and see if there is anything you could do to help."

That evening after dinner, John tried his best to address his brother's troubled state. "Come, Charley," he said, "tell me. What is the matter with you?"

First hesitating, Charles then "put forth the sad story of his love for Miss Woods and how she had jilted him." He felt certain her parents had advised her against marrying him.

"John," Charley said, "you know I have a good mind to go back to Rhode Island and see her again. She might change her mind. You know, I was and still am very fond of Miss Woods." But pride kept him from returning. His brother would later remark that, from that time forward, Charles's "attitude towards women was a cold and suspicious one."

Charley began a tour of the United States with his brother. In New Orleans, he had his fortune read from tarot cards by a Cajun woman. She predicted that he would not have a long life. Several catastrophes soon followed. A train he was riding in Birmingham, Alabama, jumped the track. His brother was seriously hurt. After Charley nursed John back to health in a hotel room, the two visited the Clover Hill Coal Mine in Virginia, a company where Charley owned some shares. Descending a mine shaft in a cage, Charley was nearly decapitated. Mindful of the psychic's prophecy, he thought it high time to return to the safe haven of Avondale.

Throughout his journey, Charley was aware of the hatred many Americans felt toward the Irish. Keenly sensitive to class differentiation, Charley did not want to be taken for a common impoverished Irish immigrant. He and his brother visited "a Southern Colonel, the coal-mining pioneer of Birmingham, Alabama," when the town's architecture consisted of a conglomeration of wooden houses. Before they reached the door, Charley said, "For God's sake don't tell him we are from Ireland, as they've never seen a real Irish gentleman, and wouldn't know one if they did." He was insulted to be cast aside because of his nationality by New England grandees and well-to-do Southern families whose Irish ancestors had come to America fairly recently themselves.

America was far from what Charley had expected. The bigotry, political hypocrisy, and rude and coarse behavior of the general population abraded his refined aristocratic sensibilities. Disillusioned with the country he had always dreamed of visiting, and heartbroken that a marriage to Abby Woods would never be, he convinced John to give up his orchards and return with him to Ireland. On New Year's Day, 1872, the two boarded a ship that sailed out of New York City.

On October 15, 1873, Abby Francis Woods married her deceased cousin's husband, Samuel Appleton Browne Abbott, a strikingly handsome, Ivy League–educated son of a Boston Brahmin family. Marshall and Anne Woods could not have envisioned a more perfect match for their daughter.

Abby had nabbed the man described in her 1870 journal. Point for point, he met her criteria. He had a broad-reaching intellect. He cherished literature, collected rare books, and eventually became president of the board of trustees at the Boston Public Library on Copley Square. There, Abbott's interests in arts and letters converged. He was in charge of overseeing the library's eight-year construction. Through this venture, he became friends with artists of his day, some of whom would contribute to the work in progress. Charles McKim, the architect whom Abbott hired to design the library, spoke of his client's charm and wit, eagerly introducing him to such artists as John Singer Sargent, Edwin Abbey, Pierre Puvis de Chavannes, Augustus Saint-Gaudens, and James Whistler.

When Abby married Sam, he was a lawyer in his father's firm and served on the boards of several family-owned companies. He was flush with money and, better still, would never have to concern himself with making it. His thoughts were neither fully occupied with business nor focused upon her. His social ease and sense of humor made him great company. There was only one glitch: Abbott loved women and they loved him, married or not.

Sam and Abby had both met on the rebound. In a short time they would both come to realize their priorities and personalities clashed. Domestic life did not suit Sam Abbott. While Abby was content in the company of her children and dogs, Sam preferred being out and about, mingling with intellectual and artistic companions with whom he could converse on a variety of subjects. During the long periods of time Abby spent visiting her parents, Abbott began to roam and fell in love with another woman.

After the birth of their fourth child, the marriage dissolved. Divorce was out of the question, as was staying in Boston as a scorned wife. In 1879, Abby moved back to Providence, children in tow, to live out the rest of her life with her parents and single brother at 62 Prospect Street. Abbott eventually moved to Italy with his mistress. There he became the first director of the American Academy in Rome.

One can only imagine Abby in 1880, reoccupying her childhood bedroom in Providence and wondering what life might have been like in Ireland had she married her old suitor.

As Abby's marriage was falling apart, Parnell was beginning to launch a political career that would make him one of the most powerful, famous, and beloved politicians of the nineteenth century. After being dismissed by Abby, Parnell had returned to Ireland to find that a comfortable and predictable future as the squire of Avondale seemed a bit lackluster—especially when more challenging opportunities now beckoned in the public sphere.

During Parnell's time in America, momentous political changes had been taking place at home. Ireland had begun to chafe under British control. In 1870, Isaac Butt, an Irish Protestant barrister and a former Member of Parliament, founded the Home Rule Party. What "Home Rule" meant specifically was open to debate, but the pressing nationalist issues of the day included the desire for a domestic parliament for Ireland, education reform, amnesty for political prisoners, and land and rent reform.

Parnell returned home in 1872, just as the notion of home rule for Irish citizens was beginning to take hold, and within two years he had "put his name forward for membership in the Home Rule League," according to Robert Kee in *The Laurel and the Ivy*, a recent biography of Parnell. It wasn't long before Parnell was adopted as the Home Rule League's candidate for the county of Dublin. Accepting the nomination for his candidacy, Parnell rose to give thanks to his supporters. A journalist writing for *The Nation* described the scene: "To our dismay he broke down utterly. He faltered, he paused, he went on, got confused, and pale, with intense but subdued nervous anxiety, caused everyone to feel deep sympathy with him. The audience saw it all, and cheered him kindly and heartily; but many on the platform shook their heads." Parnell lost the election by a landslide.

In his memoir, Charles Parnell's brother John credits Abby for catapulting his brother into public service. "His jilting undoubtedly helped drive his energies into politics," John wrote, "for he was deeply hurt at the idea of being considered a country gentleman without any special abilities."

Undeterred, Parnell ran in 1875 for the seat of Home Rule MP for County Meath. This time he was clearly the popular candidate. He was also becoming more adept at public speaking. On April 11, 1875, he spoke before thousands of supporters and received a standing ovation. Afterward, as Kee put it in his biography, Parnell "was carried on their shoulders to his carriage accompanied by enthusiastic cheering and the strains of a brass band playing national airs. He and his party were able to drive only a short distance before the crowd removed the horse from the traces and drew the vehicle themselves." The next day, Parnell arrived in Navan, County Meath, by train to attend a rally there. In a radical speech, he outlined his ambitious agenda, telling the audience he looked forward to the day when Ireland would be a free nation, governed by its own people, with its own parliament. Through constitutional means he would work in the interests of the majority of the population in Ireland by fighting for the rights of tenant farmers so that they would never be displaced from their homes. The audience, loving what they were hearing, applauded, cheered, and waved hats, scarves, and green banners in support. The mood was exhilarating. A priest, after seeing Parnell, said, with a sigh, that Ireland was "growing young again."

Parnell, now twenty-eight, won the election in April by an overwhelming margin. Once the final results were announced, tens of thousands celebrated. Throughout County Meath, "sprigs of laurel and green boughs were fastened on the fronts of houses . . . while bonfires were lit all over the county."

Two years later, in 1877, Parnell was elected president of the Home Rule Party. Among the Protestant gentry, he was considered a traitor to his class. His proposals for the redistribution of land and the idea of peasant proprietorship sounded to them very much like confiscation. And in the English Parliament, Parnell was labeled an obstructionist because of the tactics he used to stall English bills until Irish issues were addressed. "The house lies prostrate at his mere presence," one member said. His methods of achieving change can be summed up in the answer he gave to a young recruit who once asked him how a man was to learn the rules of the House of Commons.

"By breaking them," Parnell replied.

Beyond campaigning for the rights of the disenfranchised in Ireland, Parnell's calls for liberty extended to farther-flung British colonies. He introduced bills to protect human rights and led the fight for prison reform, pressing for the banishment of barbaric and routine methods of torture such as flogging, solitary confinement, and binding men in chains. He also sought to guard the welfare of women and children working in factories and shops throughout the colonial empire. Women, he believed, should be admitted to Parliament.

In 1878, bad weather and falling prices for livestock resulted in the second famine to hit Ireland in just over thirty years. On either side of the Irish Sea, an economic depression was underway as well. Credit from banks was virtually nonexistent. Small farmers were rapidly filing for bankruptcy. Poor laborers, out of work, felt the impact most severely. A large number of evictions ensued.

Parnell headed to America to raise money for famine relief and to rally support for Irish nationalism. At the age of thirty-three, he was a political star recognized around the world. Songs, slogans, and poems praising his name were on the lips of every citizen who supported the Irish cause. He was considered the real leader of the country, his role of savior unrivaled. Even as the hierarchy of the Catholic church was wary of losing its hold on political power in Ireland, parish priests loved him.

As the Cunard ship bearing Parnell pulled into a New York City dock in January 1879, two of Parnell's sisters and his American mother were present to greet him, and newspaper reporters and Irish Americans turned out in droves. The next day, he spoke to a packed audience at Madison Square Garden. In Washington, D.C., he addressed the House of Representatives. He appeared before state legislatures and visited sixty-two cities, including some in Canada. With the money Parnell raised in North America, Ireland's national treasury brimmed with cash.

In the eight years since Charley had returned to Ireland, he had never found a woman to replace Abby in his affections. Now, back in America, he sought her out. Her marriage was over, she was curious to see him again, and she happily accepted his invitation to accompany him to a charity ball. What happened that evening, no one knows.

What is known is that after Parnell returned to London, he fell in love with a woman named Katharine O'Shea. She was the wife of Captain William O'Shea, a Catholic Member of Parliament from County Clare representing the Home Rule Party. After fourteen years of marriage, the O'Sheas were somewhat estranged. They lived apart most of the time—she in Eltham, a London borough, with their three children; he comfortably ensconced in an apartment in central London. Despite the separate living arrangements (she claimed their physical attraction was dead), a great deal of mutual affection remained between the two, and both residences were paid for by Katie's conservative and rich aunt Ben (whose real name was Anna Maria Wood).

Willie was struggling to keep his constituency. Being intelligent and ambitious, he was aware that if he wished to remain in office, he needed to more closely ally himself with the dynamic Parnell. And Katie was eager to do what she could to advance her husband's career. "Her only concern was to get [Parnell] into her husband's social net."

It was almost impossible to get close to Parnell, much less hold a one-on-one meeting: the "Chairman" seldom had time to spare to mingle with friends outside the political sphere. Overworked and overbooked, he lived a stressful and lonely existence in a London hotel, in a neighborhood inhabited by artists and writers.

Katie repeatedly wrote to Parnell, inviting him to attend luncheons and dinners she hosted for her husband, but her notes went unanswered. So that summer she drove to the Houses of Parliament with her sister and sent in a card requesting Parnell to meet them outside. Her primary intention was to benefit Willie, of course, but her plan took a surprising shift. In her memoirs, Katie later wrote that Parnell "came out, a tall, gaunt figure, thin and deadly pale. He looked straight at me smiling, and his curiously burning eyes looked into mine with a wondering intentness that threw into my brain the sudden thought: 'This man is wonderful—and different.' "

Parnell joined the O'Sheas at the theater in July 1879. That night, according to Katie's account, Parnell told her about the American woman he had loved in 1870. He said he had just seen her again on his recent trip abroad and realized that he was finally over her.

Longing for the kind of loving maternal affection he craved and had never had, Parnell pursued Katie, and in the following months the two became lovers, meeting for trysts in various sleepy English towns. Within months of meeting Katie, Parnell told her he would give up his career if she would marry him, but Katie was unwilling to divorce her husband. (Nor was she eager to threaten the inheritance she was promised by her wealthy aunt Ben, who would never have sanctioned Katie's new relationship.)

In January 1880, Parnell attended the opening session of Parliament. On the third day, an American woman was sitting behind him, in a place usually reserved for Lord Randolph Churchill. It seems likely that Parnell himself had made arrangements some months earlier for Abby to 'be present, after she let him know she would be in London but before he had met Katie. *The Freeman's Journal* (an Irish newspaper that was a forum for Home Rule) noted that "several apparently gracious messages passed during the day" between Parnell and the American woman. But the time for reconciliation had irrevocably passed. Flirting with Abby may have been Parnell's way of inflicting revenge. Like the fox who walks away from the grapes, he simply did not want her anymore.

That summer, Parnell's brother John and sister Theodosia vacationed in Newport, Rhode Island. Theodosia, having known Abby Woods in Paris ten years earlier, wanted to find out what had become of her. "Come, let us call on Charley's old sweetheart," she said to her brother. Welcoming the suggestion of a spontaneous visit, John relished the opportunity to observe Abby's reaction to Charley's celebrity. It appears that neither knew of Abby's separation at the time and that they were still under the impression that she was married to Samuel Abbott, whom they sarcastically referred to as "the rich American."

In a carriage, the two made their way up the wide, fashionable thoroughfare known as Bellevue Avenue. They marveled at the splendor of newly constructed mansions perched near sea cliffs and surrounded by gardens and recently planted trees.

An elaborate iron gate hinged on stone pillars marked the entrance of the villa where Abby and her children resided in the summertime. John and Theodosia instructed their driver to park under the portico and wait for them there. At the front door, they stated the purpose of their unannounced visit to an Irish servant. They stood in the hallway while she went to fetch Abby. Moments later, Abby appeared and led her visitors into the drawing room. John described her, then thirty-one, "as still very pretty, and as usual, charmingly dressed, her vivacious manner unchanged."

"She talked rapidly," John wrote, "evidently rendered somewhat nervous by the memories we aroused."

Suddenly she raised the topic everyone was waiting to discuss. " 'Do tell me, how is your great brother Charles? How famous he has become!' " She went silent, but before anyone could answer her, sighed, and on the verge of tears suddenly cried out, ' "Oh why did I not marry him? How happy we should have been together!' " John and Theodosia felt their brother's suffering had been redressed. In an 1870 letter, Abby had been smug about a relative who had married unwisely after a short courtship: "If a girl once married in haste," she wrote, "she must repent at leisure and reap the rewards of her own folly." Her words now applied to her own situation, having settled for Sam Abbott on the rebound.

Meanwhile, a bizarre triangular relationship between Parnell, Willie, and Katie was underway. In the first phases of the love affair, Parnell often stayed under the same roof as Kitty, Willie, the children, and their servants over holidays such as Christmas and New Year's. He kept up his end of the bargain by stoking Willie's career, and the two were able to work together politically despite the fact that they virtually shared the same woman. Gradually, though, Willie faded out of the picture, coming to Eltham only on Sundays to take the children to church. Parnell moved in with Katie in a house she had rented elsewhere, and over the next eight years she bore Parnell three children without the public's being aware of the unconventional circumstances. (This was an age when privacy was afforded celebrities.)

But in December 1889, Captain William O'Shea filed for divorce, and when the case came to trial the following autumn, the suit resulted in scandalous public court hearings. In June 1891, Parnell and Katie were married in a civil ceremony, as no church would consent to perform the service. The great leader had fallen, and the woman whom he loved was derided as "the Whore of England."

Charles Stewart Parnell died in Brighton less than six months after the marriage, at the age of forty-five, his wife and his dog at his side. At his funeral, as many as 150,000 Irish citizens stood outside the church in the afternoon rain. As the coffin was carried to the cemetery, people plucked sprigs of ivy in his honor, inaugurating Ivy Day, the yearly Irish tradition of marking his death. According to Katherine Tyran, a mourner at the funeral, at Par-

nell's final resting place "the sky over the grave had cleared . . .
The stars were looking out of a quiet green and golden space. As
his coffin was lowered to earth, a woman shrieked and there was a
second's confusion. As it touched the earth, a meteor sailed across
a clearing in the sky and fell." Another mourner, Standish
O'Grady, recalled that "the sky was bright with strange lights."

In William Butler Yeats's poem "Come Gather Round Me
Parnellites," the poet invites readers to celebrate Ireland's "chosen
man" for two reasons: the patriot's love of his country *and* his
deep love for a woman. Calling forth the memory of a leader who
inspired hope in all who wished to be free, Yeats wrote, "Every
man that sings a song/Keeps Parnell in his mind."

The "lass" referred to in Yeats's poem is Katie. But it was
really through his first love, Abby Woods, that Parnell discovered
his calling in life. Comparing the love of a woman to that of one's
country, Parnell told William O'Brien, "You would never have
got young men to sacrifice themselves for so unlucky a country as
Ireland"—then added, with a smile, "only that they pictured her
as a great woman. That makes all the risks worth taking."

Parnell's code name for himself was "the Fox." In the house
where Abby Woods was raised, there was a mirror laden with
symbols of the man who exceeded her expectations. A carved fox
sits centered at the bottom of the frame. His nose points not only
to the grapes he will never have, but directly to a cluster of ivy.

PART THREE

Message in a Mirror

CHAPTER THIRTEEN

The Gerrys

Pulling myself from the deepest recesses of Abby Woods's world, I continued to collect conflicting expert opinions about the provenance of my Fox and Grapes mirror's frame. (Was it made in England, Ireland, or the United States?) It was time to look further into the families of the Woods-Gerry Mansion, where the mirror had once hung. Like the Woodses and the Browns, the Gerrys were American aristocracy, but I still knew little about them, much less whether any mirrors were mentioned in their personal inventories. Both Peter and Edith Gerry had died in Providence, which meant their wills would be stored in probate at city hall.

Providence City Hall is a nineteenth-century stone behemoth with its back to Route 95. A security guard directed me to Vital Records on the fifth floor, where I found the woman in charge sitting behind a window sealed with black iron bars, its ledge up to my shoulders. A plaque above her cell-like enclosure read, "Smile God Loves You." She directed me across the hall, toward record books indicating the numbers and files of the deceased, then to the will room, where I could flip on the light myself.

Stepping through that door, I was assaulted by the stale smell of rotting paper. I massaged the wall in the dark for the switch. I pushed a lever, heard a loud click, and the room began to flicker like a reel of a silent movie. Fluorescent fixtures hung from chains, only half their tubes in operation. The bottom halves of some windows were covered with cardboard and black plastic garbage bags, attached to the molding with duct tape. Over the top panes, punctured yellow roller shades came halfway down. Leaves of peeling paint curled from dingy beige walls and ceiling, and visitors had covered a makeshift plywood desktop with balls of used tissue and empty water bottles and soda cans. The accompanying chair was upholstered in brittle black plastic ripped to its cotton batting. A metal rotary telephone with cord cut and a rectangular portable radio appearing to date from the founding of portability sat atop a filthy steel safe, opened and empty. Rows upon rows of green filing cabinets lined the room and created aisles along the concrete floor. Wire coat hangers dangled where the copper handles were missing on drawers. Many of the drawers were left open, with papers—I assumed, wills—half out of their folders, others in piles on the floor. I thought of the time spent on wills and fees paid estate lawyers. So much for the thoughtful gesture of bequest.

Peter Goelet Gerry was number 59272, and Edith Stuyvesant Gerry, number 60192. Senator Gerry died in 1957, predeceasing Edith by one year. It appeared all he left his wife was debt. Gerry had quite a bit of real estate himself in upstate New York and New York City. His mother was the only daughter of Robert Livingston, one of New York's biggest landowners. His grandfather Ogden Goelet was a land developer in New York City and the owner of Ochre Court in Newport, a Norman-style mansion designed by the architect William Morris Hunt. From deeds concerning Peter Gerry, it appeared he and Edith had routinely sold inherited real estate for money to live on. Edith, I noticed, had owned some very fine artwork she had left to the National Gallery and to the Rhode Island School of Design. There were portraits of her painted by James Whistler and Giovanni Boldini. Another Whistler was a portrait of George Washington Vanderbilt II. I realized then that Vanderbilt had been Edith Gerry's first husband. When they married, he was the richest man in the world. Two Manets were mentioned, but no specific furnishings—or mirrors. Paintings aside, everything was lumped under one category—Contents. The mansion on Prospect Street and what was left in it went to Edith's two grandsons, with the last name of Cecil. Washington, D.C., was listed as their 1950s address. If I could find either of them, maybe he would recall the interior of the Providence mansion and some of the original furnishings.

As I read on about Edith and her first and second husbands' numerous households, it was understandable how she might have found it an overwhelming task to make lists of household inventory. It's not only that Edith and her first husband owned Biltmore House, with its 225 rooms and forty-five bathrooms, in Asheville, North Carolina. George W. Vanderbilt also owned a town house on West Fifty-third Street he had built for himself, designed by William Morris Hunt. He inherited his father's 58-room mansion and all its contents at 640 Fifth Avenue. This residence, called the Triple Palace, took up an entire block. That was not all. George inherited William Henry Vanderbilt's summer house in Bar Harbor, Maine, and Cornelius Vanderbilt's original home, New Dorp, on Staten Island. George and Edith also purchased a town house in Washington, D.C., where George, the real estate, art, and book collector, died, almost broke, at the age of fifty. With such a pedigree, George Henry Vanderbilt Cecil and William Amherst Vanderbilt Cecil would not be hard to track down.

"Where did you find my name?" George asked me over the phone.

"You might find this odd, Mr. Cecil," I said, "but it was in the vital records office in Providence, Rhode Island. I was looking for information concerning the people who lived in a house in Providence, and a mirror they owned. I noticed that your grandmother Edith Gerry resided there for thirty years. You and your brother, William, were mentioned as beneficiaries of her estate. Apparently you both inherited the Woods-Gerry Mansion. I found out about Biltmore and then looked you up in the Asheville phone book. That's how I found you."

"Well, what can I do for you?" he asked cheerfully.

I explained about the mirror trail and the fact that my attention had now veered to investigating the mansion's inhabitants. Would he mind if I asked him a few questions about the interior of the house and his recollection of his grandmother's life there?

"No, no. Go right ahead."

"Did you and your brother ever visit your grandmother in Providence?"

"Oh, yes. Many times. Sixty-two Prospect Street. They bought the house, I believe, in 1930, and we visited often until about 1938. Soon after that, we moved to Europe, where we stayed during the war. I lived in Europe for quite a while after that. When I returned with my family, we would take the children to visit my grandmother in Providence during the fifties until her death. She died in 1958."

"What do you remember specifically about the house?"

"Oh, it was the ugliest house in Providence!" George declared. "Just awful, absolutely plain on the outside, austere really. But very, very beautiful on the inside, with high ceilings and a wonderfully grand stairway." The dining room, where Piazzetta's Italian murals covered the walls, had made quite an impression, judging by the way George described the room. "You know," he said, "there was never any electricity in the dining room. It was always just lit up with lots of candles. Beautiful! And there was the most magnificent garden in the back that went on and on for quite some distance down the hill, with these marvelous statues, a whole crowd of these Italian figures. They were everywhere. We used to call it the Roman Empire."

"Do you happen to have any pictures of the inside of the house when your grandmother lived there? I'm especially interested in any photographs that might show where the large mirrors were placed."

"No," said George. "I'm afraid I don't have a thing. No pictures at all. Wish I could be of more help. Ask the Browns. They're big on these kinds of things. Don't they have a museum or something?"

I asked George what happened to the contents of the mansion.

"Well," he said, "as you can imagine, the house was very diffi-

cult to get rid of. It was so big no one wanted it. Finally a buyer
came along and bought it for next to nothing. My brother and I
took some personal things and, after, called in an appraiser. I suppose anything they could not dispose of, they left there."

I was certain Anne Brown Francis Woods must have inherited
furniture from both John and Nicholas Brown. Having become
familiar with the Brown genealogy, I felt ready to take Henry
Brown up on his offer to visit him at Warwick Point and discuss
his ancestors. I had come across his name over and over again in
the manuscripts division of the Rhode Island Historical Society,
where he had deposited papers covering the last three centuries. I
imagined Henry Brown a living card catalog of family information, as he had written books and articles about his ancestors. The
fact was, I was getting lost in my own research, my map becoming more fragmented, my intentions more vague. The business
with the mirror had made a sharp turn into an insatiable curiosity about the Woodses. I was sure Henry would be able to fill me
in on more details. Perhaps he had relevant material stored at his
house. So many family histories are still locked up in attics along
with the notion that someday, someone will sort through things.
I knew Henry Brown had carried through on his idea. I sensed
that he had the gift of organization.

In February 2002, I was in Providence and decided to call
him. He invited me to get together with him that very day. I
penciled the directions to Spring Green Farm, where Henry's
ancestors had lived for 250 years. It was the country seat of John
Brown, who had a hand in starting the Revolutionary War when
he ignited the British revenue ship *Gaspee*. I was unsure if I could
find my way through the Warwick strip malls to his house on the
"Point." He offered to meet me in the parking lot of one of
Rhode Island's franchise institutions—the Newport Creamery—
off a commercial boulevard.

Henry spotted me immediately and, with a wave, beckoned
me to follow him, driving along a twisted, two-lane road through
a 1960s, middle-class housing development. Henry slowed at an

entrance framed by a canopy of trees and tall, unclipped privet.
We entered the driveway through a split-rail gate connected to a
lopsided fence. A series of buildings were sparsely laid out on the
vast grounds of the family compound. We passed what I recognized as the original John Brown wooden colonial mansion and
stable. When we arrived at Henry's house, he signaled me to park
beside a stand of blue spruce while he continued down the hill. I
stood outside the modest, modern house, its glass walls facing
small, shallow inlets and, beyond, an open view of Narragansett
Bay, and waited for Henry.

He appeared, running up the side of the hill where I stood. I
held out my hand. "We'll have none of that," he said and gave me
a bear hug. "Gee, you're very pretty," he observed and leaned
back for a better view of my face, both hands braced firmly on my
shoulders. The familiarity did not make me feel awkward so
much as in for a treat. I looked forward to an afternoon spent
with an eccentric personality.

Henry was handsome in an old-time poetic way. With his
white hair pushed back from his face, slightly crooked nose, and
full beard, he resembled a cameo of Henry Wadsworth Longfellow. Terrier eyebrows lent further expression to hazel eyes that
widened when he smiled, his face ruddy from time outdoors surf-
casting for stripers and blues. He was in his seventies, and fairly
fit. The day of our visit, he was wearing the uniform of the laid-
back New Englander: a plaid flannel shirt tucked into corduroy
trousers, and a pair of leather boating shoes.

We headed straight for the house. Henry stood holding the
door open with arms outstretched, welcoming me inside. In the
kitchen, he introduced me to his somewhat younger wife, Ann, a
pretty blonde who taught classes in decorative painting in a separate studio on the property. The hand-stenciled borders of the
kitchen walls, the Hitchcock chairs, and trays scattered around
displayed her handiwork. She vanished just moments after I
arrived, leaving Henry and me alone to talk about our mutual
interest in his ancestry.

In the living room, he bowed and, sweeping his arm in an
exaggerated courtly gesture, directed me to sit at a cherrywood

swing-leg table near a window facing the marsh. The tide was low and the sky, a winter gray. Black ducks swam near the water's edge. Bird feeders nailed to trees and dangling from the roof of the porch attracted a steady flow of visitors. "I've put aside a box of letters and other materials for you," he said.

At the other end of the room, thick with bookcases, he shuffled through papers within built-in filing cabinets. Oil portraits of youthful, well-tailored, early-eighteenth-century Providence and Philadelphia ancestors, with pleasant faces and eyes that seemed to follow you from their places on the wall, were everywhere. I turned to see Henry bending down to retrieve a blue cardboard box from behind a Philadelphia Classical mahogany sofa (circa 1825) with cornucopia carvings. He returned, pulled up a chair to my left, plunked the box on the table in front of me, and lifted the top to reveal a series of large, marked acid-free envelopes, his collection of Anne Brown Francis Woods letters and other keepsakes from the attic of the colonial mansion next door, where he was raised and became addicted to history.

Henry dug right in. "Well, here's your girl." He leaned back for a better look at my reaction, his first exhibit a photograph of Anne Brown Francis Woods. "This is the only photo I know to exist of her," he said.

It was an exciting moment for me. I found it mesmerizing, finally to have her face staring out at me from its heavy black background tones. In the years I had looked into her life, I had not imagined what she looked like any more than one would a figure from fiction.

The photograph was a head-and-shoulders portrait. Anne wore a stiff black bonnet with a light silk ruffled lining framing her strong facial features. A voluptuous, starched bow was tied at her neck, its ends extending below her breasts, a striped shawl over her shoulders. Her dark, shiny hair was parted in the middle and pulled back tightly, covering her ears in 1850s style, a small bow at the crown of her head. She was full-featured with dark, well-defined eyebrows and puffy lips. Her eyes, large and widely set, radiated a strong will. There was a grounded intensity to her appearance that matched the opinionated character of her diaries.

Henry suggested the photograph was taken around the time of her marriage to Marshall Woods.

"Look at this," he said proudly. With both hands he raised a worn leather-bound and water-stained book held together with an elastic band. "Wait until you see what this is. I bought this at an antique store in Providence. Do you believe I only paid five dollars for it?"

"Well, are you going to tell me what it is?"

"Anne Brown Francis Woods's cookbook!" Turning his head in my direction, he found the only response I could manage, a perplexed and tight-lipped grin anchored to a few slow nods. Historic objects, I thought, do not affect everyone the same way. Henry handed me the book, and I recognized Anne Brown Francis's handwriting. The French, I thought, will eat anything with a sauce. Still, Anne was my territory and did not need defending. I had long since claimed her and liked her well enough. To Henry, she was likely little more than a research footnote on both her Brown grandfathers' side.

Together we looked through letters, mostly from the lifelong exchange between father and daughter, John Brown Francis and Anne Brown Francis Woods, periodically speaking of events in Henry's family over the past three centuries. I found Henry enthusiastic but never overbearing, our conversation occurring on a shared wavelength. "Isn't this fun?" I asked.

"Yes," Henry answered. "I am having a wonderful time. Usually, I have to do a lot more explaining. There aren't many people I can talk to about these things. I'm really very surprised at how much you know."

I had done my homework before arriving on Henry Brown's doorstep. I knew almost every story he alluded to, along with its characters. Besides the vast stash of private family documents under his roof, he had an access to and a way of looking at history that was highly emotional and personal. He seemed actually to love these people he had gotten to know through their memorabilia. Thrilled with his responses, like his eyebrows lifting and knotting as I probed his genealogy, I did not notice the hours pass.

"Are there any relatives of the Woodses still living in Providence?" I asked Henry.

"Yes," he said. "Charles Kilvert's daughter, Bay Kilvert, well, now she's married and goes by the name McClure. Charles Kilvert was a friend of mine. He was once the mayor of Providence. He died last year. That reminds me," Henry continued. "Charles Kilvert sold a Goddard Newport kneehole desk that belonged to John Brown. It broke all records at the time for a piece of furniture. That desk came from Anne Brown Francis Woods's estate and had descended to him through her. Yes, I know this for a fact."

We came to the end of all we could discuss at one sitting, with two centuries covered in an afternoon. Ann appeared from her studio, pleased Henry had a new friend to reminisce with. It was time for tea. While Ann was in the kitchen, Henry, exhausted, slumped in a Windsor armchair squeezed between a doorway and a tall mahogany case clock with ships and painted dials. His eyes stared ahead, unfixed as though his thoughts were far away. I suppose he could feel my unspoken question, which was what he was thinking.

"They wrote such beautiful love letters then." He sighed wistfully. "It didn't turn out well for any of them. It all ended so tragically."

I nodded but still didn't think the Browns had been singled out to bear love's sorrow more than any others. However wrong, it is always harder to feel sorry for the rich.

Henry, the perfect host, showed me around his house, pointing to things of interest. Some nice eighteenth-century mahogany furniture and early still-lifes captured my attention. One serpentine American chest of drawers with carved ball-and-claw feet Henry claimed had belonged to John Brown caught me off guard. It looked like Philadelphia carving, but I did not have the nerve to inspect it closely. After all, this was a private residence, not an auction preview.

Henry was a couple generations older than I, but no matter. Right from the start, his sweet smile and gentle disposition were nearly enough to make me fall a little in love with him. Already smitten, I was pushed over the top by the scent of cinnamon tea and the eighteenth-century chest. I wanted to whisper in Henry's good ear that we could spend the rest of our lives together as archivists discovering unread documents and working on his next book project: "The *George Washington*: John Brown's Cargo Ship." In my imagined future, Henry and I would spend our evenings discussing the times and lives of the dead over simple home-cooked meals, exhausted from days of cataloging.

I quickly reckoned with the fact that I had come along too late. Henry seemed to like his wife, a lot, and there was no indication he would want her replaced. Besides, as he had mentioned earlier, the love lives of the Browns seldom turned out well. I did not want to add to a family history of misery. In the end, all I wanted was for Henry to be happy.

I pointed out two paintings that caught my attention the minute I stepped into the master bedroom. "Oh, that's what I had wanted to show you," Henry said, tapping his skull with his knuckles. "These were done by Anne Brown Francis Woods when she was thirteen. She was a painter, you know. John Francis made sure all the children were given music and art lessons." Anne had tried to imitate Old Masters, just as my sister had at precisely the same age—twelve. In one appeared to be the Turks Head estate in Warwick, another mansion Anne, along with her uncle, had inherited from her grandfather Nicholas Brown.

Before I left, I wanted to ask about John Carter Brown Woods, the ultimate mama's boy.

"He died in the 1930s, didn't he?" Henry asked. Since I had been following the family chronology for years, I assured him the decade was correct. "Carter, oh yes. Him," Henry said. "My grandfather knew him quite well. The Bachelor, they called him. I have several notes from him addressed to my grandparents." Not surprisingly, Henry had the files on hand. Minutes later, he produced a bundle of letters tied together with a string. "Here are some of his letters to my parents. Look at this," he said with mild disgust. "Do you believe this? The Bachelor is still using the mourning stationery six years after his mother's death."

"What are you talking about?"

"This," Henry explained, "was the notepaper they used after a person in the family died." The stationery was cream-colored with wide, black matte borders. It looked thoroughly modern, suggestive of an understated designer perfume label. Thinking how thrifty Yankees could be, I suggested that Carter had simply overordered the bereavement stationery and was just trying to use it up for economy's sake. Henry arched one eyebrow, tilted his head to the side, and shrugged his shoulders. Neither of us cared to read the letters, so they were rebound and put away without further comment. In another of those rare instances of two people connected beyond words, it was evident Henry and I shared the same opinion: Carter was a loser.

I could sense that I was wearing Henry out, so it was time for me to leave Spring Green. At the front door, he put his hand on my shoulder and told me how much fun it had been to have me stop by to reminisce about the past. I carried a folder containing photographs of Anne Woods and Charles Stewart Parnell when they were young. Henry, driving his own car, escorted me to the highway, and we waved goodbye near the on-ramp to Route 95.

My next step was with Abby Woods's great-granddaughter Bay McClure.

"I'm the keeper of things," Bay said as I entered her shingled College Hill residence in Providence. I liked her immediately. Bay was a portraitist, and her studio, designed to look like a potting shed, was set off to the side of her house with a large perennial garden in the front. Petite, with delicate features, shoulder-length strawberry blond hair, and a trim, athletic figure, Bay was prepster pretty at about fifty; married, with several grown daughters, one of whom was named Abby. We set to work.

She had boxes of letters and photographs laid out before her Victorian sofa, all regarding Anne Brown Francis Woods and her daughter, Abby. "I remember my great-grandmother's house so well," she said. "There were rooms full of mirrors—and beautiful wallpaper. I have many things from that house, too. This sofa is from Prospect Street, as well as these green and pink Limoges plates on the wall over the sideboard, and these alabaster lamps and marquetry tables." She recalled seeing a group portrait of Anne Woods and her granddaughters sitting on and beside a dolphin sofa. She was not sure who owned the picture now.

Bay brought out a letter signed "AW" and handed it to me. "I found this in a sideboard. Who do you think it is written by?" I had an answer: Almira Woods, Marshall Woods's mother. Bay produced more letters and photographs of people she had been unable to identify. Had I any clues? Surprising myself, I did, even as to individuals in family photographs.

"If there is such a thing as reincarnation, I must be related," I joked.

"Hey," she said. "It may be true. You know, I believe in that sort of thing." Looking puzzled, she poked a finger into the side of her cheek and stared at me with her head cocked to one side. "I wonder who you could have been," she asked, contorting her face. I let the topic drop and got on with the subject of her great-grandmother.

Bay brought out a large framed drawing. "This is my great-grandmother Abby Woods Abbott." In the 1870s portrait, Abby had classical features, and her hair was worn up in the Grecian style. Long, ornate jet earrings dangled halfway down her neck. Bay then went to a cabinet drawer to fetch a scrapbook of Abby's Grand Tour. "This is a record of the places where the family traveled," Bay said.

"No," I apprised her. "These photographs and etchings are from a trip east that Abby took with her father, Marshall, in 1870. The rest of the family stayed home." Bay looked at me again as if I were psychic, but I had to set her straight. "Documents exist at the local historical society, a lot of them donated by Helen Abbott Washburn, Abby's oldest daughter."

"Oh, Aunt Helen," said Bay. "She is the person my father got the Newport kneehole desk from, and some other nice things. Helen inherited the desk from her grandmother Anne Woods. One day my father went to visit his aunt at her house in East Greenwich, and she told him to take anything he wanted out of the barn. The desk was one of the things he took. It sold at Christie's and broke a record."

I traded a copy I had with me of Nicholas Brown's will for a postcard Bay had of the Woods mansion with shutters when the Woodses had lived there. Bay explained the dissolution of Abby's marriage to Abbott. Anne had whisked away the idea that any daughter of hers should stay with a philanderer. I asked Bay if she knew anything about Abby's love affair with Parnell. She was sure Anne Woods would have discouraged her daughter's living in the boondocks of a mostly Catholic country, so far from the Providence nest.

Bay's husband walked through the front door and greeted us. Fred bore an eerie resemblance to Charles Parnell. As he was a lawyer, I gave him Nicholas Brown's will to keep him occupied while Bay and I headed for the second floor. "Wait until I show you her clothes," Bay enthused. "They are magnificent."

We ascended two flights to a small, windowed storage room containing triple-decker steamer trunks filled with dresses Abby had worn. I wondered if I might see outfits Vignon had designed for her. The nineteenth-century Parisian couture designer's costumes are now part of collections at the Metropolitan Museum of Art in New York and the Musée des Arts décoratifs in Paris.

Bay gathered a pile and placed it on a bed in the adjoining room. There were evening dresses, lawn dresses, day dresses, and serious traveling clothes made from beautiful colored textiles adorned with handmade lace still in perfect condition. A gypsy costume with red ruffles exemplified the Victorian vogue for staging tableaux. I noted a dress of emerald silk, embellished with white lace. Was this the ball gown Abby wore to Parnell's fund-raiser in 1879? If so, it surely would have given him the creeps. According to William O'Brien, one of Parnell's closest friends and his biographer, Parnell's aversion to the color green was genuine, right at the top of the list of the Irishman's many phobias. "How could you expect a country to have luck that has the color green for its color?" Parnell had said. Poor Abby. If only she had worn something other than green, they might at least have remained friends.

Bay held a skirt in front of her. It came up to her chest. "That was some tall woman who could have worn that," I said.

"Yes, they were tall. My grandmother and her three sisters were all close to six feet." To illustrate her point, Bay showed me a photograph of a family gathering featuring a group of giant middle-aged blondes—the four Abbott sisters. We then examined the way the garments were made, with amazement both at the craftsmanship and that a human body could have fit into them. If Bay's great-grandmother Abby was a fashion tower, the waist on one dress was the size of my thigh, the wrists as small as a child's. "I offered these dresses to RISD," Bay remarked. "I thought they were important because not only were some of them made in Paris but some of the day dresses were made by a dressmaker here in Providence named Mathews. But RISD was not interested. They seem to have a storage problem."

Bay then mentioned another cousin, Bambi, who lived on Nantucket. She has Woods belongings; some of Marshall Woods's capes were stored at her place, Bay said. I made a note to contact Bambi.

"I have a cousin you might want to contact," Bay said. "She lives at Spring Green next to Henry Brown, and she has most of the family portraits. She may have a lot more things, too. She is a member of the Female Charitable Society." When I laughed at the old-fashioned name of the organization, Bay frowned. "You know," she said seriously, "you have to be born into it."

One February Sunday morning, my friend Susan accompanied me to the Swan Point Cemetery in Providence, where we hoped to find Browns and Woodses. As their diaries, letters, inventories, books, and family conversations had not helped determine my mirror's precise origin, I held some hope that the dead might lend revelation—or luck. (I would leave no stone unexamined.) I knew Anne and Abby were both accomplished pianists enamored of German composers. With a mind to the memories the mirror conjured, I slid Schumann's "Scenes from Childhood" into the dashboard CD player and headed down Blackstone Boulevard.

Stone-pillar gates marked the entrance. The cemetery bordered a river, its landscape hilly and wooded. We drove around, looking out for the Victorian heroines whose lives had so occupied Susan's and my shared speculation for the past few years— Almira, Anne, and Abby, any one of whom might have laid claim to an ornate gilded mirror.

Although a main building contained a directory, it was not open on Sundays. Luckily we spotted a security guard eating a doughnut in a black sedan parked with the motor running. I drove up alongside. He rolled down his window. "Who ya looking fa?" he asked through the steam of a coffee cup resting on the shelf of his belly.

"Anne Brown Francis Woods," I replied.

"No, don't know where that could be. Here's a map you can have if you think it will be of any help."

The map indicated various types of trees and shrubs, and highlighted areas with graves of prominent Providence natives. Its topicality helped. From my grave-site experience, I have noticed that the old families have the best real estate, lucky enough to have gotten there earlier, securing choice plots with views. I was astonished that people would care where their bodies would lie, but then my father did. He referred dismissively to those with no island heritage, buried in the back hollow of the Block Island cemetery, as "just summer people." Incidentally, my father's ashes are now wedged among the gravestones of my mother's ancestors, a privilege he felt he was entitled to through marriage, even though he was raised in New York City and as a kid only "summered" on Block Island himself.

On the Swan Point map, I located some prime land. Instinct told me Anne had to rest on the point overlooking the Seekonk River. In an attempt to stir the spirit of Anne Woods, I switched the music to Brahms's Liebeslieder Waltzes. As we crawled along, I was feeling optimistic.

"Okay," I announced. "It's got to be around here." I parked off to the side. Both of us stopped to admire Joseph R. Brown's pyramid, a geometric sculpture of deep red stone conjuring ancient ruins and Grand Tours past. Looking like charades players acting out roles as FBI agents, Susan and I scurried in half circles with heads down and hands clasped together as if pulled by dogs on invisible leashes following the scent of a missing person. To entertain Susan, I impersonated a diviner entranced by the magnetic field of Woods spirits by shaking my arms and tilting my face to the sky.

"Anne, where are you?" I called to the wind in the trees. "Direct us to the plot in which you lie." I randomly stopped to examine the wintry ground at my feet. There I stood, at Anne Brown Francis Woods's grave. "Here she is!" I shouted.

"Look," Susan said sternly, pointing. "There's Marshall! What a pain in the neck!" Susan never liked Marshall. He was too self-involved, his gout and temperament so disruptive to Anne's life and everyone's travel plans. He had not been much fun, beginning with the honeymoon, and Susan held it against him. Furthermore, he had not liked Parnell, a muse for Irish literature.

"There's Almira, the family decorator," I said, "and her lovely husband, the Reverend Alva Woods," the kind, intelligent father-in-law. I felt reunited with the persons whose letters I had combed over for the last few years as I stood above their remains.

The Woods cemetery section was as contained as their genteel world, cordoned on four sides with purplish brownstone edging. Only seven were buried in the plot. A pair of tall weeping hemlocks planted on either side of Carter's grave leaned toward each other in a sad, protective gesture, as in a mourning needlepoint from the early nineteenth century. Leaning over his stone, I lashed out at Carter: "Your mother specifically asked you in her will not to sell family real estate short of dire circumstances, but you did, even though you didn't need the money. It was unforgivable to hand over Nicholas Brown's Cranston farm, acres of beautiful land, for the purpose of creating a golf course, Mr. Clubman. Yes, I saw your golf cart listed in the house inventory."

Susan had sore points of her own. I noticed she was quiet and looked down in the dumps. "What's wrong?" I asked.

"Well," she said, "to tell you the truth, I don't care for Anne's stone." Rectangular and raised above the ground, its flat limestone lid was inscribed with Anne's dates, nothing more. "I'm

disappointed. I just thought she would have something . . . well
. . . different. Marshall must've picked it out."

I rose to his defense, deeming it austere and thematic. It
reminded me of medieval tombs of kings in European cathedrals,
minus the effigies in repose on the lids. The Woods stones were
unembellished. No statues, no angels, no towering obelisks
called out for recognition. I studied the lettering as Susan tidied
up the grave site, removing twigs and leaves.

"We'll be back later," Susan said over Anne's stone, as if to
someone trapped in a well. Then she added, "Next time I come
I'll bring something nice to leave for you."

I wondered what Susan planned to show up with, but now
that she had developed her own private relationship with Anne, I
did not want to butt in by asking.

I placed my hands on Anne's tomb. "Come on, Anne. Where
did you get that mirror? It's been nice getting to know you, but
I need to wrap this up." The next day I called my brother Bobby
to tell him of our quick location of the Woods burial ground and
the short graveside séance.

"Did they say anything to you?" he asked.

"Stone-dead silence," I said, "which shouldn't surprise a biol-
ogist like yourself."

"You should have brought along a Ouija board."

"Hadn't thought of it."

CHAPTER FOURTEEN

Nantucket

In October 2004, I drove to Cape Cod to catch the commuter plane to Nantucket from the Barnstable airport in Hyannis. Bay McClure had spoken to her cousin Bambi (née Priscilla) Mlecsko about my interest in the Woods family and the mirror. One day Bambi, a year-round Nantucket resident, had called me. Her mother, Wit Gifford, now in her nineties, had recently gone into a nursing home. Bambi was responsible for clearing her parents' house in Nantucket, where the family had spent summers. The house was to be sold. In addition to Marshall Woods's capes, she had discovered a suitcase full of old Woods photographs, letters, and diaries. She thought I might have some idea what to do with the documents. Would I be interested in taking a look at what she had?

It was a cold, overcast day, prelude to the next six New England months. I boarded the small plane with the kinds of passengers who fly it every day: a Massachusetts Department of Environmental Management employee, a contractor with a toolbox, an architect toting a long cardboard cylinder containing house plans, and a panting Labrador retriever with a red bandanna tied around his neck. From the sky I was amazed at how large Nantucket was compared with Block Island. I had heard much about development there, but it seemed the Nantucket Conservation Foundation had done an excellent job of protecting large tracts of land.

At the Nantucket airport, Bambi's husband, Tom Mleczko, owner of a fishing charter business, greeted me. From his russet complexion and muscular build, it was easy to tell he was the outdoorsy type. As I passed through the gate, he stuck out his hand and introduced himself.

We headed in the drizzle to his pickup. Tom swung my overnight bag onto the bed of the truck, depositing it beside lobster traps, rope nets tangled up with lightweight fishing lines, and an old pair of patched rubber waders. I climbed into the passenger's side and tried to ignore the tufts of dog hair combined with sand covering the upholstery. When Tom heard it was my first time on Nantucket, he gave me a guided tour of the historic district, enthusiastically pointing out areas of interest.

Off-season the town near the main ferry landing was quiet, most of its shops closed. "For those of us who live here," Tom said, smiling, "this is the time of year we all wait for." Adjusting the brim of his fishing cap, he looked over at me and continued, "It is so nice when all the tourists leave and we have the place to ourselves." He had never heard of the hotel where I was staying, which surprised me. What kind of hole in the wall could the place be if even a native did not know where it was? I reached into my purse for the address. Very slowly, we drove by the inn. From the outside, the building looked like an old summer boardinghouse. I was right when I intuited that the rooms would be small, gloomy, and smelling of mildew. Just across the street was another hotel, the one I wished I were staying in. It was a brick mansion with black shutters, described by the plaque on the fence as having been built in the 1700s for a whaling merchant. Here was the real-life version of how I had always pictured Nantucket. Beyond a hand-forged iron gate, a wildflower garden was planted on either side of the entrance walkway. Large maples with generous branches looked virtually eternal. The bedrooms undoubtedly were furnished in American reproduction furniture and Williamsburg fabric, a style that I usually loathe but that at this moment seemed just the cozy place with first-class amenities I craved to come back to on a rainy day. I did not know Tom well enough to ask him to wait while I ran in the merchant's house to upgrade my lodgings. Fussy though I could be, I didn't need him thinking "spoiled New Yorker."

The more I looked around, the more I realized how precious this part of town had become. The houses were indeed historic, but their mystery had been stripped away by overrestoration. Not one roof sagged; no cedar shingle curled, no joist buckled, and no corner beam perched out of kilter. The structures were probably straighter now than when they were first built. Not a chip of paint was missing on a window, door, or beaded clapboard. As we bumped along the cobblestone streets, I saw the culprits engaged in various stages of "upkeep" with their ladders, buckets, and hammer holsters. The hotel perennial garden that I'd found so delightful moments ago began to grate on me as I noticed so many others just like it. No plastic toys in backyards here. Trellises were covered in every expected creeper, vine, and rose, hydrangeas placed according to color and time of bloom; shrubs had been pruned to look just a little wild amid knee-deep hybrid grasses, household herbs, and tall-stalked lilies and irises. There was not a leaf bitten by bug or besmirched with fungus. Everything stood, ready for the van to pull up and unload the photography crew from a home magazine. Most of the houses were vacant. Few people lived in this summer community all the time.

"Tom," I asked, "has every antique house on the island been restored to perfection?"

"No, not really," he said. As we left the historic district, the houses spread out. "For instance, here's Bay's father's house. He died several years ago, and it's been on the market for a long time." I swooned at the sight of the two-story colonial with center chimney and weathered shingles, where "improvements" had obviously never been done and the inside would be original. Its large front yard was devoid of shrubbery. Old Yankees did not make unnecessary repairs, but Mr. Kilvert had allowed the house to degenerate to a stage that was not good even to my taste. Right away it needed a jack and a couple of new foundation beams.

We drove along a coastal road for a while before Tom turned into a long driveway cut through the dunes. It loomed ahead—

the Gifford summer residence, a massive Victorian structure. Several modern windows were stuck in awkward places. "There is no heat in the house, and it's a little cold inside," Tom said apologetically as we climbed a stairway to a side porch. "Maybe I can find an electric heater." He opened the door, calling out his wife's name as we entered.

Bambi appeared, wearing a plaid flannel shirt, blue jeans, and sturdy hiking boots. She was in her mid-fifties, tall, with long gray hair parted in the middle and loosely held back with a barrette. "I'm glad you could come," she said in a husky voice. "This is going to be a busy day for me. Nino, the family appraiser from Providence, is coming this morning, too. He ought to be here any minute. In the meantime, I'll show you where the photographs and letters are so you can get started."

Tom left, and Bambi led me through a wide hallway into the dining room. She pointed out two oil portraits. Over the fireplace was the one of her mother, "Wink," looking like a 1940s society figure. She posed in a kelly green ball gown sitting upright on the edge of a chair, hands folded in her lap. Her blond hair was styled in a pageboy, her facial expression pinched. Over the sideboard hung the portrait of a balding Mr. Clarence Gifford, nicknamed Bud, dignified and serious in corporate suit and tie. Bambi confided that her mother's parents, one of whom was one of Abby Woods's daughters, had not approved of the marriage. They did not think Bud Gifford would amount to much, since he had not come from the right background. For starters, he had not been born in New England. "But," Bambi said, staring up proudly at her father's image, "they were wrong. He ended up becoming the chairman of the board of the Rhode Island Hospital Trust Company."

She disappeared to tasks upstairs, leaving me with a trunk of old family photographs and a white pigskin suitcase trimmed with red leather she said held "some old letters." Before I started to work, I tried to get my bearings by gazing out a large picture window facing the sea. Several massive shingle houses, all recently built, sprouted from the dunes.

When I stepped back to get an overview of the room, I

couldn't help but notice a blue marlin hanging crookedly over a long wooden ledge crowded with sporting trophies and pewter and porcelain plates, platters, and cups. Corner cupboards were stacked with china. I walked around the first floor for a few minutes, soaking up the beach-life vibes and decor that could only be described as "genteel bohemian." There was just the slightest semblance of order to things. The Giffords had lived hard here, their furniture of different styles deposited from other residences. Old magazines, chairs in faded floral slipcovers, and random tables lent the spacious rooms a fallen, clubby feeling. A vintage freezer chest with a corroded chrome-plated handle had been slathered in coats of blue enamel paint to hide rust. The Giffords, old-style WASPs, could not care less about showing off status or heritage. Unless something was beyond repair, it was wasteful to pitch it out. If there was any doubt, objects were relegated to the purgatorial attic. Many families did not consider old family papers and photographs worthy of storage, but here it seemed that some had been spared by inertia.

I opened the trunk first. White tags were strung to daguerreotypes, identifying the subjects. One by one, I took them from the trunk and organized piles on the table by name. The daguerreotype cases were made of stamped leather and opened like books; tiny gold side hinges held them closed. The photographs inside were covered in glass and surrounded with gold engraved frames, opposite each a cut-velvet cushion, its wear indicative of viewing.

I reached for the case marked "Anne Brown Francis Woods." Henry Brown knew of only one photo of her, but here was a treasure trove. Rotating the case in my palm, I pulled her full-length portrait into view. It was an early image, from the 1840s; she may have been a teenager. The era's obligatory hairstyle—middle part, hair pulled back to cling to the contours of the head—so severe on most women, flattered Anne. It showed off her oval face, wide eyes, and sensuous mouth. It was easy to see why Marshall was smitten. Judging from the long, black dress, she was extremely tall. She had grace and presence. There were many pictures of her. It was unusual to find an image from 1849 of someone smiling, but here was one. Anne Woods beamed into the face of the infant she held dressed in christening finery.

A picture of Marshall Woods taken around the same time had him looking like a more dignified version of Edgar Allan Poe; Almira, his beloved mother, was a dead ringer for Emily Dickinson.

It appeared Carter had owned some home camera equipment starting in the 1870s. With so few pictures of him in any group, I figured him to be the one behind the lens. He had recorded the family's casual existence on Prospect Street and on the city streets of Europe through the evolving methods of photo processing. Large glass plate negatives of his mother and sister were even more beautiful with the scratches they had received uncovered in the trunk. Posed as they were under the shadow of the porch roof, dressed in fitted coats and giant plumed hats, one could make out just the outlined edges of the two against an afternoon sky, like a pair of black cut-out paper silhouettes.

Many pictures were taken of Abby after she had left Boston and returned to Providence. As she aged, her hair became darker, and she was so thin as to look unhealthy. Voluminous hair framed a gaunt face. Surprisingly, I did not find one photograph of Abby with any of her daughters. There were many images of her in the yard, squinting in the sun as she knelt beside groups of out-of-focus pug dogs.

Finally, I came to an interior shot of the house on Prospect Street. In a wallpapered room filled with Victorian furniture, Anne and Marshall Woods sat in matching rockers in front of a fireplace. After thirty years of marriage, they had grown to look alike, both in body and in countenance. Anne, in her portly fifties, smiled contentedly into the lens as she held a baby granddaughter on her lap. I riffled through the bottom of the trunk to see if there were more photographs of the rooms but was out of luck. It was no use looking for an image of the Fox and Grapes mirror. It seemed logical that if the photographer's intent was to take pictures of people, he would stay away from any mirrors, where flashbulbs would ruin the portraits. Mirrors are common enough in old photographs, but their subjects are decor. Carter Woods's purpose was to create family picture albums.

My hands had begun to get numb from the raw dampness of the Giffords' house, and I thought it best to see inside the suitcase before all I could think of was getting warm. I clicked open the brass hinges. Letters were matted to the top of the frayed lining and bunched below. I found the original agreement between the builder and Marshall Woods for the Prospect Street mansion; an 1824 diary of Nicholas Brown's daughter, Anne, from Spring Green. There was correspondence between Anne Brown Francis, as a child living with her grandfather Nicholas Brown on Benefit Street, and her sister, Abby Francis, at boarding school in Boston. A Paris diary, written in pencil by the ten-year-old Abby Woods in 1860, had a few entries and references to her cousin and best friend Hope, whose wedding dress she would eventually select. All described the day-to-day existence of privileged nineteenth-century American girls. Early documents by females are rare in archives and those written by children even more so. I hoped to convince Bambi to donate the papers to a place where they could be properly kept.

I heard the back door open and a man cry, "Oh! Oh! What a fabulous table!" Bambi flew down the stairs to greet Nino, who had brought along his young male assistant. She brought them into the dining room. The appraiser was in his sixties, neatly attired in a sport jacket and tie.

Right from the start, there was tension between us. I was under the impression that he saw me as an interloper, while I was wary of one who proclaimed the Federal Pembroke table in the hall "fabulous" when it was not. Although, like Nino, I did not turn it over to inspect it, to my eye it appeared to be a reproduction. But I couldn't have cared less about the table. When Nino saw me riffling through letters, he seemed displeased and suspicious. After mildly saying hello, he and his assistant went into the living room to list the silver (which I surmised was his area of expertise) on the bookcases while Bambi stayed with me. Tom reappeared with a twelve-inch electric heater that had power enough to warm only one's hands, but I was grateful to have it. "How are you doing?" Bambi asked softly. I told her I had separated the family photographs and explained who the people were with a short biography of each. "Here's a picture of Marshall

Woods in Europe," I said. "Look at that great double-breasted coat with frog fasteners."

"That coat is very warm, too," said Bambi. "I wear it all the time on cold days on Nantucket."

Talk about a hand-me-down! I thought of the curious sight of Bambi at the local grocery dressed in this practical period costume made so well that several generations were able to get wear out of it. I was not so sure Marshall would have approved.

"Best of all," I said to Bambi, "are the documents in the suitcase, some close to two hundred years old." This did not elicit much of a response, as—at that moment, anyway—she was not as interested in her remote family history as I. Understandably, she got more out of going through her own generation's memorabilia, from the 1960s and '70s. Disappointed that Bambi did not share her cousins' enthusiasm for more distant times, I began to wonder why I was there. When I asked what she planned to do with the papers, Bambi said she might like to have a look at them over the winter, curled with a blanket on a couch by the fire. At the thought of antique documents within range of a fireplace, I flew into rescue mode.

"The historical society in Providence has at least ten generations of your ancestors' papers," I said. "It would be remarkable to add more material to that kind of American collection. To go through what you have would take months, and I don't think I'm the one for the job. What is needed is a professional archivist. Someone up to the task might be found at the John Nicholas Brown Center or at the Rhode Island Historical Society—that is, if you would be willing to donate the papers. Then if anyone in your family wanted to read these things in the future, it would all be there, organized and filed in acid-free folders."

Before Bambi could respond, Nino pranced through the doorway to intercede, holding a silver platter. "I would not recommend doing that!" he wailed. I looked at him in disbelief. It wasn't as though these were the sorts of papers which, alone, would be worth much. Referring to the historical society, he said, "I worked there once, and I can tell you, a lot of things disappeared. Those people don't know how to keep anything."

I rose to the defense of the librarians there, vastly underpaid for their efforts. People are trained to be archivists, I told him. The availability of such documents is crucial to scholars and writers. Maybe that was the way things were when he worked there, but since then perhaps the situation had improved. I did not mean what I said as a personal attack on Nino, but he heard it that way.

"I take great offense at that statement," he replied indignantly. With that, he clicked his heels and huffed out of the room.

Bambi, trying to diffuse the atmosphere, invited me to go with her to buy a take-out lunch for everyone. I jumped at the chance to ride in her heated van. On the way into town, I restated my position about the suitcase of archival material. Bambi was a reserved person. I could not tell if my recommendations had any effect on her.

I had originally planned to stay on Nantucket for two days but had already seen everything I cared to and now decided to leave early the next morning. Although I did not go through everything, I had not found a Woods household inventory from Providence. Alan Miller, the American carving expert, was probably right. I would never find mention of the Woods mirror. It seemed pointless to continue searching on Nantucket.

We went back to have lunch in the guest cottage, which was connected to the main house by a wood-planked walkway. It was at least fifty-five degrees there, and the water had not yet been turned off. Nino stayed in the main house while his apprentice, Bambi, and I sat around a table eating chowder. Bambi told me that, because her parents' house was historic, whoever bought it could never tear it down. She showed me a picture of what it had looked like sometime in the 1890s. It was unrecognizable. The two major hurricanes in the last century had blown away the original turrets and porches.

I spent another hour going through photographs in the dining room with Bambi, who was becoming a bit more interested in what I was up to. We both admired how handsome Samuel Abbott had been when her great-grandmother Abby Woods married him. I could hear Nino in the next room, going on about silverware and porcelain with his protégé. Bambi said that she wished she could have dinner with me that night, but she was the coach of the local ice hockey team and had to show up at their game. The whole family were star athletes; her daughter was an Olympic gold medal ice skater.

The idea of spending the evening alone was not particularly appealing to me and made it even more apparent that researching dead people was a lonely activity. I wanted to join the living again and be done with the Woodses. When I told Bambi I had had enough for one day, she offered to drive me to my hotel. Would I be back tomorrow? she asked.

"No," I replied. "I'll be leaving in the morning. But thanks for offering."

As I followed Bambi toward the door, I noticed the appraiser sitting on a skirted chintz living room chair, staring through a magnifying glass at a maker's mark underneath a punch bowl. "Goodbye, Nino," I called, waving limply at his back. "I'm leaving now. Nice to have met you."

"Goodbye, madam," he drily replied, not bothering to look up.

CHAPTER FIFTEEN

Seller's Remorse

By 2004 I was spending most of my time helping decorators locate antique furniture for their clients. I roamed through New York antiques shops and was paid to go to Europe to buy things with other people's money. It was time to give up my restoration space, which I barely used. Before I handed the keys back to the landlord, decisions had to be made about everything I had collected for over twenty-five years.

My enormous studio had come to be a storage warehouse for antiques that I had bought to sell to the trade and personal items that I did not want in my apartment. I bequeathed all my restoration equipment and supplies to one of my former employees. Easy. The big problem was what to do with the mirror, its maker and country of origin still undetermined. To get the mirror out of my mind and life for a while, I thought it best to put it away somewhere else. So, for thousands of dollars, I had it crated, moved, and stored in a climate-controlled warehouse.

The moving company had agreed to keep it for a limited time. To spur me into action, they slapped me with punishing storage and insurance fees over several months. I had a dream of buying an Italian Renaissance building in Providence, like the Woods-Gerry Mansion, where the mirror could properly hang, but the idea seemed increasingly unrealistic.

I had never grown tired of looking at the mirror. When I was working in the shop, almost every day my employees, clients, and I would catch a last glimpse of ourselves in it before heading for the street. I thought of the Woodses and the Gerrys doing the same and all the different costumes worn before it in various eras. It was a romantic idea, I know, but I began to feel that perhaps I had owned it long enough. I thought it deserved a proper place. It needed a real home. The most rational option would be to let the mirror go, enter it in a good auction where it would have the widest exposure. I was uncomfortable with the thought of its loss but could not come up with another plan.

I felt as strongly as ever that the mirror was American. But even had that been established for certain, not many experts seemed to care. Neither the date nor the size was sexy. Regardless of who had made them or where they came from or what they looked like, nineteenth-century mirrors were still held to be of little value. Market-driven experts had concluded objects of that period were just not old enough. End of story.

My relationship with the mirror was similar to one with a beloved. I had fallen in love at first sight, and the feeling had stayed with me for nine years. Oh, I had had my doubts. My constancy was at times shaken by the insults experts had hurled its way. But what they considered its faults, I regarded as its virtues. I liked that it was one of a kind. I liked the amateurish feeling the mirror had. The carver had tried to push himself forward artistically but had not quite made it. He had overestimated his ability, and yet had finished what he'd set out to do. In this way the mirror represented a metaphor for life itself. Specialists were bewildered by the odd juxtaposition between a mirror they found nearly worthless and someone like me, who, after so many years in the business, should have known better than to fall for something so unworthy of attention. No one actually came out and said I should have my head examined, but I could feel them thinking it.

This is not to say that everyone disliked or was blasé about the mirror. There were other people willing to be labeled wrongheaded for their attraction to it. Some had spontaneous reactions to it and made substantial offers to purchase it. But while I was facing the idea that every relationship has an expiration date, I did not know whether that day had come. On several occasions, I thought the hour of our parting had arrived, but then I would notice something compelling about the mirror and about the feeling of owning it. In the late afternoon, a sunbeam would pierce the windowpane, making its way through a parting in my curtains to strike a tiny golden fist clutching a cluster of grapes, and I would submit again to the mirror's charm. I could see myself reflected in the glass, framed by a fable that had applied to the lives of almost all who had owned it.

I fantasized about simplifying my life, getting rid of anything I did not need as a way to glide into the future unfettered. Giving up my studio was a step forward. New collectors did not understand how long it takes to restore things properly, nor were they willing to pay for the right job. It was hard to make a living when decorators skimmed off 30 percent of wages. Many highly skilled antiques restorers were leaving the business. It was too expensive to maintain a shop in Manhattan. I planned to take a sabbatical.

I sent pictures of the Fox and Grapes mirror to the English Furniture Department at Christie's. A lot had changed since I had started out in the business. Although American decorative arts was still a boys' club, current membership included women at higher levels in auction houses. There were at least three high-end American women dealers.

For a long time, women had been heads of European furniture departments. They had proven pretty good at running the art business. Melissa Gagan headed the European furniture department at Christie's. She had worked there for ages. I assembled a package of photographs and information, as I had done so often before for an expert opinion, and sent it off to her. She called me with an estimate of $25,000, which wasn't close to covering my costs, but I wasn't surprised.

Melissa's second call brought even dimmer news. Having had a chance to see the mirror—then not fully assembled; some of the larger elements were made to come apart for storage—in their warehouse, she said her original estimate would have to be adjusted. Perhaps $10,000 to $15,000 would be more realistic. "I think your best option would be to put it in one of our very good house sales," she offered. She did not think the carvings good enough for the English sale. She had a fair argument there, I admitted. The reason they did not look English to her, I explained, was that I was almost certain the mirror was from America, where the carving style was quite different from Europe's.

Melissa confessed that she did not know much about American mirrors and that I might know more. "Aren't mirrors usually described as 'American or English' in catalogs and books because of the uncertainty of origin?" she asked.

"Yes, that seems to be true in general," I agreed. "Confusion exists on the premise that mirrors were imported from England in the eighteenth century and sold through colonial shops. We do know, however, that there were a few carvers here who advertised their own creations. Reynolds in Philadelphia is one example, although I am not suggesting him as the maker. The Chippendale style of frame I assume you are referring to was made in the 1780s. They are the fretwork mirrors, veneered in walnut, with a gilded phoenix on the upper scroll board. Most have carved and gilded festooning of leaves and fruit wired into the sides. Those are almost always listed as 'American or English,' but the consensus now is that almost all of them are English."

Melissa agreed that those were the models she had in mind. But she was not aware of many early American mirror frames carved entirely of wood in the Rococo manner. "There is one," I said, "although now I'm sure it's earlier than mine, based on the scale." This particular eighteenth-century example was displayed in the American Wing of the Metropolitan and had been created by James Reynolds.

With that, Melissa went to work. "Now what about the date? Let's say it is nineteenth century. That way you are safe. If you give it a specific time period, and it turns out you're wrong, the buyer can come after you later." I told her that just about every museum expert I had spoken with had set the production date in the 1830s. Melissa wanted to make sure I had the wood analysis paperwork in order. I did. Seeming convinced by my arguments, she asked what I thought of listing the mirror as an American-made example of a British design. I felt that description was correct but dreaded the response such a statement might trigger in American decorative arts circles: those experts would never commit to listing it as American because so far no one had come up with any other examples. Too sticky a situation. I told Melissa that I thought the less said the better. The presence of white pine was the standard guarantee of American manufacture despite new insistences that it was not a prime factor. To my knowledge, there were no examples of early English frames made entirely of that wood. Melissa brought up the pine ballast argument.

"Yes," I said, "I know the wood is sometimes called mast pine, but a sailing vessel was not in the same category as a mirror's frame or furniture."

"Well," she said, eager to get on with her day, "this is all very interesting, but what are we going to say?"

"Say it's second quarter of the nineteenth century after a Thomas Johnson design, and include the original Johnson illustration and plate number. A mention in the text that the frame is of American white pine may generate some interest in American collectors."

Once my disappointment at the lower estimate had settled in with that of a house sale instead of a fine furniture auction, my instinct told me to withdraw the mirror from Christie's. When I spoke to other American furniture restorers about my notion to sell, they were shocked; the frame was just too good to give away for near nothing, especially after all the work I had put into it. They all loved it, too, and tried to persuade me to reconsider. One who had helped with the restoration said that he would store it for me for free, in his garage.

The next day, I got back in touch with Melissa. I told her I had decided to have the mirror picked up from Christie's warehouse. I was unwilling to put it in a house sale, even a very good one, rather than the fine English furniture sale in October, where it would have exposure to a wide audience.

To my surprise (and dismay) Melissa instantly changed her

mind. To make me happy and spare me the trouble and expense of moving the piece again, she would place it in the October sale. She was being very earnest. Feeling slightly better, though confused, I finally said okay. Melissa is a first-rate copywriter. When I asked how she planned to handle the American versus English dilemma, her finesse put me at ease. "Believe me," she said, "we know we have to be very careful how we word these things. I plan to say, '*Interestingly*, the mirror is constructed of *Pinus strobus* (North American white pine), which may indicate American manufacture.'"

When the Christie's catalog came out, all I noticed was how great the photograph of the mirror looked, the gilt frame popping out of a black background, to its right the Thomas Johnson plate. Then came the call from Ron De Silva, the dealer who had helped broker the sale of the dolphin sofa. He had seen the mirror in the catalog and knew I owned it.

Christie's had made a mistake concerning dimensions, he said. The mirror was listed as 247 inches or 20.5 feet instead of 8.5 feet high. The width was off, too, although this error was minor in comparison—approximately half a foot. In centimeters, however, the dimensions were accurate.

Because its size had always been one of the mirror's main deterrents, I was not pleased. In addition, as its theme was the Fox and the Grapes, it was puzzling that the four-legged creature sitting at the base was described as a howling wolf.

In Rhode Islandese, De Silva asked, "What the hell is an American mirror doing in an English sale? And the provenance. My God! The Woods-Gerry Mansion!"

Only someone from Providence would take that to heart, I thought.

"That mirror belongs back in Providence," he declared. "They [Christie's] should have at least put it in an American sale," he said.

"Why?" I asked, knowing the answer.

"Money!" he answered. "I really have no idea what they are thinking," Ron continued. He added that he had called the auction house to complain, to no avail. After speaking to Ron, John

Hays called the Rhode Island School of Design Museum to see if there were interest in buying the mirror for Woods-Gerry, which the school still owned. No was their answer. They already had enough mirrors and didn't have room.

Once I sold the mirror, I figured I would never see it again. Was there more yet to find out? Had I not looked in all the right places? With such thoughts, I shot back up to Providence three weeks before the auction was to take place. Over the years, I had become familiar with almost every branch of the Brown and Woods families. Since my initial research at the historical society, the manuscript collection had been reorganized. Helen Abbott Washburn, Abby Woods's eldest daughter, had donated the bulk of the Woods papers, which I had not thoroughly looked through.

At my request, Karen, a research assistant, delivered Helen Washburn's personal file marked "Inventory" to my table. I felt Helen, the self-appointed custodian of family papers, had been overzealous in her donations. For instance, letters from her grandchildren at summer camp had been deposited. Among the papers were articles of interest, though. I savored people's sentimental attachment to heirlooms. Small envelopes from 1894 in Anne Brown Francis Woods's hand were addressed to Helen. Inside were notes that told the tale of objects she had either inherited or purchased herself. Helen was assigned the responsibility of handing down these heirlooms to the next generation. Among the treasures was an embroidered cashmere shawl from the East, a wedding gift from Nicholas Brown I to his wife, Ann Carter. It had arrived aboard the ship the *Ann and Hope* in 1790. A jet chain with balls and diamonds and a coral necklace Anne Woods had bought on her first trip to Naples, in 1852, were mentioned, as were an assortment of ladies' fans from France and a Carter family silver loving cup, all from 1788. There, too, was a ring belonging to Joseph Brown's daughter, Eliza, which purportedly had once been owned by Marie Antoinette.

In 1950, when Helen Abbott Washburn was seventy-six years

old, she began to assemble and distribute the heirlooms. She never called an appraiser to guide her. No sums could be attached to what she called simply "remembrances." Helen had her own way of doing things. "All things in the house have markers and stickers," she wrote in pencil on a plain sheet of white stationery. A painting of Governor John Francis and John Brown's maple armchair were meant for her son Jack. Nicholas Brown's bed and inlaid sideboard were left to her grandson Kenny. "Maurice," she wrote, of her mentally handicapped son, "must have anything to make him happy." Nicholas Brown's secretary was left to Helen's only daughter, who ended up predeceasing her.

Wait a minute, I thought. How many secretaries did Nicholas Brown have beside the one that sold at Christie's for $12.1 million? Apparently the answer was "a few." I wondered how the auction houses would go about promoting another. The whale oil label had been used too often.

I had looked haphazardly through Carter Woods's files when beginning my research. Now I decided they warranted another pass. Sidetracked again from my search for the mirror, I began to examine Carter's personal history. His obituary photograph must have been taken forty years before his death: young, his hair dark, his face a bit round. Large, intelligent eyes looked straight ahead from beneath thick brows.

Carter turned out to have been an oddball. Here was a man born to the Victorian age, devouring literature concerned with psychology. The brooding bachelor pondered the source of his melancholic moods. Winter evenings he could be found in the library, seated on a heavily trimmed chair beside a fire, pipe at hand, under the spell of titles such as *Alterations of Personality* by the French psychologist Alfred Binet.

A pampered Victorian from a well-traveled family, Carter found life in Providence static. "I have puzzled to know why it is that the people whom I used to like so much no longer interest me," he wrote in 1897, at the age of forty-seven. "It must be that I have grown tired of the same people day to day without much variation in the scenes." He missed the company of men of his own generation. "If I could only," he thought, "have a few merry times with some of my old Hopkins friends, I think I should enjoy life more." In the meantime, Carter could not delude himself that any of the four girls he was seeing concurrently interested him. Alone, he missed their company; with them, he was bored. "What does it matter to me whether May went downtown today, or Helen took a walk, or Hallie played golf?" he complained. "If they have a good time I'm glad, only do not bother me with the details. If I could only meet some new attractive people I should feel the same burst of energy as before."

Carter's lifelong interest in photography led to his installing a darkroom in one of the underused rooms in the Prospect Street mansion. In the 1920s he was also communicating with the Museum of Fine Arts in Boston to determine who may have made a silver pitcher inherited from his mother's side and what city it came from. He was obsessed with the pitcher for about three years. I found the process strikingly similar to my mirror escapade and followed with interest as he called on silver specialists, sending them photographs and getting nowhere.

Carter Woods did not see much to celebrate about the Irish on Saint Patrick's Day as stated in a letter to his favorite niece, Helen, on March 17, 1927. "The Irish," he wrote, "are a treacherous race, unreliable, hot headed, unreasoning, and without judgment or balance. There may be exceptions, but they are rare and none have come under my observations. It is claimed that there are Irishmen with gentlemanly instincts, but I have never happened to meet any. The first and only great Irishman I ever knew was Charles Stewart Parnell, who wanted to marry your mother. In the end he ran true to his people's form, and proved to be a bad lot, although he laid the beginning of Ireland's Independence. You see I have little use for the Irish, although I may be tarred with that brush, remotely."

I found Carter's personality amusing but had to get going again with the investigation of where my mirror could have been made. In a box containing Carter Woods's personal papers, I discovered a folder marked "Household Inventory." There, in a subfolder, was a tag with the words *Picture Frames and Paintings Certificates of Authenticity from 1843–1916.* Carter's handsome script recorded information he had found written on the backs of family portrait picture frames. Carter noted: "On the John Brown Francis and Abby Francis Woods portraits are small printed labels bearing the following: WHOLESALE AND RETAIL LOOKING GLASS AND PICTURE FRAME MANUFACTORY, JAS. S. EARLE & SON, No. 816 Chestnut Street nearly opposite Girard House, Philadelphia." He goes on to note: "On Mrs. Woods' Healy portrait is the following label: JAMES S. EARLE, 212 Chestnut Street, opposite Girard House, Philadelphia." (So, after two years at 816 Chestnut Street, the frame makers apparently moved down the street to this last address in 1857, and there they remained until 1906.)

In all the years I had been sifting through the Brown and Woods family papers at the Historical Society, this was the first and only time the term *looking glass* had appeared in an inventory. This seemed very promising indeed.

I clicked on Google and searched *James Earle*. What appeared was an article on the American portrait painter Thomas Sully, written for the Wooster Art Gallery. What I learned from it was this: In 1819, James Earle, a gilder and carver, and Thomas Sully, a painter, started Earle and Sully's Exhibition Gallery on Chestnut Street in Philadelphia. Sully painted the pictures, and Earle made the frames and handled the books. The partnership lasted twenty-seven years. When the gallery closed in 1846, Earle and his son, James S. Earle, proceeded to open yet another frame shop, and as time went on, this establishment—already known for its picture frames from the early days with Sully—began to be known as well for the elaborate Rococo revival mirrors they were manufacturing. The enterprise lasted through the nineteenth century and was sponsored by a group of robber barons.

Earle and Sully were also connected with George Peter Alexander Healy, the Healy mentioned in Carter's inventory. A leading portraitist of the time, Healy painted all three of the portraits (two of the Woodses, and one of Governor John Brown Francis) that Carter had described.

Originally from Boston, Healy had, by the time he was eighteen, displayed such aptitude for portrait painting that it attracted the attention of the daughter of the famous portrait painter Gilbert Stuart. Jane, too, painted portraits, and she urged Healy to move to Philadelphia, where her Rhode Island–born father had a studio. In Philadelphia, Jane introduced Healy to the man who would become his lifelong mentor: Thomas Sully. Healy moved to Europe in 1834 and spent most of the rest of his life working there, but he traveled back to America now and then to paint the portraits of the rich and famous, and he continued to use Sully's studio to do so. (In his illustrious career he would paint John Quincy Adams, Abraham Lincoln, Henry Wadsworth Longfellow, Nathaniel Hawthorne, and John James Audubon.)

Thinking back, I recalled that the Brown family had also employed Sully. He had been commissioned to paint Nicholas Brown II's posthumous portrait in the 1840s, a picture that is owned by Butler Hospital, an institution for the mentally ill that Brown funded. And in the Providence home of one of the Brown/Woods descendants I visited, a man by the name of Ken Washburn, I'd seen an 1820s portrait of a young Governor John Brown Francis that looked as if it could have been painted by Sully—or possibly even by Gilbert Stuart. Governor Francis had been married to Nicholas Brown II's daughter, and had fathered Anne Brown Woods. This portrait was stored in the Washburns' attic (along with some of Healy's work), and was still in its original frame. It was gilded, an ogee in shape, with small, compressed grapes and leaves squished into the four corners.

Since John Francis was born in Philadelphia and often visited the city during his lifetime, evidence was mounting that the family had shopped in the City of Brotherly Love for a very long time. More specifically, it was becoming clear that the Browns and Woodses had known the painters and framers working in Earle's studio. And it is not at all far-fetched to assume that they bought a few mirrors there, too. Studying illustrated books on nineteenth-century mirrors, I found that the Rococo revival mirror I had bought at the Clayville auction and sold to a decorator looked much like the models offered at Earle's shop in the mid–nineteenth century. But it wasn't until I came upon Earle's "fireman's trophy frame" that I discovered a true relative of my Fox and Grapes mirror.

I spotted it in an article by Margery Schwartz in the Decem-

ber 1997 issue of *Picture Framing Magazine* about a traveling
frame show called "2001: A Frame Odyssey." Studying the photo
of the mirror, I was amazed to see two funny little carved men
carrying axes and other firefighting tools. The delightful folk
art characters looked as if they could have climbed right off
my Fox and Grapes mirror and onto this one, finding a spot
beneath the carving of Poseidon, the sea god, seated grandly at
the crest of the mirror, holding his trident and pouring water
from a jug.

The mirror had been commissioned in 1856 for the Friendship Firehouse in Alexandria, Virginia, and was now in the collection of the Virginia Lyceum and displayed in the Friendship
Firehouse Museum. The caption under the photo read: "Fireman's Trophy Frame, c. 1856; Fabricated by James S. Earle and
Son, Philadelphia (attri.). Pine, composition, wire and 23k gold
leaf, 45" x 25"." While the scale of this mirror was very different
from that of mine, the treatment of the figures—their forearms
and gestures, the shape of the tiny hands, the way the fingers
were carved and held tools—was almost identical. It seemed clear
to me that they were either carved by the same person or by two
carvers who worked together (or one for the other).

The likeness didn't stop there. The base of each was American
white pine. The carvings of twisted grapes and leaves on the fireman's frame were in composite (a form of casting material, usually plaster), and attached to the frame by wires. These carvings
shared the primitive aspect of those on the Fox and Grapes mirror. The dark gray color of the bole used as the ground for the
gold leaf was the same shade on both frames. (Black or gray
clay—versus red—was routinely used on American mirror frames
and Empire furniture after 1810, until the third quarter of the
nineteenth century.)

I was now convinced that the Fox and Grapes had been made
in Earle's studio at some point between the 1830s and the 1840s
and that Anne Brown Francis Woods had more than likely inherited it from one of her grandfather Nicholas Brown's homes—
either from the house on Benefit Street in Providence (where a
very expensive mirror was listed as hanging in the southeast parlor) or from the Turks Head estate in Warwick—the Italianate

mansion that Anne owned jointly with her uncle Carter Brown. Why did it seem out of the question that the Gerrys had brought the mirror with them to 62 Prospect Street? Because it had become clear that—as dealers and experts had intuited from the start—Philadelphia was my mirror's city of origin. And while Senator Gerry represented the state of Rhode Island, he was New York–born, and the Gerrys, from my research, shopped mainly in New York and in Europe. Whoever purchased the Fox and Grapes mirror was a loyal patron of Philadelphia artists and the craftsmen working there.

William Adair was mentioned in the article. In the past, we had spoken on the phone about gilding. Bill's background in frames is impressive. He worked for ten years as a frame conservator for the Smithsonian Institution and won the Rome Prize in Design for his studies on the subject. He has published numerous articles, is a frequent speaker on the museum lecture circuit, and is president and founder of the Decorative Arts Trust International Institute for Frame Study. His firm in Washington, D.C., is called Gold Leaf Studios.

When I asked Bill if he knew anything about the Earle frame makers of Philadelphia, he quickly said yes. "They made the firehouse trophy frames. I love those frames. The figures of people are so eccentric, quirky, and charming." That said it all.

I told him about my mirror frame and how similar the figurative carvings were to those of the frames illustrated in the Wooster Art Gallery article, and I told him that Earle frames were mentioned in the Woods inventory. Based on the fact that my mirror was fully carved out of wood and not composite, Bill offered a theory of his own: "Maybe you have one of the very early Earle frames [meaning when Earle worked with Sully, before 1846]. You know, the Earles were in business for a long time." He had three more photographs of the fireman's trophy frame at his office, he said. Anxious to compare more images of Earle's handiwork to the carvings on my mirror frame, I set up an appointment to meet Adair the following week in Washington.

Gold Leaf Studios is a large brick four-story carriage house in the D.C. museum district. In every room and corridor rows of period frames of various sizes, styles, and finishes are hung on warm-toned walls. Another floor had been partially constructed over rafters. Sections were created out of two-by-fours for enormous plaster pier mirrors in need of restorations.

The light was subtle and the atmosphere peaceful. I asked Bill how he managed his own ideas about his field if they didn't conform to those of the academic community. "I keep my head low," he said, laughing. I sat in a frayed upholstered wing chair opposite my host, who sat behind his desk. He flipped through the photographs I had brought of my mirror. What was the color of the clay used as the base for the gold leaf in the Fox and Grapes mirror, and how was the back constructed? he asked. After answering these questions, I asked if he thought my frame was American.

"Definitely," he replied. "It is made out of American white pine and it has American-type carvings." Whether these were by Earle he was not certain, but he was not ruling out the possibility. The only Earle frames he had seen were the firehouse ones, but he reiterated that the Earles had been in business long before those were created. Based on the Woodses' purchase of so many other frames from Earle's shop, Bill thought it very likely my mirror may have been made there as well. Frame studies was a new area, but at such conferences, he had found fresh information slow to surface; the same topics recurred, he said.

It was late afternoon when I left Gold Leaf Studios. In heavy rain, I hailed a cab to the National Gallery, where the largest collection of Thomas Sully's paintings is kept. Might any original Earle frames still be on them? I knew the frames on portraits were plain but often had carved composition designs in the corners. These pressed carvings of fruit or leaves, popular in the 1830s, were what I was looking for. I wanted to see how closely they resembled the elements on my mirror.

Just around closing, I appeared before the information desk. Which room held Sully's work? I asked. I was on the right floor, the woman behind the desk said, but every Sully in the collection had been taken down, she was not sure why. When I explained it was not the paintings I wanted to see but the frames, she made a call to the basement. The conservator there was not familiar with the Sully frames, nor did the name Earle ring a bell with him. Defeated, I went to the cafeteria and moped over a cup of coffee.

That night I stayed with friends in Washington. I simply could not stop wondering about the mirror and had a bad case of seller's remorse. I wanted to snatch my mirror from the Christie's sale but didn't know how to do so at this late date. Melissa Gagan was doing me a favor by putting it in her best fall auction.

William Jay Iselin's was just the kind of impartial advice I needed. Not a close friend, Will was more of an acquaintance from my years in the antiques business. I respected his judgment, and his love of art and antique furniture was genuine. An honest businessman with highly refined taste, Will lives in Paris and is the founder of an international art advisory firm.

After graduating with honors in fine arts from Harvard, he began his antiques career in Christie's American Decorative Arts Department. He became senior vice president of the European and English Furniture Department in New York, then in London, and when Christie's opened its galleries in Paris, in 1995, Will was named director of the European Furniture Department, supervising hundreds of auctions throughout England, the United States, and Europe.

Despite Will's blue-blood background and years of recognition in the art field, he is refreshingly modest. His wry sense of humor is mixed with a contagious optimism. Will's main objective in his career is to have fun with it. As an art adviser and not a dealer, he works tirelessly for his clients, an antiques detective who seems to know everyone and where to find anything of the best quality anywhere in the world. If the search for just the right object turns out to be unfruitful, Will simply moves on with perfect detachment. Particularly in this last respect, I wanted to learn from him.

The next morning, from my friend's house on the Potomac

River, I called Will. He was at his Right Bank office and seemed
glad to hear from me (that cordial charm). Will had patiently
endured my mirror saga when our paths crossed in Paris. I half
knew the subject would rattle him even before I dialed. With my
D.C. hosts' dog barking in the background, I explained that I
had placed the mirror in Christie's Fine English Furniture Sale
and now wanted to withdraw it. What would the penalties be? I
sheepishly asked. I told him how Christie's had incorrectly published the size, that they had thrown out the $2,500 crate I had
had made for it, that I was considering donating the mirror to
RISD, that Bill Rieder at the Met thought it was American, that
I believed I was close to determining its maker, and last, that I
had discovered that *no one* really knows much about mirrors. I
thought it prudent not to mention my mystical alliance with the
Woodses. I was sure this would cause Will to write me off as a
lunatic.

It took him just seconds to image the mirror on his computer
screen. How much would I have to pay Christie's to withdraw it
from the sale? I asked again. "Ten percent," Will said. He paused
for a moment before asking the question that puzzled him most.
"What is it with you and this mirror anyway?" To this I had no
logical answer, and he did not wait to hear it. Speaking so rapidly
I dared not interrupt, Will began to address every lame point I
used as an excuse not to sell the mirror.

"Maryalice," he said, "you are right that no one knows all that
much about mirrors. First of all, Bill Rieder doesn't know it's
American for sure. So what, anyway! Look, it is too bad that
Christie's threw out the crate, but they do not have room to store
such things, and furthermore that is not their responsibility. If
you withdraw the mirror now, you will have to pay ten percent
plus commission and insurance, the photo expenses of $900 on
top of that. Then, with it out of there, you are going to have storage fees again. Say you donate it to RISD. Even if they were willing to take it, the best you will get is a $25,000 tax deduction,
and, really, come on, what would that do for you? It certainly
doesn't help the sale that Christie's had the size wrong in the catalog, but what does it matter? *Listen. To. Me.* What you are doing
just doesn't make sense! Look," he said, "I hate to say this to you,

but I feel I must. Here are the facts. It is a nineteenth-century mirror that has been regilded, and the glass has been replaced. *Get real!* I could see it if it were an eighteenth-century mirror worth lots of money. *But. It's. Not!*" Speaking slowly and firmly, he delivered his final advice. "Maryalice. Leave the mirror in the auction," and then, raising his voice, he added rapidly, *"And pray to God it sells!"*

I felt relieved that someone had made the decision. For me, asking Will's advice was more like a toss of a coin, whereas he based his assessment on raw facts. "Okay. Okay," I relented.

When I got back to New York, I had an e-mail from Will. "Sorry I was so brusque, but you know I meant well! Good luck, and let's hope the mirror sells for lots of money!" I smiled at the thought of Will's not-so-investment-driven record of antiques bought for himself. Once, when I was in Paris shopping for a New York client, I stayed in a hotel on the Left Bank without Internet connections. Will offered to let me use the computer in his home office. His apartment has a view of the Eiffel Tower and is spacious enough for him to live with three children and their nanny. The rooms contain a superb collection of artwork and antiques. Hudson River landscapes inherited from his family and French still lifes (one of tulips and goldfish swimming in a glass bowl stuck in my mind) were everywhere. Aubusson carpets covered the floors, woven in rich blues, crocus yellow, and vibrant reds. French and English eighteenth-century furniture was placed around the rooms, as well as pieces not so precious.

One of the days I was there, he walked in after having just stopped by the Drouot auction house. He carried a paper bag, the contents of which he could not wait to show me. "Well, what do you think?" he asked, beaming. He held up a mahogany French Empire mantel clock missing a bit of its molding and one of its tiny and intricately cast bronze astrological dials. It was indeed marvelous, but as a restorer I knew, but did not point out, that he would never find anyone with the skill to replace the sign of Virgo, numeral 6 on the face. His other purchases of the day included a dozen or more identical silver saltcellars with blue glass liners, not so remarkable or valuable. In response to my quizzical expression at the number, he said he was all out of salt holders for his apartment, and those he could not use would always make handy gifts. It was comforting to know that even the pros can get caught up in the undertow of an auction.

Thanks to Will, my mind was slightly more at ease on auction day than it might have been. I knew it was not the best time to be selling my mirror. Styles were moving in their predictable twenty-year cycles, and the historical revival popular since the 1980s was quieting down. Modern design, especially retro twentieth-century furniture, was back. Chrome was in. Gold was out. The antiques business was changing, and I was growing a little tired of the politics and the market in general. The theme of the sour grapes now hit home. I half convinced myself I didn't want the mirror anymore and began not to care if I ever saw it again. The fruits it bore, the allure of its former owners, I believed no longer interested me. There was always something else to fall in love with.

On the afternoon of the Christie's auction, I called the automated auction hotline to hear how much the mirror had brought. "Lot number seventy-six did not sell," the computerized voice announced. I sat at my desk in a daze. The mirror had not made the reserve. I pressed in numbers of some other lots. Other high-estimated mirrors and furniture also featured in full-page photographs remained unsold. Even pieces without reserves went below the low sides of their estimated prices. The auction had been a bomb. I was thrilled.

I called Christie's to find out how much the fiasco was going to cost me. They said they would be happy to put the mirror in a future sale. I was not interested. The mirror was going to follow me to the grave, it seemed. In the end I came out of the experience relatively unscathed, the penalties not as high as they would have been for withdrawing earlier. And there was a place for the mirror to go until I could figure things out. My friend's offer to store it in upstate New York was still good.

In the meantime, I went to the Christie's warehouse in Queens to see if the mirror had made it off the auction floor in one piece. As workers wheeled it toward me on a long wooden dolly, I felt my entire body soften at the sight of the glittering, playful figures.

My attraction to the Victorians had begun in childhood, and through them my earliest connections to art were founded. There was a hauntedness to the citizens of that era; their dark clothes, gothic architecture, spidery handwriting, all these things inspired me. One of my lifelong occupations has been to visualize the way the land looked then, miles of farmland with its bordering shores full of vessels, powered by sails. I admired the Victorian urge to preserve heirlooms, which could be interpreted as a lesson in the importance of memory. For them, moving forward meant bringing the past along, whereas our modern psychology is focused on living fully in the present.

One reason the mirror's investigation had taken me so long had to do with the journey into one of my favorite periods in history. Letting go for me, I suppose, would have meant ending my relationship with the Woodses, and when I got right down to it, I liked having them around. The mirror had led me to a variety of speculative possibilities. Its history was now part of my own. Was it made in Earle's workshop in Philadelphia? The striking similarity to the fireman's trophy mirror and the swirl of other factors made me confident that it was. The tobacco heiress Doris Duke had an embroidered pillow in her house in Newport good for summing up provenance and attribution as well as any other of life's questions never tidily resolved. It said, "The answer is maybe, and that's final."

There was perhaps nothing so remarkable about the Woods family. Marshall and Anne Woods, who persuaded their daughter not to marry Charles Parnell on grounds of his not having a public name, have been forgotten. The Woodses were merely representative characters of a certain class in a particular period of New England history. They were like characters in a novel one becomes attached to. Yet it was that moment in time which had made me love everything about the Woodses and the things they owned.

In the Christie's warehouse full of prized objects, I marveled at the mystery of why we are affected by one work of art and not another. Despite the use of technology in determining value, art's effect cannot ever be explained factually. It is really very simple. If a piece has life, people respond to it. What takes place between artist and viewer is a highly personal and mysterious experience. Thinking is not required.

What was the point of hunting for clues that could lead to a particular certainty or, worse, trying to convince the art world there was something redeemable about what I appreciated and others did not? I did not need experts to define what art meant to me. I was on the wrong track when I brought authorities into that process. I had been, as Anne Woods would have put it, "a poor deluded mortal." I had never wanted to be part of a team that examined finishes under microscopes or wished I had earned a doctorate in American decorative arts. What did it really matter if my mirror was worth more than a policeman's oak refrigerator and far less than John Brown's Newport kneehole desk, neither of which would have excited me to own?

The American abstract painter Agnes Martin wrote, "The response to art is the real art field." The artist, who used Victorian poetry, Buddhist discipline, and Transcendentalism in her work and life, wrote, "The value of art is in the observer. When you find out what you like, you are really finding out about yourself." Her philosophy resonated with me. After years of investigation, there was really nothing to be proved that could enhance the experience of seeing something I found beautiful. Everything I needed to know about the Fox and Grapes mirror, I knew the moment I first saw it.

CHAPTER SIXTEEN

The Fox Gets the Grapes

There was something the Woodses and I shared besides the mirror. All of us had spent time living in European cities and entertained the possibility of becoming permanent expatriates. This in itself is not so remarkable. Many travelers have felt this way. The idea of reinventing life for oneself, the freeing aspect of anonymity, adds to the illusion that you can change who you are. But for the Woodses and me, this fantasy was not an option. Once its roots get used to the soil, a plant may not thrive when moved. We were native Rhode Islanders and would always return.

I had experienced the best of Block Island in the first half of my life but came to see its character, like that of so many places, eroded by tourism and overbuilding. In summer the constant run of ferries from the mainland deposited thousands of tourists on a fragile island. Screeching mopeds took over the roads, while outdoor music from dozens of bars provided a new background. A town council composed largely of citizens in the building trades was unsurprisingly ineffective in enforcing zoning. There was even discussion of a golf course. It was beginning to look a lot like suburbia.

The town government applied for every grant available, all of which came with concessions. The independent philosophy of life upon which the island had been founded was long gone. I decided it was time to leave if I did not want to spend the rest of my life grumbling about the changes. I felt guilty selling inherited land and a house my brother Bobby had lovingly designed for me, but the place was feeling claustrophobic. With my mother's blessing, I put my house on the market.

I knew it would not take long to sell. Every room claimed views of the ocean, rocky coves, and clay cliffs. Old Harbor Point is a famous fishing spot. Before the sun rises and just after dusk in spring and fall, men in waders stand on wave-splashed rocks to catch record striped bass. From my porch at night, I could see the Newport Bridge lit up like a diamond necklace across Block Island Sound.

It was a blissful place off-season and when the wind was not howling, which was frequently not the case. Its exposed northeast site met with storms that made the whole house shake. Windows buckled, and anything not securely nailed or tied was likely to blow off and float away. I wanted my next house to be near the ocean, but not right on it. There was a reason why the old-timers never built near the beach. I wanted to live in a protected valley where there was a good chance I could plant trees and see them grow.

I was happy to be single; I did not have to consult anyone about the major changes I was preparing to make. But this was not to say there were no constraints on my decision. For two years my mirror had been swathed in Bubble Wrap in my friend's garage. A home for both object and owner would have to be found.

After combing the Connecticut coast and the Hudson Valley, even scrolling the Internet to sites as far away as Santa Barbara, California, I realized I could never leave Rhode Island. On Aquidneck Island, the towns of Newport, Middletown, and Portsmouth had the historic architecture I craved, but it appeared unlikely I could find a house there restored to my standards. I was resigned that, when I found something, I would have to do the work myself.

For several months my heart had been set on an Italianate house built in 1848 in Newport, its interior spared renovation by the poverty of its past owners. The house had a soul, and the mirror could be hung with room to spare on any first-floor wall. As negotiations dragged on, I changed my mind. It was too close to Bellevue Avenue, almost always thick with traffic. My Newport broker had not shown me anything else appealing, so I looked around myself from my apartment in New York. On my computer screen appeared a stone Cotswold-style gatehouse, offered by her company. I recognized it immediately as being on an estate in Middletown called Gray Craig. I had been there before.

The year was 1986. I was living in New York City, and Christie's asked me if I would be interested in doing some restoration work for them in Rhode Island. The Gray Craig estate was for sale, and Christie's had been chosen to auction the contents of the main house. I spent over a week there that June, sprucing up the antique furniture for a heavily advertised on-site event. During that time I learned of the property's past owners.

In the 1880s, a group of Newport robber barons bought the seventy-seven-acre parcel of land to use as a hunting preserve. It was then called Gray Craig Park and was amply stocked with wild game. It was sold in 1901 to Mr. and Mrs. Mitchell Clark of New York City, whose family fortune was made in the steel industry. They built a pudding-stone castle (complete with drawbridge), which was the appropriate setting to showcase their collection of armor. In 1915, Mr. and Mrs. Jordan Mott of Chicago bought the estate. Three years later it was gutted by fire. The site, being well known and near Newport, was not on the market long before it was scooped up by another wealthy American family.

In the early 1920s, the Van Beurens, heirs to Standard Oil, had hired the architect Harrie T. Lindeberg to scout locations and build them a house. Lindeberg had trained with the firm McKim, Mead, and White in New York City and had been commissioned by America's elite to create domestic, rustic-style houses of the Tudor genre. He persuaded his Rhode Island clients to buy the Gray Craig property, a dramatic setting for the five buildings he had sketched in his mind to be erected there.

The steep bluestone ledges on one side of the property lent

the perfect site for Lindeberg's designs, which resembled manor houses in rural English county seats and on the Normandy coast. Constructed of local materials, his buildings were elegant, sophisticated, and idiosyncratic.

On my Christie's mission in 1986, I passed a massive turreted structure built into a hill—Gray Craig's stable and garage, with living quarters for the help above and no apparent need to drive to a gas station what with pumps just outside. A rambling greenhouse attached to the stable rivaled in size the New York Botanical Garden's. The hothouse had once provided fresh flowers and fruit year-round, but now random branches seeking sun had broken through the glass panels. Wedged into a valley and cradled by bluestone ledges stood a pink stucco house called the Engineer's Cottage.

The terrain was so inviting I parked my pickup on the roadside and made my way to the main house on foot. Budding trees and mowed paths leaked their scents into the air. In a clearing another stone house with dormered windows shared the terracotta-tiled roofing of the other buildings. This was Kennel Cottage, where the family's Pekingese dogs had once lived. Just beyond lay fruit orchards planted in rows to either side of a tri-arched pavilion where the cherished pets were trained and exhibited. The roof of the pavilion had caved in; the oak beams lay on the floor amid huge plant containers resting on their sides.

The buildings melded seamlessly with their terrain, lending an organic unity even to the enormous manor house poised on the highest hill. As with many revivalist buildings from its day, the house's interior was an eclectic mix of highbrow Georgian, medieval English, French Normandy, and American colonial. French doors opened onto the slate terrace. Elephantine yews and clipped topiaries grew close to the house in semiformal intimacy. Peacock statues recalling eighteenth-century porcelain were placed at either end of a balustraded retaining wall. From the patio, a broad lawn framed by bright green deciduous trees rolled toward a large pond where swans floated in a line. Beyond a marsh in the distance lay a beach with a white cliff and natural breakwater that jutted out into the Atlantic Ocean: Purgatory

Chasm. It was easy to imagine having been transported to a baronial park in another century. I went back to the truck for my camera. Never expecting to return, I wanted to record these last vestiges of Scott Fitzgerald's American era.

I did not attend the auction of Gray Craig. I had heard that it was sold to a real estate investment company but that the townspeople were attached to the land. Many had trespassed there as children and teenagers and wanted the site to be preserved. A conservation-minded family purchased the land from the initial investors. Plans for a Gray Craig Association were approved. Lindeberg's buildings would be saved and sold separately. Large lots were donated to the abutting Norman Bird Sanctuary, and the town acquired the rest for open space, adding to an already established wildlife corridor.

There was no way to know in 1986 that just shy of twenty years later, I would find the Gray Craig gatehouse while scrolling through real estate websites. A house where deed restrictions prohibited large-scale development was a dream, not to mention that it was an English stone house set near a stream, and so close to the ocean one could hear the surf. I concurred with Anne Woods on copies. If the real thing were impossible to procure, a beautiful reproduction was the next best thing. My Rococo English revival mirror would hang in a Tudor revival cottage.

My brother Bill still worked in real estate and still coached me on money matters. When I told him about the gatehouse, he lent me his advice. "Don't let the Realtor at Gustave White know you love the house. It's an awkward situation. Remember, real estate agents work for the seller first. Any enthusiasm will be reported back to them immediately. And don't make any offers before you have spoken to me."

My friend Susan and my sister-in-law Heather went with me to view the property. The listing agent, whom I had never met, was in the office on Bellevue Avenue. He might have spotted us pulling up to the curb in my mother's Block Island car, an old, rusted-out Plymouth sedan. I looked like a swamp Yankee dressed for yard work. Glancing at me with barely concealed contempt, he clearly thought I was not a serious buyer for such an expensive property. Walking up to his desk, I asked him if I might take a look at the gatehouse in Middletown. No, he replied flatly. He was too busy. I insisted. He riffled through his desk. Without a word and with his eyes kept on the computer screen, he held the keys in the air for my agent. The four of us headed out the door.

Following the agent in my car, I arrived at the marked entrance. The long driveway was lined with trees beginning to show their autumn colors. Enchanted by the beauty and mystery of the place, we all crawled from the car in slow motion. Susan and Heather stayed together while I entered the house with the broker. Through a diamond-leaded-glass window, I could see Susan in the courtyard, jumping up and down and raising her fists like a sports fan at a stadium. Heather, an avid gardener, was gazing up at a holly tree with a fond expression generally reserved for babies and puppies. As for me, I had already compromised myself with the broker, who picked up on my displays of delight like a dog in heat. I flashed back to Bill's earlier warning and realized I would be financially punished.

When the agent rushed off to another appointment, the three of us stayed behind in the yard. It was unanimous. This was the perfect match of person to house. Susan, the English professor, who compared everything in life to books she had read, crooned, "It is soooo Virginia Woolf!" Standing on a hill in front of the house, I could see Paradise Rocks. This was where the nineteenth-century American Luminists all came to capture the serene light of sky and shoreline. These were my favorite American painters. The Woodses were among their patrons. Where my gatehouse now stands was once a house where John La Farge, the nineteenth-century American painter, muralist, stained-glass maker, and travel writer, lived. From this very spot he ventured outside to draw and paint dozens of local landscapes. The views he captured of ledges and water remain almost unchanged to this day.

Seduced by the land's romantic past, I ended up paying full price for the house I found out later had lingered on the market for five years without a single offer close to the asking price. After the closing, with keys in hand, I entered the house by myself. Within minutes it became very apparent why I had not been allowed to stay too long the two times the house had been shown to me. Neither love nor money had touched it in ages. I was in for a mammoth restoration project.

The renovation began in November 2005. There was so much work to do I left New York to oversee the progress. Tradesmen took over, hacking and drilling into the three-foot-thick walls. One late January afternoon, I left the Portuguese work crew in plaster dust to walk to the beach and remind myself why I had moved there. Two houses down from my driveway on Paradise Avenue I spotted Mike Corcoran. He was unfolding himself from his car, plainly exhausted from a day's work at his auction house in Portsmouth.

"Hi, Mike," I hollered, waving from the curb.

"Maryalice," he said cheerfully, "how ya doin?" I told him I was now his neighbor. "I'm sorry my voice is a little hoarse," Mike said. "We had an auction today."

"That's right. I forgot about it. How did it go?"

"Pretty well," Mike replied. "Better than expected. We got $45,000 for a chaise longue made in 1780 or something."

"Where was that?" I asked. "I didn't see it at the preview."

"You didn't see it? It was right near the front door! And we sold a highboy for $15,000. So, overall, the day went pretty good." Mike broke off to pat his two waiting Airedales. "By the way," he asked, "whatever happened to that sofa you bought at Tracy's? How much was it sold for, and who bought it?"

I knew Mike knew who bought it, because he never forgets a name. But he did not necessarily know where it had ended up.

"Leigh Keno bought it from me and sold it to the Detroit Institute for $160,000 to $190,000, I think."

Furrowing his brow, Mike thought for a moment. "Is that right? Well, you didn't pay that much for it, right?" I did not respond. He let it drop. "About Gray Craig," he said. "You know the Van Beurens hired Christie's to do the auction."

"Yes, I remember."

"Well," Mike continued, "I think Christie's made a big mistake in the way it was handled. People say I was just jealous the family didn't hire me. That is not true at all," he said, flicking his wrist. Standing still and looking at the sky, Mike thought back. Using his hands to mimic a frame, he began to fill the canvas of the auction setting as it would have been had he been in charge.

"In the main house there is a big terrace with a wide stairway in front that faces the pond and the ocean. They [Christie's] should have had a long, narrow tent going out to the lawn, where the audience would have been seated." Mike, an expert in crowd psychology, pointed out that when people are seated close together, it creates more energy and excitement, which in turn triggers faster and higher bidding. "There was a tent," Mike admitted, "but it was too big! And instead of bringing all those wonderful things outside and holding them up for people to see, everything was displayed on a video screen." He closed his eyes in disgust. The memory of a mismanaged sale two decades earlier still got under his skin.

From Mike's standpoint, technology was partially responsible for taking the fun out of his job. The country auctioneer liked to run his business the old-fashioned way, on a personal level. For Mike, money was not the motivating factor. The thrill of his job was in the exchange.

By spring my gatehouse renovation was almost complete. I had not thought much about the mirror—no doubt to the relief of my family, friends, and colleagues in the antiques business. My plan had been to send for it once the house was finished. In the meantime, people who had seen the cottage in its debased state were curious about the improvements.

On a rainy day, a group of real estate agents dropped in. I laughed when most of the women commented that everything looked so English. One woman separated from the others and stood below an arch in the hallway. Arms folded, she stared out a window to a walled courtyard. Her thoughts appeared miles away. As I passed by, her trance was broken. "You know," she murmured in a thick Irish brogue, "this place makes me a little homesick." She looked at the floor and rocked her body. "The house is so much like an Irish house."

The house and mirror, I realized, had a lot in common.

A few weeks later, Charlie, the mover who had carted my possessions from Block Island to storage, called me from upstate New York. "Mary, I'm here at your friend's house. I gotta tell you, this mirra is a monsta!"

"Charlie, I told you it was big. The question is, will it fit in your truck?"

"Yeh, we can do it." Charlie sighed. "But it's going to cost more than I quoted you. I'll need more guys just to lift this thing." The next day, the movers pulled into my driveway. I got a few hostile looks from the tattooed crew as they descended the rig's steps and went back to unfasten the container gate. Four men groaned as they lifted the mirror from the truck bed and hoisted it onto the two-by-fours that were screwed to the back so it could be picked up. "Where's this thing goin'?" a young one gasped. I hesitated to answer, as I was unsure it would make the turn from the hallway and through the narrow doors of the dining room.

"What is this anyway?" another chirped, gasping for breath. "Some kind of valuable antique or something?"

"It is an antique," I said, "but perhaps only valuable to me."

When they left, I looked at the mirror leaning on a wall in its new home. I recalled what Ron De Silva, the antiques dealer, had said when it was displayed at the Christie's auction: that it belonged back in Rhode Island. Could I interpret my own past and future in its gold-flecked symbols? Were there forces at work in its frame to determine its place? Could mirrors really serve as conduits to one's own ancestors? To all these questions the answer appeared to be yes.

It did seem odd that, with so much mobility at work in the world, I would come to live on the island my ancestors had first settled with Anne Hutchinson, before moving to Block Island. I wondered if there is something imprinted in our brains that draws us to the land our families were familiar with for generations. I could never be away from the ocean for long. I was addicted to island living and had been since childhood. The familiar line on the horizon, the indigenous plants and trees, the changing colors of the seasons were things that made me happy. Finding a place for the mirror brought me home again. The Woodses' spirits were back where they belonged, too.

The mirror's Rococo carvings had literally prophesied my new surroundings. The ivy was duplicated on my stone house's exterior. The cross-hatchings on the swags matched the shape of the leaded windows, and more fortuitous yet, the apple blossoms presently blooming in my small orchard were the essence of their carved counterparts. The whittled spilling water mimicked the flowing springs originating from the Maidford River that pass under and over the rock ledges at Gray Craig. The prominent goat stood in conveniently for my sun sign of Capricorn, while a gray vixen lived in a hedge of juniper. Wild grape vines wound around the brambles near a stream bordered by willows. The babies with baskets? Soon to arrive were my nephew's four-year-old daughter and six-year-old son from Boston. On Good Friday, when their mother opened the car's back door, two cherubs with stringy heads of hair stepped onto the pavement, in their hands holding empty baskets for Easter. The Rococo tableau was now complete.

Notes

All quotations by the Woods family, including the telegram from Charles Stewart Parnell to Abby Woods, were taken from their letters and diaries in Alva Woods Family Papers and Washburn Family Papers. Rhode Island Historical Society, Providence, R.I.

Correspondence (1860 to February 1864) from Marshall Woods to Richard Upjohn is from the Gowdy Collection, Providence Preservation Society, Providence, R.I.

Prologue
4 When raised, the mirror: encyclopedia.jrank.org/mic_mol/mirror_through_o _fr_mirror_mod_.html.

1. A Rhode Island Auction
15 "Furniture of quiet elegance": Charles F. Hummel, "Queen Anne and Chippendale Furniture in the Henry Francis du Pont Winterthur Museum, Part III." *Magazine Antiques* (January 1971): 98–107.

25 "From antiquity onward": David L. Barquist, Elisabeth Donaghy Garrett, and Gerald W. R. Ward, *American Tables and Looking Glasses in the Mabel Brady Garvan and Other Collections at Yale University* (New Haven, Conn.: Yale University Art Gallery, 1992).

2. Imagining the Past
27 "no authority was able": Arthur Kinoy, *The Real Mystery of Block Island: The Origins of the Island Colony* (Block Island Historical Society, 1961).

36 "the earliest known": Marlia Schwartz, "Discovery on Block Island: 2500-Year-Old Village Predates Agriculture." *Nor'easter: Magazine of the Northeast Sea Grant Programs* 2 (1990): 32–37.

3. A Hands-On Education

44 "bought for and sold": "Harold Sack, 89, Connoisseur of American Furniture, Dies," *New York Times*, July 10, 2000.

4. The Fox and Grapes Mirror

61 " 'You're not as mighty . . . always a lion' ": Aesop and Anne Gatti, *Aesop's Fables* (San Diego: Harcourt Brace Jovanovich, 1992).

61 "Rare is an offensive": Myrna Kaye, *Fake, Fraud, or Genuine? Identifying Authentic American Antique Furniture* (Boston: Little, Brown, Bulfinch Press, 1991).

62 "The art of carving": Jeanne Schinto, "The Art of Woodcarving in America: A Symposium." *Maine Antique Digest* (2007).

64 made of polished obsidian: Mark Pendergrast, *Mirror Mirror: A History of the Human Love Affair with Reflection* (New York: Basic Books, 2004).

64 Hathor, the goddess of love: Ibid., 116.

65 "image reflected in a mirror": Ibid., 9.

65 "full length mirror cost more": Ronald Phillips Ltd., *Reflections of the Past: Mirrors 1685–1815* (London: Ronald Phillips, 2004).

65 "were used as amulets": Pendergrast, *Mirror Mirror.*

66 "the masters of mirror making": Ibid.

66 "just as the samurai sword": Ibid.

68 "A Venetian mirror": 1911encyclopedia.org/mirror.

69 "Bigger is better . . . splitting the universe apart": Dennis Overbye, "Mirror, Mirror," *New York Times*, August 30, 2005, "Science: Space & Cosmos."

70 "a pair of eight-foot mirrors . . . displayed between windows": Barquist et al., *American Tables and Looking Glasses*, 13.

70 "Large expanses of plate glass": Ibid., 27–28.

71 "be of the solid kind": Ibid., 30.

71 For the popularity of fables as teaching devices, see David Stockwell, "Aesop's Fables on Philadelphia Furniture." *Magazine Antiques* (December 1951): 522–25.

72 "Tho' these designs were meant": Thomas Johnson, preface, *Collection of Designs* (London, 1758).

72 *Beware of flattery*: David Stockwell, "Aesop's Fables on Philadelphia Furniture," 522–25.

73 "The 1794 Philadelphia directory": Peter L. L. Strickland, "Documented Philadelphia Looking Glasses, 1800–1850." *Magazine Antiques* (April 1976): 784–94.

73 "James Reynolds, Carver and gilder": Luke Beckerdite, "Philadelphia Carving Shops: Part I: James Reynolds." *Magazine Antiques* (May 1984): 1120–33.

74 " 'a very large and genteel' ": Ibid.

76 "HERCULES COURTNEY, Carver and gilder": Luke Beckerdite, "Philadelphia Carving Shops: Part III: Hercules Courtenay and His School." *Magazine Antiques* (May 1987): 1044–63.

76 "the insidious arts": Clive Edwards, *Eighteenth-Century Furniture*. (Manchester, U.K.: Manchester University Press, 1996).

77 "the soul of the departed": Barquist et al., *American Tables and Looking Glasses*.

5. Provenance in the Marketplace

84 "every Saturday": James Blaine Hedges, *The Browns of Providence Plantations: Colonial Years* (Cambridge, Mass.: Harvard University Press, 1952), 199.

85 "a man of magnificent projects": *Dictionary of American Biography*, "John Brown of Providence Plantations."

85 "a person of extraordinary intelligence": Antoinette Forrester Downing and Helen Mason Grose, *Early Homes of Rhode Island* (Richmond, Va.: Garrett and Massie, 1937).

88 "that any article described . . . WHICH MAY CHANGE": Christie's catalog.

89 "In 1776, a letter": Wendy A. Cooper, "The Purchase of Furniture and Furnishings by John Brown, Providence Merchant. Part I: 1760–1788." *Magazine Antiques* (February 1973): 328–39.

90 "The only certain documentary reference": Christie's catalog.

90 "very highly valued at L95": *L* stands for "lawful money."

90 "introductory essay": Christie's Catalog.

93 "Last Tuesday evening . . . such a moving multitude": Letter from Eliza Goddard to Mrs. Abigail Goddard, January 7, 1788. Henry A. L. Brown Collection, mss 1031, box 1, folder 1, Rhode Island Historical Society.

95 "The house and everything": Martha W. Appleton, "Mrs. Vice-President Adams Dines with Mr. John Brown and Lady: Letters of Abigail Adams to Her Sister Mary Cranch." *Rhode Island History* (October 1942), 103.

6. John Brown's Mansion

101 "There is a kind": J. Carter Brown, interview, titled "The Art of Creating Culture," San Antonio, Tex., May 5, 2001, available at achievement.org/autodoc/page/bro1int_4.

102 "a looking glass . . . 16 pair cotton do": Nicholas Brown II, will and codicil #A6141, City of Providence Archives, City Hall, Providence, Rhode Island.

7. The Woodses: A Nineteenth-Century New England Family

110 "developed tastes that": James Blaine Hedges, *The Browns of Providence Plantations: Colonial Years* (Cambridge, Mass.: Harvard University Press, 1952).

110 They were part: James Blaine Hedges, *The Browns of Providence Plantations: The Nineteenth Century* (Providence, R.I.: Brown University Press, 1968).

111 "clothes were not ironed": Diary of Anne B. F. Woods, July 1848. Alva Woods Family Papers, series 3, mss 816, box 11, folder 6, Rhode Island Historical Society.

111 "Both of us are perfectly happy": Ibid.

112 "that his whole frame ached": Letter from Anne B. F. Woods to Rev. Alva Woods, July 30, 1848. Alva Woods Family Papers, series 1, mss 816, box 7, folder 553, Rhode Island Historical Society.

112 "I am almost frantic . . . wants his mother": Telegram from Anne B. F. Woods to Alva Woods, July 31, 1848. Alva Woods Family Papers, series 1, mss 816, box 7, folder 554, Rhode Island Historical Society.

112 "Dear ones": Ibid.

112 "I advise friction . . . 3 times a day": Letter from Dixie Crosby to Alva Woods, August 21, 1848. Alva Woods Family Papers, series 1, mss 816, box 7, folder 566, Rhode Island Historical Society.

112 "exquisite taste . . . lifted to a wall": Letter from Anne B. F. Woods to Almira Marshall Woods, April 1848. Alva Woods Family Papers, series 1, mss 816, box 10, folder 530, Rhode Island Historical Society.

113 "When I got married . . . love spirited and sick": Letter from Anne B. F. Woods to Almira Woods, October 1848. Alva Woods Family Papers, series 1, mss 816, box 7, folder 569, Rhode Island Historical Society.

113 "Anne was beautiful": Diary of Marshall Woods, January 2, 1849. Alva Woods Family Papers, series 3, mss 816, box 16, folder 5, Rhode Island Historical Society.

114 "Anne . . . is fatigued": Ibid., January 6, 1849.

114 "Anne has been through": Ibid.

115 "the surroundings seemed wonderfully strange": Diary of Anne B. F. Woods, January 15, 1852. Alva Woods Family Papers, series 3, mss 816, box 11, folder 7, Rhode Island Historical Society.

115 "horrid faces": Ibid.

115 "Mothering makes me extremely happy": Diary of Anne B. F. Woods, March 1852. Alva Woods Family Papers, series 3, mss 816, box 11, folder 7, Rhode Island Historical Society.

115 "motherless child": Ibid.

115 "cared for and loved": Ibid.

115 "Marshall was not nice": Ibid.

115 "I have much fatigue . . . bear it with patience": Ibid.

116 "dark, dismal and filthy": Ibid.

116 "foot passengers": Ibid.

116 "superb marble floors . . . have any idea of": Diary of Anne B. F. Woods, January 24, 1852. Alva Woods Family Papers, series 3, mss 816, box 11, folder 6, Rhode Island Historical Society.

117 "If only a greater part . . . stifling to me": Ibid.

117 "I have no knowledge": Charles Dickens, *Pictures from Italy* (1844; reprint, New York: Ecco Press, 1988).

118 "Oh what a filthy": Diary of Anne B. F. Woods, May 1852. Alva Woods Family Papers, series 3, mss 816, box 11, folder 6, Rhode Island Historical Society.

118 "the amount of trash": Ibid.

120 "I fear the wooden connection . . . the walls were up?": Anita Glass, "Early Victorian Domestic Architecture on College Hill" (master's thesis, Brown University, 1960).

122 "desire . . . as long as possible": Anne B. F. Woods will and codicil, 1890. Alva Woods Family Papers, mss 816, box 1, folder 26, Rhode Island Historical Society.

123 "old fashioned furniture": Ibid.

8. A Scientific Matter and Opinions from Experts

127 "Antique pieces containing": Donna J. Christensen to Maryalice Huggins, December 28, 1995.

128 "The small nail/sprigs": Michael Sandor Podmaniczky to Maryalice Huggins, January 5, 1996.

129 "chimneypieces, looking glasses, and pier tables": Luke Beckerdite, "Immigrant Carvers and the Development of the Rococo Style in New York, 1750–1770." In *American Furniture* (Hanover, N.H.: University Press of New England, for the Chipstone Foundation, 1996).

9. The Irish Question

140 "As one of the greatest": Lewis F. Hinckley, *The More Significant Georgian Furniture* (New York: Washington Mews Books, 1990).

141 "Chippendale . . . Irish country landscapes": Lewis F. Hinckley, *Queen Anne & Georgian Looking Glasses: With Supplement on the Distributors of Colonial and Early Federal Looking Glasses* (New York: Washington Mews Books, 1987).

141 "Irish furniture was not popular": Lewis Hinckley, *The More Significant Georgian Furniture* (New York: Washington Mews Books, 1990).

10. The Scryer

149 "see what ordinary mortals": Pendergrast, *Mirror Mirror*.

152 "Outside the fog": Letters from Abby Francis Woods to Anne B. F. Woods, January–October 1870. Alva Woods Family Papers, series 1, mss 816, box 12, folders 20–24, Rhode Island Historical Society.

153 "Alexandra limp": Alison Gernsheim, *Victorian and Edwardian Fashion, a Photographic Survey* (New York: Dover Press, 1981).

154 "I must get a maid": Letters from Abby Francis Woods to Anne B. F. Woods, January–October 1870. Alva Woods Family Papers, series 1, mss 816, box 12, folders 20–24, Rhode Island Historical Society.

154 "You may be sure . . . places for everything": Ibid.

156 "Every woman today": Joanna Richardson, *La Vie Parisienne 1852–1870* (New York: Viking Press, 1971).

156 "Take what precautions": Gernsheim, *Victorian and Edwardian Fashion*.

156 "Grecian bend": Ibid.

157 "from peasant girls . . . artificial flowers": Ibid.

157 "had to sell": Richardson, *La Vie Parisienne*.

157 "I dislike company . . . stupid evening": Letters from Abby Francis Woods to Anne B. F. Woods, January–October 1870. Alva Woods Family Papers, series 1, mss 816, box 12, folders 20–24, Rhode Island Historical Society.

158 "*Voici l'entrée* . . . out of [her] head": Ibid.

158 "Well, how are you . . . my advice sincerely": Ibid.

159 "very handsome, rich . . . in her place": Ibid.

159 "I always envy girls": Ibid.

159 an opulent limestone mansion: Letter from John Read to Marshall Woods, September 17, 1858. Alva Woods Family Papers, series 1, mss 816, box 5, folder 23, Rhode Island Historical Society.

161 "His name was Charles Stewart Parnell": Interestingly, if you go looking for Charles Parnell's name in Abby Woods's letters, you will not find it. At the Rhode Island Historical Society, there is a cache of seven months of letters

written by Abby in 1870 to her mother, Anne Brown Francis Woods, and the correspondence reveals Abby's involvement with a man she is thinking about marrying. But the original handwritten letters have been copied and typed by someone, presumably a family member—and the suitor's name has been omitted. On page after page of the transcriptions, there is a blank space where the man's name once was. Why was his name erased? I believe the most logical explanation was Victorian shame. Abby died a few years after Parnell, and as the family sorted out her papers and passed them on to her daughters, I assume they sought to rewrite Abby's history. The Woodses did not want their daughter's name associated with Parnell after he was accused of adultery in the scandalous divorce proceedings covered in the press.

The Parnell biographers were less discreet. In all accounts, from Parnell's brother's and sister's biographies to memoirs by fellow politicians, to the most recent biography by Robert Kee, it is universally acknowledged that the jilting, in 1870, by "the Rhode Island heiress, Miss Woods," had been the catalyst for launching Parnell into a career in politics.

Even with the missing name, Parnell's steely personality emerges unmistakably in Abby's letters. In one, she vividly records complaints made by her friend, George Bradley. Originally from Albany, New York, Bradley came to visit Abby one summer afternoon at her hotel in London, having fled Paris shortly before the Franco-Prussian War. He told Abby that he had observed the Irishman during brief social interactions and thought him distant, aloof, and cold. Abby confessed that she understood what he meant.

The truth is, Parnell was always a mystery. No one except his wife knew him intimately. He was an enigmatic figure who didn't leave behind a large volume of papers for posterity, and he kept his personal emotions to himself. In fact, recounts one of his biographers, when Parnell was in Kilmainham Gaol, he was so concerned that someone might intercept or read his letters that he wrote to Kitty O'Shea in disappearing ink.

162 "I shall enjoy myself": Letter from John Read to Marshall Woods, September 17, 1858. Alva Woods Family Papers, series 1, mss 816, folder 23, Rhode Island Historical Society.

164 "offering little stability": F.S.L. Lyons, *Charles Stewart Parnell* (New York: Oxford University Press, 1977).

165 "liked the games there": Ibid.

165 "visiting the ruined fort": William O'Brien, *Parnell of Real Life* (London: T. F. Unwin, 1926).

166 "We are a peculiar family": Ibid.

166 "outdated editions to do": Ibid.

166 "his academic deficiencies . . . from a confrontation": Lyons, *Charles Stewart Parnell*.

166 "one of the three or four": Robert Kee, *The Laurel and the Ivy: The Story of Charles Stewart Parnell and Irish Nationalism* (London: Hamish Hamilton, 1993).

167 "once [Parnell was] entrapped . . . best man at chess": O'Brien, *Parnell of Real Life*, 58–59.

167 "a complete impatience . . . through his children": Ibid., 46.

168 "In every shady nook": Emily Monroe Dickenson, *A Patriot's Mistake: Reminiscences of the Parnell Family* (Dublin: Hodges, Figgins & Co., 1905).

11. Travels East
169 "All quotations in this chapter are from correspondence between Abby Francis Woods and Anne B. F. Woods, January–October 1870. Alva Woods Family Papers, series 1, mss 816, box 12, folders 20–24, Rhode Island Historical Society.

12. Parnell Comes to America
185 "May 6, 1871 / THE WESTERN UNION": Abby Woods Abbott commonplace book. Abbott Family Papers, mss 783, box 4, folder 1, Rhode Island Historical Society.
186 "he was only": R. F. Foster, *Charles Stewart Parnell: The Man and His Family* (Hassocoks, U.K.: Harvester Press Limited Humanities Press, 1976), 124.
186 "sullen and dejected": John Howard Parnell, *Charles Stewart Parnell: A Memoir* (New York: Henry Holt and Company, 1916).
187 "holding his face": Ibid.
187 "John," she insisted: Ibid.
187 "Come, Charley," he said: Ibid.
187 "put forth the sad story": Ibid.
187 "John," Charley said: Ibid.
187 "attitude towards women": Foster, *Charles Stewart Parnell*, 124.
187 "For God's sake": Parnell, *Charles Stewart Parnell*.
190 "put his name forward": Kee, *The Laurel and the Ivy*.
190 "To our dismay": Ibid., 39.
190 "His jilting undoubtedly helped": Parnell, *Charles Stewart Parnell*.
190 "was carried": Kee, *The Laurel and the Ivy*, 73.
191 Ireland was "growing young again": Ibid.
191 "sprigs of laurel": Ibid., 75.
191 "The house lies prostrate": Ibid., 136.
191 " 'By breaking them' ": O'Brien, *Parnell of Real Life*, 73.
193 "Her only concern": Kee, *The Laurel and the Ivy*, 246.
193 "came out, a tall, gaunt figure": Ibid., 246.
194 "Several apparently gracious": Ibid., 311.
194 "Come, let us call": Parnell, *Charles Stewart Parnell*.
194 "the rich American": Ibid.
194 "as still very pretty": Ibid.
194 "She talked rapidly": Ibid.
195 "Do tell me . . . we should have been together!": Ibid.
195 "If a girl once married": Letters from Abby Francis Woods to Anne B. F. Woods, January–October 1870. Alva Woods Family Papers, series 1, mss 816, box 12, folders 20–24, Rhode Island Historical Society.
195 "the Whore of England": Kee, *The Laurel and the Ivy*.

196 "the sky over the grave": Ibid.

196 "You would never": O'Brien, *Parnell of Real Life*, 143.

13. *The Gerrys*

211 "How could you expect": O'Brien, *Parnell of Real Life.*

15. *Seller's Remorse*

234 "All things in the house . . . make him happy": Note by Helen Abbott Washburn, undated. Washburn Family Papers, mss 783, box 1, folder 10. Rhode Island Historical Society.

234 "I have puzzled . . . energy as before": Diary of John Carter Brown Woods, June 14–20, 1897. Alva Woods Family Papers, series 3, mss 816, box 16, folder 8, Rhode Island Historical Society.

235 "The Irish . . . I may be tarred with that brush remotely": Letter from John Carter Brown Woods to Helen Washburn, March 17, 1927. Washburn Family Papers, series 1, mss 783, box 1, folder 6, Rhode Island Historical Society.

236 "On the John Brown Francis": Note by John Carter Brown Woods, November 11, 1916. Alva Woods Family Papers, series 6, mss 816, box 12, folder 33, Rhode Island Historical Society.

245 "The answer is maybe": J. Carter Brown interview.

246 "The response to art . . . about yourself": Holland Cotter, "Agnes Martin, Abstract Painter, Dies at 92," *New York Times*, December 17, 2004, "Arts: Arts & Design."

Bibliography

Aslet, Clive. *The American Country House.* New Haven, Conn.: Yale University Press, 1990.

Barquist, David L., Elisabeth Donaghy Garrett, and Gerald W. R. Ward. *American Tables and Looking Glasses in the Mabel Brady Garvan and Other Collections at Yale University.* New Haven, Conn.: Yale University Art Gallery, 1992.

Barratt, Carrie Rebora. *Queen Victoria and Thomas Sully.* Princeton, N.J.: Princeton University Press in Association with Metropolitan Museum of Art, 2000.

Beckerdite, Luke. "Immigrant Carvers and the Development of the Rococo Style in New York, 1750–1770." In *American Furniture,* edited by Luke Beckerdite, 233–65. Hanover, N.H.: University Press of New England, for the Chipstone Foundation, 1996.

Beckerdite, Luke. "Philadelphia Carving Shops: Part I: James Reynolds." *Magazine Antiques* 125 (May 1984): 1120–33.

————. "Part II: Bernard and Jugiez." *Magazine Antiques* (September 1985): 498–513.

————. "Part III: Hercules Courtenay and His School." *Magazine Antiques* (May 1987): 1044–63.

Beckerdite, Luke, ed. *American Furniture.* Hanover, N.H.: University Press of New England, for the Chipstone Foundation, 1996.

Blum, Stella. *Victorian Fashions and Costumes from Harper's Bazaar, 1867–1898.* New York: Dover Publications, 1974.

Brown, Henry A. L. *John Brown's Tract: Lost Adirondack Empire.* Canaan, N.H.: Phoenix Publishing, 1988.

Brown, Malcolm Johnston. *The Politics of Irish Literature: From Thomas Davis to W. B. Yeats.* Seattle: University of Washington Press, 1973.

Carpenter, Ralph E. "The Magnificent Nicholas Brown Desk and Bookcase." *Christie's Catalog,* June 3, 1989.

Cooper, Wendy A. "The Purchase of Furniture and Furnishings by John Brown,

Providence Merchant. Part I: 1760–1788." *Magazine Antiques* (February 1973): 328–39.

———. "The Purchase of Furniture . . . Part II: 1788–1803." *Magazine Antiques* (April 1973): 734–43.

Cotter, Holland. "Agnes Martin, Abstract Painter, Dies at 92." *New York Times*, December 17, 2004, "Arts: Arts & Design."

Dickens, Charles. *Pictures from Italy.* 1844. Reprint, New York: Ecco Press, 1988.

Dickenson, Emily Monroe. *A Patriot's Mistake: Reminiscences of the Parnell Family.* Dublin: Hodges, Figgins & Co., 1905.

Downing, Antoinette Forrester, and Helen Mason Grose. *Early Homes of Rhode Island.* Richmond, Va.: Garrett and Massie, 1937.

Edwards, Clive. *Eighteenth-Century Furniture.* Manchester, U.K.: Manchester University Press, 1996.

Fabian, Monroe H. *Mr. Sully, Portrait Painter: The Works of Thomas Sully (1783–1872).* Washington, D.C.: Smithsonian Institution Press, 1983.

Foreman, John, and Robbe Pierce Stimson. *The Vanderbilts and the Gilded Age: Architectural Aspirations, 1879–1901.* New York: St. Martin's Press, 1991.

Foster, R. F. *Charles Stewart Parnell: The Man and His Family.* Hassocoks, U.K.: Harvester Press Limited Humanities Press, 1976.

Gatti, Anne. *Aesop's Fables.* San Diego: Harcourt Brace Jovanovich, 1992.

Gernsheim, Alison. *Victorian and Edwardian Fashion, a Photographic Survey.* New York: Dover Press, 1981.

Glass, Anita. "Early Victorian Domestic Architecture on College Hill." Master's thesis, Brown University, 1960.

Goff, Lee, and Paul Rocheleau. *Tudor Style, Tudor Revival Houses in America from 1890 to the Present.* New York: Universe, 2002.

Hayward, Helena, and Douglas Ash. *World Furniture: An Illustrated History.* London: Hamlyn Publishing Group, 1965.

Heckscher, Morrison H. *American Rococo, 1750–1775: Elegance in Ornament.* New York: Metropolitan Museum of Art, 1992.

Hedges, James Blaine. *The Browns of Providence Plantations: Colonial Years.* Cambridge, Mass.: Harvard University Press, 1952.

———. *The Browns of Providence Plantations: The Nineteenth Century.* Providence, R.I.: Brown University Press, 1968.

Hewitt, Mark. *Domestic Architecture of H. T. Lindeberg.* New York: Acanthus Press, 1996.

Hinckley, Lewis F. *A Directory of Queen Anne, Early Georgian, and Chippendale Furniture.* New York: Crown, 1971.

———. *The More Significant Georgian Furniture.* New York: Washington Mews Books, 1990.

———. *Queen Anne & Georgian Looking Glasses: With Supplement on the Distributors of Colonial and Early Federal Looking Glasses.* New York: Washington Mews Books, 1987.

Howarth, Herbert. *The Irish Writers, 1880–1940.* New York: Hill and Wang, 1959.

Hummel, Charles F. "Queen Anne and Chippendale Furniture in the Henry Francis du Pont Winterthur Museum, Part III." *Magazine Antiques* (January 1971): 98–107.

Kaye, Myrna. *Fake, Fraud, or Genuine? Identifying Authentic American Antique Furniture*. Boston: Little, Brown, Bulfinch Press, 1991.

Kee, Robert. *The Laurel and the Ivy: The Story of Charles Stewart Parnell and Irish Nationalism*. London: Hamish Hamilton, 1993.

Landrey, Gregory. "The Conservator as Curator: Combining Scientific Analysis and Traditional Connoisseurship." In *American Furniture*, edited by Luke Beckerdite, 147–59. Hanover, N.H.: University Press of New England, for the Chipstone Foundation, 1996.

Lyons, F.S.L. *Charles Stewart Parnell*. New York: Oxford University Press, 1977.

Martin, Agnes, and Dieter Schwarz. *Writings: Schriften*. Stuttgart: Cantz, 1991.

McAlester, Virginia, A. Lee McAlester, and Alex McLean. *Great American Houses and Their Architectural Styles*. New York: Abbeville Press, 1994.

Melchior-Bonnet, Sabine. *The Mirror: A History*. New York: Routledge, 2001.

O'Brien, William. *Parnell of Real Life*. London: T. F. Unwin, 1926.

O'Connor, T. P. *Charles Stewart Parnell: A Memory*. New York: Ward, Lock, Bowden, and Co., 1891.

———. *Memoirs of an Old Parliamentarian*. 2 vols. London: Ernest Benn, 1929.

Olson, Stanley. *John Singer Sargent: His Portrait*. New York: St. Martin's Press, 1986.

Overbye, Dennis. "Mirror, Mirror," *New York Times*, August 30, 2005, "Science: Space & Cosmos."

Parnell, John Howard. *Charles Stewart Parnell: A Memoir*. New York: Henry Holt, 1916.

Pendergrast, Mark. *Mirror Mirror: A History of the Human Love Affair with Reflection*. New York: Basic Books, 2004.

Randall, Richard H., Jr. "Designs for Philadelphia Carvers." In *American Furniture*, edited by Luke Beckerdite, 57–62. Hanover, N.H.: University Press of New England, for the Chipstone Foundation 1996.

Reif, Rita. "Harold Sack, 89, Connoisseur of American Furniture, Dies." *New York Times*, July 10, 2000.

Richardson, Joanna. *La Vie Parisienne 1852–1870*. New York: Viking Press, 1971.

Ronald Phillips Ltd. *Reflections of the Past: Mirrors 1685–1815*. London: Ronald Phillips, 2004.

Schinto, Jeanne. "The Art of Woodcarving in America: A Symposium." *Maine Antique Digest* (2007).

Schwartz, Marlia. "Discovery on Block Island: 2500-Year-Old Village Predates Agriculture." *Nor'easter: Magazine of the Northeast Sea Grant Programs* 2 (1990): 32–37.

Stockwell, David. "Aesop's Fables on Philadelphia Furniture." *Magazine Antiques* 60 (December 1951): 522–[25].

Strickland, Peter L. L. "Documented Philadelphia Looking Glasses, 1800–1850." *Magazine Antiques* (April 1976): 784–95.

White, Elizabeth. *Pictorial Dictionary of British 18th Century Furniture Design*. Woodbridge, Suffolk, England: Antique Collectors' Club, 1990.

Acknowledgments

I would like to thank the following people:

Susan Vander Closter, Professor of English at the Rhode Island School of Design. Her assistance with the initial research, her ongoing engagement with the story, and her unfailing faith that I could write this book were invaluable.

Chris Calhoun at Sterling Lord, my agent and longtime friend. Over many dinners together in New York, he was brutally honest about the rewrites I had to make. He always countered my resistance with a hefty dose of positive reinforcement. By insisting on my best work, Chris fufilled his initial promise, which was that ultimately he would find the perfect publisher for my manuscript.

Sarah Crichton, my editor at Farrar, Straus and Giroux. It was an honor beyond my wildest dreams to have had the opportunity to work with her. Her amazing intuition and talent made the process of completing this book a joyful experience.

Katie Hall, who helped me organize the structure of the manuscript and put me back on track when I was lost.

Stephen Sink, for translating French passages in Abby Woods's 1870 letters to her mother.

My good friend Henry Steele. He read the early versions of the manuscript and offered me many insightful suggestions.

The Brown/Woods descendants, Henry A. Brown, Bay

McClure, Bambi Mlecsko, John Gifford, Ken Washburn, and David Merriman. All of them graciously welcomed me into their homes and shared with me their knowledge of family legends.

Bill Rieder and Morrison Heckscher at the Metropolitan Museum of Art. Carolyn Sargentson at the Victoria and Albert Museum. I am extremely grateful for their scholarly opinions, time, and efforts on my behalf.

Dean Failey, John Hays, Melissa Gagan, and Susan Kleckner at Christie's, and Simon Redburn at Sotheby's. I believe all of them had my interests at heart and tried to steer me in the right direction with regard to the mirror.

My mother, Alice Mott Huggins, for her loving encouragement and her assistance in gathering information about the early settlers of Block Island and Aquidneck Island.

Karen Eberhart, Rick Stattler, and all the rest of the dedicated staff who assisted me in special collections and the manuscript department of the Rhode Island Historical Society.

Jeff Beardsley, DonWon Song, and Diana Throw at Sterling Lord Literistic, each of whom spent long hours poring over the chapters. I am grateful for their intelligent comments and suggestions.

Special thanks to Cailey Hall at Farrar, Straus and Giroux.

CPSIA information can be obtained at www.ICGtesting.com
Printed in the USA
LVOW071128240313

325746LV00001B/1/P